The New Phenomenology

Also available from Bloomsbury:

Basic Problems of Phenomenology, Martin Heidegger
Phenomenology: An Introduction, Michael Lewis and Tanja Staehler

The New Phenomenology

A Philosophical Introduction

**J. AARON SIMMONS AND
BRUCE ELLIS BENSON**

B L O O M S B U R Y

LONDON • NEW DELHI • NEW YORK • SYDNEY

Bloomsbury Academic
An imprint of Bloomsbury Publishing Plc

50 Bedford Square
London
WC1B 3DP
UK

1385 Broadway
New York
NY 10018
USA

www.bloomsbury.com

First published 2013

British Library Cataloguing-in-Publication Data
A catalogue record for this book is available from the British Library.

ISBN: HB: 978-1-4411-1711-3
PB: 978-1-4411-8283-8
ePub: 978-1-4411-3328-1
ePDF: 978-1-4411-7273-0

Library of Congress Cataloging-in-Publication Data
Simmons, J. Aaron, 1977-
The new phenomenology : a philosophical introduction /
J. Aaron Simmons and Bruce Ellis Benson.
pages cm
Includes bibliographical references and index.
ISBN 978-1-4411-8283-8 (pbk.) – ISBN 978-1-4411-1711-3 –
ISBN 978-1-4411-7273-0 (pdf) – ISBN 978-1-4411-3328-1 (epub)
1. Phenomenology. 2. Philosophy, French. 3. Phenomenological theology.
I. Title.
B829.5.S483 2013
142'.7–dc23
2013005643

Typeset by Newgen Imaging Systems Pvt Ltd., Chennai, India
Printed and bound in India

For David Wood and Merold Westphal

CONTENTS

ACKNOWLEDGMENTS

Writing a book is never a process that is simply the product of the author(s). It owes to the generosity of a host of others. To those who have given us their time, energy, support, and encouragement while we were working on this book, we can only say "thank you." In particular, Aaron would like to thank Vanessa and Atticus.

We would also like to thank the editorial staff at Bloomsbury for their support of this project from the beginning. It arose out of an innocent question in the book exhibition hall at a professional meeting: "Does Bloomsbury have any plans to publish a book on new phenomenology that would be accessible to non-specialists and could be used to teach courses on French phenomenology?" We never thought that the answer would be: "No, but are you interested in writing such a book?" At the end of this long process, though, we are thankful for that surprising response, which literally called out to us and laid claim on our time and our thought. It has been an enormously productive process and one that has helped us to get clear on exactly what we think about when what we think about new phenomenology. Thanks also to Jessica Corey for preparing the index.

Finally, we would like to offer a special note of appreciation to David Wood and Merold Westphal for their friendship and scholarly example. It is with pleasure that we dedicate this book to them.

A NOTE ON THE COLLABORATION

This book is a product of long hours of conversation between us. That said, Simmons is the primary author of all of the chapters (except for Chapter Two and portions of Chapter One). Benson then edited and revised the entire manuscript. Accordingly, it is very much a collaborative effort, but with a division of labor being separated along these lines.

Introduction:

Welcome to the family

In their book *Pragmatism: A Guide for the Perplexed*, Robert B. Talisse and Scott F. Aikin (2008) quite sensibly begin by laying out what the book is about. However, as they explain, pragmatism doesn't easily map onto the notion of school, theory, trend, or movement (Talisse and Aikin 2008, 1). Rather, the main philosophers "who embrace the term pragmatism disagree over central and substantive philosophical matters." Even more surprisingly, "they also disagree about *what pragmatism is*" (2008, 2). Instead of viewing this definitional difficulty as an objection to the viability of pragmatism as a contemporary philosophical perspective, Talisse and Aikin understand it to highlight the fact that pragmatism is "a *living philosophy* rather than a historical relic," which means that pragmatism "is still working itself out, still trying to figure out what it is" (2008, 3).

So how does one define a living philosophy that continues to develop? Talisse and Aikin note that pragmatism is "a collection of more or less loosely connected philosophical themes, arguments, and commitments" and although "each version of pragmatism has its distinctive insights and virtues, none can claim to be the last word on the philosophical problems to which it is addressed" (2008, 3–4). Such a description is quite apt for *new phenomenology*, since it too displays a unity amid diversity. By "new phenomenologists," we mean those French philosophers in the latter half of the twentieth century who all think in the wake of Edmund Husserl (1859–1938) and Martin Heidegger (1889–1976)—namely: Emmanuel

Levinas (1906–95), Michel Henry (1922–2002), Jacques Derrida (1930–2004), Jean-Luc Marion (1946–), Jean-Louis Chrétien (1952–), and to some extent, but in importantly different respects, Jean-Yves Lacoste (1953–), and Paul Ricoeur (1913–2005). All of the new phenomenologists go beyond the specifics of Husserlian and Heideggerian thought in key ways.[1] Most famously, as explained by Dominique Janicaud (2000), the new phenomenologists "go beyond" historical phenomenology in their willingness to consider God and religious existence. Yet, as we will argue in this book, they should not be read as exclusively, or even as primarily, engaged in a theological project. Although they all do engage in significant reflection on topics of concern to philosophy of religion, they also deal with a wide range of central matters for philosophical inquiry and human existence more broadly.

Whether *classical* phenomenology can be viewed in a meaningful way as a "school" is open to question. That question is even more complicated for *new* phenomenology. Although it does have historical and philosophical "sources" (viz. the thought of Husserl and Heidegger) such that there are discernible common threads that run through much of new phenomenology, the work of the new phenomenologists is characterized as much by differences between the different thinkers as it is by their commonalities. For example, despite all the new phenomenologists recognizing in the work of Husserl a distinctive and robust possibility for philosophy, none of them entirely agree about where the main pressure points and problems lie within Husserlian phenomenology.

Further, new phenomenology is *not* united by a specific set of doctrines such that it could be considered a unified philosophical theory. While there are frequently points of theoretical resonance among the new phenomenologists, the relationship between them is best thought of as a complicated Venn diagram in which there are regions of intersecting trajectories, but without an obvious area in which they all overlap such that a substantive list of necessary conditions for being a new phenomenologist could be specified. Further, there is no easily articulable claim upon which they will all agree that is specific enough to stand as the basis for such a set of doctrines or even as a manifesto for a movement. So, new phenomenology is not clearly definable as a historical trend or movement. Further, although it has its roots in twentieth-century France, its influence has not remained isolated there. And, even though some (following the lead of Janicaud) have tried to identify new phenomenology with a "theological turn" in French phenomenology, which might indicate something of a "trend" in recent phenomenology more broadly, none of the thinkers usually identified as new phenomenologists accept this characterization. Indeed, as we will consider at length, they have all in one way or another challenged the idea that there has been such a "turn" to theology.

According to the new phenomenologists, the primary "turn" in their thought is toward the implicit possibilities of the original phenomenological framework laid out by Husserl and critically developed by Heidegger, even if such possibilities push beyond the specifics of classical phenomenological formulations. For the new phenomenologists, classical phenomenology is better thought of as a source of inspiration that opens onto phenomenological novelty, even if in sometimes *heterodox* directions as we will discuss in Chapter Two, than as an outline of limitations beyond which phenomenological inquiry cannot go. In this way, the new phenomenologists are all faithful to Husserl in a variety of ways and all unfaithful to him in a variety of others (though this "unfaithfulness" to Husserl is done in the name of faithfulness to phenomenology itself). Yet, this ambivalence might be an expression of a deeply phenomenological tendency insofar as it reflects the complexity of phenomenality itself as located and expressed in historical contexts and lived situations. Indeed, if staying true to Husserl were required in order for one to be a phenomenologist, then, given the rather significant development in his own thought over the course of his authorship, Husserl's own bona fides as phenomenologist could be questioned.

As a living philosophy, new phenomenology is not something upon which we can look back with the clarity of historical hindsight. Rather, our proximity to it is such that "it" remains at issue in the contemporary debates. Indeed, given the continued philosophical activity of such new phenomenologists as Jean-Luc Marion and Jean-Louis Chrétien, "it" is continuing to develop and expand. Additionally, as contemporary scholars begin to engage the work of these thinkers more frequently and with more depth, in particular those who have often been less prominently considered in the continental literature—namely, Henry and Chrétien—the stakes and entailments of their thought continue to get worked out. Accordingly, what "new phenomenology" *is* is still, to some degree, a matter of what "it" will *become*. François-David Sebbah puts this complication as follows:

> There must be no question of throwing oneself into an endless quest for resemblances and differences; a great deal of insipidity and coarseness would inevitably result from any attempt to demonstrate that in some sense Levinas, Henry, and Derrida [and we might add Marion, and Chrétien] are saying the same thing; immense naïveté would be required to make such a claim despite their many differences. (2012, 7)

In light of such claims, it might seem odd to attempt to write a book specifically trying to provide a philosophical introduction to new phenomenology while recognizing that *new phenomenology* is not a rigid designator of a stable philosophical perspective. Nonetheless, we do think that there is value in viewing recent French phenomenology as a coherent and distinctive philosophical *family*. And, like all families, there are sure to be robust disagreement as well as underlying shared values and commitments. In this way, we are following Sebbah himself who, while discouraging any attempt to lay out points of resonance and dissonance across these thinkers, chooses to focus on a particular "*family* of contemporary French phenomenology" made up of Levinas, Derrida, Henry, and Marion (2012, 6). As with all families, there is not an identity across the membership, but simply an underlying connection and set of commitments. While it is sometimes possible to offer stable accounts of such connections and commitments, it is often the case that the members of a philosophical family are "related," as it were, by their shared engagement about what being part of a particular family would even mean. Specifically, the new phenomenologists are all engaged in working out what phenomenology itself requires, assumes, and supposes.

Importantly, Sebbah goes on to say that "just as there is thus no 'essential' common denominator for the different elements composing a 'family', the borders of a family are not clean ones: they are susceptible to modification from other adopted perspectives" (2012, 7). As in most families there are usually those distant cousins who are rarely invited to reunions, Sebbah rightly points out that in the new phenomenological family there are individuals who are closer to some sort of fragile center and others who are farther away. Crucially, though, how the center itself is conceived is a matter of continued discussion and debate within the family.

There is a further complication: the term "new phenomenology" is not itself used with any regularity by the figures associated with it. Indeed, the first usage of the term to describe those French phenomenologists who attempted to think at, and occasionally push beyond, the limits of Husserlian phenomenology seems to be by Dominique Janicaud who, in his (in)famous 1991 essay, *Le tournant théologique de la phénoméologie française*, distinguishes between the "historical phenomenology" of Husserl and (the early) Heidegger on the one hand, and the "new phenomenology" of Levinas, Chrétien, Marion, and Henry on the other hand (Janicaud 2000, 81, 86n52).[2] Following on Janicaud, in the 2000 English translation of *Le tournant théologique*, the translator Bernard G. Prusak also refers to this "second generation" (as opposed to the first generation that includes Jean-Paul Sartre and Maurice Merleau-Ponty) of French phenomenologists as the "new phenomenologists" (Prusak 2000, 3).

An alternative moniker for the work of these recent French phenomenologists might be "radical phenomenology," given the way in which all of the new phenomenologists claim in one way or another to "radicalize" some aspect of Husserlian phenomenology. In some ways, such a term would be quite appropriate, for "radical" comes from the Latin term "*radix*," meaning root or origin. As we will see in Chapter Two, all of the phenomenologists we will be considering here view their work as going back to and questioning the true origin or root of phenomenology. However, in a contemporary context where "radical" carries the connotations of both over-the-top extremism and also fundamentalist dogmatism, we find that "new phenomenology" is a better designation. On the one hand, it remains descriptively true—the phenomenology under discussion refers to the family of French phenomenology that continues to be considered and productively elaborated in the work of contemporary scholars. On the other hand, it avoids the problematic affiliations (and just simple overuse) faced by the "radical" descriptor.

Of course, we are then faced with contributing to the very naming of the "living" philosophy of new phenomenology itself, which has not yet received enough scholarly attention to stand as an uncontested designator in the first place. Although the publication of Janicaud's essay (and even more so the English translation of it) has caused a flurry of articles and books to be written wading into the debates concerning whether the thought of Jean-Luc Marion, Michel Henry, Emmanuel Levinas, Jacques Derrida, and Jean-Louis Chrétien blurs the boundaries between phenomenology and theology, and whether and how such boundaries should be erected in the first place, few of these essays have considered new phenomenology as a coherent philosophical *trajectory*.[3] We believe that such coherence (the unity in the diversity) can be articulated without forcing new phenomenology to be merely unitary and static. For this reason, we will describe this family of phenomenologists as displaying a shared "trajectory" rather than as forming a philosophical school or affirming a set of beliefs that could stand as something of a criteriological or doctrinal litmus test that must be a passed in order to gain membership to the club, as it were.[4]

Consider the following example. Multiple people can be unified insofar as they are on their way to Boston, say, but diversified insofar as they are coming there from slightly different starting points. Moreover, people could be unified insofar as they are all leaving Boston, but diversified insofar as they are heading in different directions. The idea of a "trajectory" nicely expresses this ambiguity: it can mean the direction that something is taking as it moves toward a common goal and it can also mean the commonality of the source of motion that propel one outward. Both of these aspects are present in new phenomenology. While all the members of the family are starting out from the same point given their shared parental lineage, as it were, they are all moving in different directions as they variously push against the constraints laid down by this very lineage.

Accordingly, this book aims to be an introduction to new phenomenology insofar as it seeks to argue for the coherence of the new phenomenological trajectory by looking at some of the primary philosophical perspectives defended by the new phenomenologists and considering the central debates that attend their thought. However, rather than merely survey the existing literature on the topic, this book is offered as a contribution to the expanding new phenomenological literature itself as this "living tradition" continues to grow and develop. For that reason, there are times we go into a bit more detail and depth than might be expected from an introductory book. Since it is our guiding belief that the key questions asked by new phenomenology very much remain questions for contemporary philosophy, we think that such depth is needed to demonstrate that continued relevance. We might say, then, that this book is an "advanced introduction" in that it both *introduces* new phenomenology to nonspecialists while also *advancing* the debates concerning new phenomenology.

In the attempt to make the book as accessible as possible, though, we have chosen to avoid an exclusively figure-driven historical presentation, whereby each chapter would focus on a particular new phenomenologist. Instead we attempt to unpack new phenomenology by looking at the various ways it offers distinctive contributions to contemporary philosophical debates especially in the philosophy of religion, but also concerning methodology, hermeneutics, ethics, politics, social theory, and even epistemology and aesthetics. We will be quite open about places where we think problems remain for new phenomenology as propounded by specific thinkers and, hence, we want to be quite open about the seemingly obvious fact that we are not neutral when it comes to new phenomenology itself: we think that there is much therein worthy of continued assent and also some aspects worth abandoning as a result of serious consideration of other relevant philosophical alternatives.

Overall, in this book we will be arguing for three main theses.

Thesis 1: *New phenomenology can be legitimately considered an heir to historical phenomenology when understood as a general path of inquiry into phenomenality, rather than a rigid perspective that holds a set of stable doctrines regarding phenomenality and the modes in which particular phenomena appear.* We are depending on an important distinction between *phenomenality* and *phenomena* here. By *phenomenality*, we simply mean the conditions of presentation, givenness, appearance, and intuition that would then get concretized in a particular phenomenon (e.g. this pencil on the table or that cup filled with ice, etc.). Sometimes phenomena are rather straightforward (as in the pencil or cup), but they can also be exceptionally complicated (as in the phenomenal possibilities presented in the encounter with others, God, the invisible, the impossible, and such abstract notions as life, difference, and even givenness itself). The new phenomenologists are especially interested in these difficult cases and, as such, their focus on the philosophy of religion is a result of the notion of "religious phenomena" being a large umbrella term for these difficult phenomena (though it is likely that a notion of "ethical" or "ethico-religious" phenomena would be a better category for Levinas and Derrida). Yet, rather than directly considering ethical or religious phenomena, many new phenomenologists find it more productive to consider the stakes of phenomenality, as such, in order better to understand the specific phenomenological challenges that such ethical or religious phenomena present. In particular, the new phenomenologists are interested in the ways in which phenomenality might overflow or remain excessive of discrete phenomena. Getting clear on how such "excess" occurs across the range of perspectives that share the new phenomenological trajectory will be one of the tasks of this book. That said, for those familiar with phenomenology as defined by Husserl, considering new phenomenology will require some significant questioning of Husserlian assumptions. Namely, we will suggest that new phenomenology (a) displaces the centrality of intentionality, (b) transforms the role of the "horizon," and (c) rethinks the ways in which the phenomenological "reduction" ought to function. All of these points will be considered in what follows, but for now it is sufficient to say that the ways in which such displacement, transformation, and rethinking occur will differ depending on which new phenomenologist one considers.

Thesis 2: *New phenomenology should be weighed and considered in light of a variety of contemporary philosophical problems.* Although we will contend that the focus on the "theological turn," even if important, has been overblown as the unifying thread of this phenomenological family, it is crucial that we not move past it too quickly. Accordingly, we will directly address Janicaud's influential reading of new phenomenology and yet do so in order to move beyond it as an adequate lens for understanding the key points of the philosophical trajectory under consideration. In order to give it careful consideration, however, we will spend quite a bit of time working out the various aspects of new phenomenological *philosophy of religion* as distinct from postmodern *theology*.

Thesis 3: *New phenomenology can be productively put into conversation with other contemporary philosophical perspectives regardless of whether those perspectives are traditionally associated with "continental" philosophy.* In the *Cartesian Meditations*, Husserl laments the fact that often there is a splintering within philosophical dialogue: "To be sure, we still have philosophical

congresses. The philosophers meet but, unfortunately, not the philosophies" (Husserl 1999a, 5). The same could be said of the contemporary philosophical landscape—only now we might also add
that, often, philosophers intentionally choose to meet at different
places and in different societies such that, in many cases, *not even
the philosophers* representing different philosophies meet, much
less their philosophies. As Shaun Gallagher and Dan Zahavi note
regarding phenomenology and analytic philosophy of mind, in particular, "very little communication is going on. . . . In fact, on both
sides, the habitual attitude towards the other tradition has ranged
from complete disregard to outright hostility. Indeed, up until the
1990s, it was unusual to find philosophers from these different
traditions even talking to each other" (2012, 2). In agreement with
Gallagher and Zahavi about the importance of cross-traditional
dialogue, we have chosen to break up the chapters in this book
according to areas of philosophical inquiry rather than by specific figures. That said, given the particular foci that concern the
different thinkers, it is understandable that various chapters will
focus more prominently on some new phenomenologists instead
of others.[5]

None of these three theses are philosophically innocuous. That
is, they all reflect our particular stands on matters of continued
debate. However, our minimal hope is that the arguments that
we provide for these theses will allow those who would challenge
them to have a clear and lucid account as a target against which
counterarguments could then be given. In the attempt to focus on
arguments in this way, we will consider not only the main views
propounded by new phenomenologists, but also the main objections to those views that should also be considered. Though we
will occasionally have to get into some detail regarding the specific thought and technical vocabulary of a particular thinker,
in such cases we will attempt to keep the jargon to a minimum
while attempting to present the view of the thinker under consideration as charitably as possible. That said, we want to stress
the fact that this book was intentionally conceived and written as
an *introduction* to new phenomenology. Though we have tried to
balance breadth and depth, we recognize that in an introductory
book such as this there are going to be frequent places where much
more could and should be said about the thinkers being considered
but, in the name of clarity and accessibility to nonspecialists, we

have had to be judicious about how deep to wade into the specific terminology and nuance of their texts. That said, while we have attempted to simplify the notoriously difficult thought of the new phenomenologists, we hope that we have not *oversimplified* it. For those who would like to dig deeper into the specific debates, issues, and thinkers being considered, we have tried to provide suggestions for further reading. Our goal in writing this "philosophical intro-duction" to new phenomenology is hopefully to stimulate further interest in the important philosophical resources offered by recent French phenomenology. Although new phenomenology is a com-plicated philosophical trajectory that demands serious attention and rigorous reading, we believe that such attention and rigor is repaid in full for those who devote the time to do so. Accordingly, this book is not meant to replace reading the primary texts by the new phenomenologists or the technical scholarship that has been written about those texts. Nonetheless, for those readers who are not already versed in the history of continental philosophy and the vocabulary of Husserl and Heidegger, we hope that his book will serve as a good place *to start*.

This book progresses as follows. In Chapter One, we provide a basic introduction to the classical phenomenology of Husserl and Heidegger in order to have some of their most important ideas (and the technical vocabulary in which they express those ideas) on the table. This classical context will allow us more closely to situate our discussion of new phenomenology as importantly consistent with key Husserlian and Heideggerian commitments. Focusing on the debate between Marion and Derrida about what should count as phenomenological orthodoxy and phenomenological heresy, Chapter Two will lay out the key philosophical views of the indi-vidual new phenomenologists in order that we can then use this as background for going deeper into their thought as it concerns the specific topics considered in later chapters. While we will admit that new phenomenologists are rightly considered phenomenologi-cal heterodox in important ways, their heterodoxy itself might be closer to phenomenological orthodoxy than is frequently realized. That is, they trespass traditional boundaries and push against tra-ditional limits while recognizing those limits, in particular, as the ones of relevance to their thought.

Given the centrality of the notions of excess, invisibility, and impossibility to the new phenomenologists, we will spend quite a bit of time working through such notions as framed by concerns in the philosophy of religion. This discussion will unfold over the course of four chapters. In Chapter Three, we look directly at Janicaud's charge that new phenomenology is simply a turn to revealed theology. In order to situate his charge and to understand its weight, we look to Husserl's "exclusion" of God from phenomenological inquiry in *Ideas I* as well as Heidegger's important critique of "onto-theology." Following this philosophical stage setting, in Chapter Four we look at the ways in which new phenomenologists deploy God-talk in their philosophy. Along the way, we consider the important role that the apophatic theological tradition (which emphases what we *cannot* say about God) plays on their thought. Importantly, Chapter Four offers a detailed rationale for why, and an explanation of how, phenomenology should not be confused with theology. In particular, the new phenomenologists suggest that theology is about actuality, while phenomenology is about possibility; and they contend that theology appeals to evidentiary sources unavailable, as direct evidence, to phenomenological analysis. Chapter Five goes deeper into new phenomenological philosophy of religion by looking at new phenomenological discussions regarding the existence and nature of God, with special attention paid to Marion's account of "God without Being." Chapter Six continues the analyses of Chapter Five by turning to prayer and the relation of faith and reason as deployed in the notion of "Christian philosophy." We look closely at Chrétien's conception of prayer as a "wounded word" and Marion's suggestion that Christian philosophy should be read as a heuristic device rather than a hermeneutic lens. These foci situate new phenomenology in ways that, we believe, make it a productive conversation partner for contemporary debates in analytic philosophy of religion. Accordingly, in Chapter Seven, we offer a series of constructive proposals in what we term "mashup" philosophy of religion. In particular, we look to new phenomenological resources for addressing the problem of evil, the relationship of apophatic and kataphatic religious discourse, and even the fate of apologetics in a postmodern world. Since it is frequently suggested that analytic philosophy of religion and continental philosophy of religion are fundamentally at odds, we also offer a critical assessment of such an opposition as proposed, in particular, by the postmodern philosopher of religion, John D. Caputo.

Chapter Eight moves beyond new phenomenological philosophy of religion but in directions that are consistent with the centrality of the theme of "excess" as it concerns normative questions dealing with ethics, politics, and society. As we see it, new phenomenological accounts of philosophy of religion, ethics, and politics are all specific ways of thinking about philosophy as more than merely a speculative enterprise, but as a lived activity. In our concluding chapter, we wrap up our discussion of new phenomenology by briefly suggesting other areas in which productive further research might occur: aesthetics and epistemology.

Meant as an introduction to new phenomenology, we spend a lot of time in this book looking back into the history of twentieth-century French philosophy. However, along the way, we attempt to make this history of continued relevance to present philosophical inquiry. Yet, we do not see this book as the final word on any of these possible points of relevance. Accordingly, we conclude the book by looking forward rather than looking back. In the brief concluding chapter that considers the possible future(s) of new phenomenology—including its promise and its challenges—we suggest that, when read as a coherent philosophical "trajectory," new phenomenology ought to be seen as more than merely a blip on the map of continental thought. Instead, new phenomenological investigations of God, self, other, and world are all of profound importance to philosophy, more broadly. However, as we will indicate, this importance is best seen when those working in continental philosophy stop assuming that French phenomenology is an exclusively "continental" tradition and those working in analytic philosophy stop assuming that French phenomenology is largely irrelevant because of its "continental" heritage. Not all philosophy is phenomenological, nor should it be, and so phenomenologists would do well to be in deep dialogue with those outside this particular philosophical family. However, such dialogue will hopefully demonstrate that philosophy, in general, is better off when it attends to new phenomenology.

CHAPTER ONE

The sources of new phenomenology in Husserl and Heidegger

"Classical" phenomenology: The Husserlian basics

In order to make sense of new phenomenology as essentially a trajectory that continues and alters classical phenomenology, it is important to lay out a few of the basics of classical phenomenology, especially as articulated by Husserl. Without attempting to give a thorough consideration of Husserl's complicated thought, which many other scholars have done elsewhere,[1] we will focus on five of his most fundamental ideas that are all appropriated and yet put into question (in various ways) by new phenomenologists: (1) intentionality, (2) horizonality, (3) the *epoché*, (4) the phenomenological reduction, and (5) subjectivity and intersubjectivity. Consider the following scenario.

You are sitting in front of your computer writing a book on new phenomenology. On your desk are a variety of books and papers, behind you are several bookcases full of books, over your left shoulder is a window through which can be seen trees and sky. On the left wall, is a large red painting. Near your right hand is a cup of tea (Earl Grey, say). Coming through the speakers of your computer is a guitar-heavy song with lyrics that sound like a lament for a lost lover. As you listen to the song, you are reminded of a rather disappointing lunch that you ate a few hours ago.

This is no hypothetical example: it describes one of our offices and a specific experience. But any of us could imagine ourselves in such a scenario, or at least a very similar one. So how might one make sense of this scenario? Immediately a host of alternatives present themselves. A sociologist might investigate the situation as it stands as a manifestation of the practices of the twenty-first-century scholar. Alternatively, a research psychologist might investigate the scenario as a case study used to explore the complicated neurological processes that allow for the brain to perceive such things as the computer screen and the books on the desk, to interpret the tea as pleasurable to the taste, and to hear the music as not merely an auditory illusion. An audiologist might investigate the ways in which the music is a result of one's eardrum receiving sound waves and vibrating in particular rhythms. A historian might approach the scenario as a manifestation of the way in which academic life tends to be a solitary one as a result of the individualism of academic production. Of course, the list of various ways of considering this scenario could go on: biological, cognitive scientific, anthropological, technological, linguistic, cultural theoretic, theological, and so on.

While all of these different ways of engaging this scenario are important, there is one basic aspect that is missed by them all: the "experience" of *hearing* the music, *typing* on the computer, *allowing* the tea to cool off, *wishing* to be outside enjoying the trees, and *remembering* that one's lunch that day was not as good as one had hoped. And, crucially, it is not just that *one's* experience is missed, but *your* experience is. It is here that phenomenology begins to make sense as a distinctive perspective from these other sciences. For the phenomenologist, underlying biology, psychology, anthropology, and, indeed, all positive sciences is *the experience itself as experienced.* One of Husserl's guiding insights is that just as there are sciences to deal with the things that are experienced, so there ought to be a science that investigates the experience itself. One way of getting a handle on what is going on in a phenomenological approach as distinguished from the approaches of other sciences is by considering the difference between "what" appears and "how" it appears. Of course, as we will see, this distinction between the "what" and the "how"—that which appears and the appearing itself—increasingly becomes a contested issue as phenomenology develops.

Phenomenology is the attempt to make sense—by way of description and analysis—of experiences as they are actually experienced.[2] In this way, phenomenology (as much as possible) tries to offer a first-person account of experience. Instead of the third-person accounts offered by positive sciences that depend on data that is often understood as "objective," "neutral," and "repeatable," phenomenology is informed by the evidence of one's own experience.[3] Central to this idea of experience is what Husserl calls "evidence" [*Evidenz*], which he claims is "in *an extremely broad sense*, an '*experiencing*' of something that is, and is thus; it is precisely a mental seeing of something itself" (Husserl 1999a, 12, emphasis in original). This phenomenological account of evidence is important because it distinguishes between the sort of "data" that would be used in the positive sciences and that which is used in phenomenology. Indeed, Husserl will even use this conception of evidence to articulate what he terms the "principle of all principles," which he defines as follows:

> *Every originary presentive intuition is a legitimizing source of cognition . . . everything originarily* (so to speak, in its "personal" actuality) *offered* to us in "*intuition*" *is to be accepted simply as what it is presented as being,* but *also only within the limits in which it is presented there.* (Husserl 1982, 44, emphasis in original)

Husserl insists that phenomenology must start with what we know by way of intuition or experience. In slightly more phenomenological terminology, we could say that we must take seriously and inquire into things that give/present themselves (or appear) in the very way that they are given/presented (or appear). Husserl's goal to get beyond all assumptions, presuppositions, theoretical frameworks, and metaphysical commitments such that we move "back to the things themselves!" As Husserl says: "Away with empty word analyses! We must question things themselves. Back to experience, to seeing, which alone can give our words sense and rational justification" (1981, 176). To turn to experience is to turn to consciousness. Husserl terms this the "personal character" of consciousness (1975, 26).

Yet how is it that phenomenology allows us to get back to the things themselves (*zu den Sachen Selbst*) and not simply the appearances of those things? Isn't there an insidious appearance/reality distinction operative in phenomenology that would threaten to land Husserl squarely in skepticism? Husserl's answer is "intentionality." Simply put, consciousness is never only a matter of immediate subjective life, but instead describes our relationship to the transcendent world. As Husserl explains, "the stream of consciousness is permeated by the fact that consciousness relates itself to objects" (1975, 18). Or, more famously, "consciousness is always consciousness of something" (1975, 13; 1982, 75). To "intend" something is simply to direct one's consciousness toward it in such a way as to make it the object of thought. So, as I look at the computer screen, the phenomenologist would describe this as "intending" the screen. Importantly, intentionality is not limited to straightforward perception; I can intend something in the mode of *remembering, desiring, hoping*, and so forth. As Husserl explains,

> We must distinguish, in relation to the intentional content taken as object of the act, between *the object as it is intended*, and the *object* (period) *which* is intended. In each act an object is presented as determined in this or that manner, and as such it may be the target of varying intentions, judgmental, emotional, desiderative etc. (Husserl 2001 v.2, 113, emphasis in original)

Nonetheless, in light of this passage, it might seem that all intentionality would yield is the object *as intended* rather than the object *itself*. In response to such a worry, Husserl claims that it is a misunderstanding of intentionality to think that it reintroduces a *representational theory* of perception. According to a representational theory, things in the world affect my cognitive apparatus in such a way as to produce a mental representation of the thing itself, which is then the proper object of consciousness. But, if this is case, then there are two entities, a mental one and one "out there." In contrast, an intentional theory does not introduce this dualism. The computer screen that I intend is the actual computer screen itself and not simply a mental image of it. Husserl speaks of "the *self-appearance*, the *self-exhibiting*, the *self-giving*" of the object to consciousness. He insists that it is "itself there," "immediately intuited" (Husserl 1999a, 57). Yet, this does not mean that all intentional directedness gets everything right about the object itself. Indeed, one's intentional gaze is always limited, and in a number of ways. For the sake of brevity, we will just consider three of them: (1) types of intentionality, (2) adumbrated perspectives, and (3) horizons.

From the beginning of western philosophy, the goal of knowing can be characterized by what medieval philosophers term "*adaequatio intellectus et rei*." Literally translated, the phrase simply means "adequation of the intellect and the thing." According to both Plato and Aristotle, we know something when our understanding of the thing by our intellect is "adequate" to the thing. The more I know about, say, cricket, the more I can be said to have an "adequate" knowledge of it. In this case, "adequate" means something like an "exact equivalence." My intentional relation to what I experience, however, generally does not meet the high standard of adequation. For instance, if I am standing in St Peter's Basilica in Rome, I have a kind of immediacy of experience of what I see and hear. That experience is much superior to having a mere "signative" intention, in which I intend St Peter's by way of a sign, perhaps one that reads "St. Peter's Basilica this way." It is also superior to a postcard showing the façade of St Peter's.

So there are different "levels" of intentionality and this has to do with the notion of *adumbrations*. Let's assume that you are looking at a small statue of Socrates that is sitting on a desk. From one perspective, you can see his face, complete with a prominent brow and full beard. From another perspective, you can see his profile, which allows for a good view of his ear, the shape of his nose, and angle of his neck. From yet another perspective, you can see the back of his head, which is largely bald. Although these are only three perspectives from which one might look at this statue, there are infinitely more perspectives that could be considered: from directly above, from many yards away, while laying down looking up at it, etc. The point is that it is impossible to perceive the statue in its "wholeness," that is, from every perspective at once. All that is ever available is an "adumbrated" perception that necessarily leaves other perspectives out. In this way, we might say that we only get slices of the world at any one time. So this means that the ideal of an *adaequatio intellectus et rei* is only going to be realized to a limited degree (and much of philosophy has debated exactly what those limits are and how significant they turn out to be).

This reference to "at any one time" brings up the other notion of limitation that is important to consider: *horizons*. I do not look at the Socrates statue at just any time in general, but rather only always at a very specific time, which itself stands in relationship to times before and after. Accordingly, consciousness is always temporal. I look at the bottle of water and now at the statue, but remember having looked at the bottle of water. Husserl explains that it is this temporal quality of lived experience (*Erlebnis*) that allows me to always be situated in the "present." The present itself is not a discrete moment unto itself, but is constituted in part by standing in relation to what has gone before and what is yet to come. Husserl describes these temporal aspects as retention and protension (see Husserl 1991). Perhaps the best way of making sense of this is to think of a melody in music. For example, consider the first four notes of Beethoven's Fifth Symphony. The melody itself only occurs *across* the notes—no note, by itself, is sufficient. Yet, even though I hear each note, I hear them as constituting the melody, which is itself a matter of retaining the previous notes (retention) as ordered in expectation of the notes to come (pretension). In addition to this temporal horizon for intentional consciousness, there is also a spatial horizon as well that serves to situate the way in which adumbrations are manifest. For example, I can only perceive the statue of Socrates by standing in some spatial relation to it—near, far, under, over, etc.

Most important, anything that we perceive has a horizon behind it in a general sense. If I perceive the trees out the window, I do so in relation to the sky behind them. Of course, I can change my focus: I can concentrate on the sky instead and then the trees become part of the horizon. All of our perceptions—all thoughts in general—thus, have a kind of horizon to them, which seems innocent enough. Phenomenologists often refer to this as the "as such." For instance, if I see a book on my desk, I see it "as" a book (and as lying on my desk and perhaps "as" something that I've been meaning to read).

Yet this "as such" extends in other kinds of ways. If I see someone who looks or sounds different from me, then I see that person "as" *different*. If that book on my desk is from another time or place or culture, then I may see it "as" *foreign*. Suddenly, the "as such" does not seem quite as innocent—our descriptions seem to convey normative gestures (we will return to the question of the relation between description and normativity in Chapter Eight). Earlier, we noted Husserl's "principle of all principles," which states that phenomena must be accepted simply as they are. Importantly, though, Husserl goes on to add the phrase "but *also only within the limits in which it is presented there*." Exactly what those limits might be is open to question. Are they limits that come from the phenomena that appear to us? Or do we "add" them in such a way that the phenomena cannot really appear exactly as they are? These kinds of questions will become of increasing importance as phenomenology develops. Such questions are particularly significant in that the goal of a phenomeno*logy* is that the "*logos*" by which we make sense of the phenomena is supposed to be provided the phenomenon itself, rather than being superimposed upon it by us. Whether this is actually what happens becomes a matter of significant debate among the new phenomenologists.

While ancient skeptics like Sextus Empiricus might have claimed that the complexities that arise due to our perceptions being shaped by adumbrations and "as such" should invite a skeptical outlook on whether one could ever really know whether one's perceptions were accurate or not, Husserl does not follow this skeptical path. Rather, Husserl suggests that his account of intentionality is able to account for such perspectival and horizontal limitations. Even if my intentional experience of the statue of Socrates occurs now in one way and in a few minutes in a slightly different way, for example I might get up and move around the room, say, it is still the same statue of Socrates that is the object of my intentional consciousness. "*All differences in mode of objective reference*," Husserl notes, "*are descriptive differences in intentional experiences*" (Husserl 2001 v.2, 120, emphasis in original). Yet, I never perceive the statue as only a slice of a statue such that I genuinely wonder if it has a backside and exists in three dimensions, etc. Instead, I perceive it as a complete statue even if I can't ever perceive the completeness itself as part of the perception. My consciousness "fills in" the remainder of the statue that is not presented to consciousness. Husserl distinguishes, therefore, between something that is presented (the particular slice I intend) and something that is co-presented (the other slices that are merely implied).

This idea of co-presentation is important as it relates to the notion of horizon itself. We have already discussed the temporal and spatial horizons that operate in the perception of some object. Yet, as I sit in my office intending the computer screen and the specific words on it, I do not conclude that it is the only object that exists. I intend the screen as internal to the office such that were I to open my office door, it would lead into a hall, which would lead to another door, which would lead outside, which would lead to the campus gates, which would open onto a road that would lead into town, and so on, and so on. If we take this conception of an expansive horizon of objects that are implicitly co-presented along with any specific presented object, then we arrive at what Husserl means by the "world" as itself functioning as a horizon. By "world," Husserl doesn't mean the planet Earth, but instead the totality of all things that serve as the co-presentational context in which anything, in particular, could be presented to consciousness. Hence, things are never perceived in their singularity, but always in the context of the world itself as a horizon of meaning. Summarizing this important perspectivalism of all adumbrated perceptions and horizonally located phenomena, Husserl writes:

> I can change my standpoint in space and time, turn my regard in this or that direction, forwards or backwards in time; I can always obtain new perceptions and presentations, more or less clear and more or less rich in content, or else more or less clear images in which I illustrate to myself intuitively what is possible or likely within the fixed forms of a spatial and temporal world. (Husserl 1982, 53)

It might seem at this point that Husserl is able to overcome the dualism of representationalism only at the cost of presupposing the reality of a mind-independent objectivity—namely, the "world." Yet, such a presupposition would mean that phenomenology is only *relatively* different from other positive sciences, but fails to achieve the presuppositionlessness required if it is to be the "rigorous science" (*strenge Wissenschaft*), which is Husserl's hope for phenomenological philosophy as the *foundation* for all other sciences. Such a reading would be warranted if Husserl is offering a rival metaphysical theory to Cartesian substance dualism, say, but his goal is different.[4] He means to provide an account of how consciousness operates when we attend to experience without any prior commitments that might affect our untrammeled reception of the givenness of phenomena, not simply to offer an account that is different than the accounts already on offer in the history of philosophy. In order to leave the ordinary assumptions that we find ourselves starting from, Husserl stresses the need for a change in our basic orientation or attitude.

Originally, we find ourselves operating according to what Husserl terms the "natural attitude" (see Husserl 1982, 50–7). What he means by this is simply that we make certain kinds of metaphysical assumptions about how things "are." To move to the phenomenological attitude means that we put these assumptions into question. Husserl claims that we need to "bracket" or "suspend" the ordinary way that we relate to the world—namely, as *"simply there for me"* (1982, 50)—and instead to focus on the lived experience of objects as they are given to intentional consciousness, rather than as we might otherwise receive them according to our commonsense assumptions about their existence and constitution. In order to see the world phenomenologically, we "bracket" our assumptions about the natural world and consider the phenomena simply as we experience them.[5]

Husserl uses the term *"epoché"* for this "bracketing" (he also sometimes calls it the "phenomenological reduction," but we will explain why these are not exactly the same thing in what follows). This term is the same used by ancient skeptics to describe the suspension of belief in light of conflicting evidence. So why is Husserl not simply advocating the same thing as the skeptic Sextus? Husserl avoids giving into the skeptical temptation because he claims that the *epoché* does not amount to a denial, or even a doubting, of the actuality of the world, but instead merely a "modification" of the way in which this actuality is taken for granted. It is bracketed precisely in order to make it a matter of phenomenological inquiry itself, as guided by the evidence of experiential intuition and not theoretical assumptions. As Husserl explains:

> We do not give up the positing we effected [in the natural attitude], we do not in any respect alter our conviction [regarding the actuality of reality] which remains in itself as it is

as long as we do not introduce new judgment-motives: precisely this is what we do not do. Nevertheless the positing undergoes a modification: while it in itself remains what it is, *we, so to speak, "put it out of action" we "exclude it," we "parenthesize it."* It is still there, like the parenthesized in the parentheses, like the excluded outside the context of inclusion. (Husserl 1982, 58–9, emphasis in original)

In this sense, Husserl is neither a metaphysical/ontological skeptic (i.e. there is no external reality) nor an epistemic skeptic (even if there is an external reality we can't know it).[6] He does not negate the reality of the world assumed in the natural attitude, but merely claims:

We *put out of action the general positing which belongs to the essence of the natural attitude*; we parenthesize everything which that positing encompasses with respect to being: *thus the whole natural world* which is continually "there for us," "on hand," and which will always remain there according to consciousness as an "actuality" even if we choose to parenthesize it. (Husserl 1982, 61)

Indeed, Husserl goes on to explicitly claim that "I am *not negating* this 'world' as though I were a sophist; I am *not doubting its factual being* as though I were a skeptic" (Husserl 1982, 61). However, it is important not to lump all skeptics together here. Whereas Husserl seems to have in mind modern external-world skepticism, he advocates a method that is quite close to ancient skepticism, as proposed by Sextus. Unlike some modern skeptics, ancient skeptics did not deny or doubt, but simply suspended belief. While Husserl will quickly go beyond where the ancient skeptics were willing to go, when it comes to the *epoché* there is reason to think that the similarities are deeper than the simple usage of a word.[7]

For Husserl, the *epoché* allows for an exclusive focus on the very thing that we earlier saw as problematically forgotten by the positive sciences: *lived experience as experienced*. This is the return to the things "themselves." As Husserl puts it: "*It makes no difference what sort of being we give our object, or with what sense or justification we do so, whether this being is real (*real) *or ideal, genuine,* *possible or impossible, the act remains 'directed upon' its object"* (Husserl 2001 v.2, 120, emphasis in original). Oddly, it is only by bracketing the objective mode of positing essential to the natural attitude that Husserl claims phenomenology can achieve "the pure objectivity of research" (1982, 62). Yet, this need not to seem so odd if we consider the way in which Husserl fleshes out his idea of the phenomenological reduction. It is important to remember that Husserl is aiming at phenomenology as a "rigorous science" and, as such, he claims that his "purpose is to discover a new scientific domain, one that is to be gained *by the method of parenthesizing* which, therefore, must be a definitely restricted one" (1982, 60, emphasis in original). As a result of the *epoché*, phenomenology *"exclude[s] all sciences relating to this natural world"* (1982, 61).

Let's return to our original example in order to get a sense of what is going on here. As you sit in your office looking at the computer with the music playing and the tea steeping, none of the positive sciences "related to this natural world" are able to access the your experience as experienced, but instead assume certain things about your experience as located internal to the mode of positing of the natural attitude: namely, we take for granted the commonsense objectivity of the world itself. Now, having engaged in the *epoché*, such things are no longer taken for granted. Instead, we are left with only that which is given/presented to consciousness (now understood as intentionally related to objects themselves rather than simply to a mental representation of the object). We literally "reduce" the world to that which appears to consciousness in some sense. If we understand the *epoché* to bracket the general mode of positing essential to the natural attitude, then it is the first step in the move toward taking up the phenomenological attitude: once we bracket, we have to engage. In this way, we might think of the *epoché* as the negative moment that sets the stage for the positive moment of walking onto the stage to begin the performance. The complete phenomenological reduction should be understood as involving these two aspects, of which the *epoché* is only the first moment.

Yet, in light of these two dimensions of the reduction, Husserl asks the right question: *"What can remain if the whole world, including ourselves with all our cogitare, is excluded?"* (1982, 63). As a result of the foregoing, Husserl's answer might be guessed at this point: "We shall therefore keep our regard fixed upon the sphere of consciousness and study what we find immanently within it" (1982, 65). The remainder that is left over after the reduction is what Husserl terms the "*phenomenological residuum*," or the "essence of *any consciousness whatever*" (1982, 65). It is important not to miss Husserl's move here. He is not saying that we are inquiring into "my" consciousness, alone, but instead looking to my own consciousness such that it might reveal what is constitutive or essential to consciousness, *as such*. In this way, Husserl's first-person perspective and inquiry opens onto a potential third-person theoretical account. Objectivity becomes possible on the basis of subjectivity. Again, Husserl does not see phenomenology as merely separate from all the other sciences, but as foundational to, or undergirding, them all. Just because we bracket the natural attitude and the mode of inquiry operative therein does not mean that we remain subsequently unable to shift one's focus back to what had been previously excluded. The point is that what was excluded is now better understood and engaged as a result of having been excluded. Husserl notes that "it must be continually borne in mind that all transcendental-phenomenological research is inseparable from undeviating observance of the transcendental reduction, which must not be confounded with the abstractive restricting of anthropological research to purely psychic life" (1999a, 32). Yet he does not think that such anthropological research should be abandoned, but instead undertaken in light of the phenomenological insights that are achieved by phenomenological research. In this way, Husserl offers phenomenology as both *a rigorous science* and also as a *rigorous basis for* the sciences.

Finally, all of these aspects lead us to Husserl's view of subjectivity, intersubjectivity, and objectivity. If there is anything that phenomenology makes clear, it is that the subject and the object go together in such a way that the one cannot even be thought—and certainly not made sense of—without the other. This is a fundamental insight of intentionality. As we have seen, intentionality is the idea that consciousness is always conscious "of" something. Yet there can be no consciousness of something without a subject. Husserl only comes to realize the deep implications of this point over time. In *Ideas I* (German original in 1913; cited as Husserl 1982), he makes the claim that a subject without a world is perfectly imaginable, whereas a world without a subject is simply not. Rather famously, he insists that the world could be annihilated, but the subject's existence *"would not be touched"* (Husserl 1982, 110, emphasis in original). Eventually, though, Husserl came to see that the two are really inseparable and that a third element—other subjects or "intersubjectivity"—was equally indispensable.

In his later philosophy, Husserl has no question that this triad—self, other, and world—always go together, even if working out exactly what that means becomes an abiding and difficult issue. His concept of the "lifeworld" [*Lebenswelt*] increasingly becomes central to his thought. Much of the time Husserl uses the term *Lebenswelt* to denote the prescientific world that surrounds us. Everything in the lifeworld can, of course, be theorized and systematized. But we encounter it on a daily basis in a non-scientific way: it is just there for us, surrounding us at every moment. Yet it is also true that we encounter culture in the lifeworld in the form of traditions, tools, works of art, and architecture. Earlier, we noted that Husserl speaks in terms of the "world," the sum total of all that we encounter. But the lifeworld is an expansion and deepening of this idea. The lifeworld also ultimately includes other consciousnesses or subjectivities, since they likewise constitute the world (or "co-constitute" the world) and are also part of the lifeworld for us. Hence, the lifeworld is deeply intersubjective. Indeed, it is this fundamentally intersubjective aspect of human experience that makes for the "objectivity" of our experience, according to Husserl. Whereas the scientific attitude sees objectivity or normativity in terms of scientific formulae, Husserl thinks it is much more basic than this. Thus, when we say that something is "objectively true," we mean that we all experience it in the same way, which makes it transcendentally true (since it transcends any particular experience). Ultimately, Husserl's overcoming of subjectivism, relativism, and reductionism is because of the intersubjectivity that makes transcendence a reality.

Such is Husserl's mature view, particularly as articulated by texts that were published after Husserl's death. Yet such texts were not widely available until somewhat later and so do not figure nearly as prominently into the "reception history" (i.e. the texts that proved influential) for the new phenomenologists. Thus, some of the questions that Husserl raises—and which he later thinks he has adequately addressed—are ones that are taken up by the new phenomenologists, who are not always fully aware of Husserl's later thought on these issues. The most prominent of these problems concerns the transcendental ego. Earlier, we noted that the world could be annihilated and the subject would be untouched. That subject is what Husserl terms the "transcendental ego," which stands behind all of these various acts of consciousness. Exactly what the status of this ego—or "pure self"—is becomes a topic of considerable discussion in Husserl. But the identity of the ego relates closely to the problem of "otherness," which can be worked out as follows. First, in order for phenomenology to be a truly "transcendental" philosophy (i.e. scientific and systematic), it must be all encompassing. Thus phenomenology must be able to describe the phenomena, as well as provide the very possibility conditions for the appearance of phenomena (not to mention the possibility conditions for the doing of phenomenology).

Second, Husserl's transcendental possibility condition for the appearance of the phenomena is the transcendental ego, which is the unidentified consciousness standing behind all apprehensions of phenomena. But, if the transcendental ego is the possibility condition in the sense of being the horizon and ground of consciousness, then how can any kind of "otherness" be constituted from this perspective? How it is possible for us to encounter another person "as" other, rather than simply another object that has been given to us in consciousness. Essentially, this is a problem of the "as such," since I encounter the other as there "for me" (just like I encounter everything else). Husserl insists that we truly encounter the other in a real way—as opposed to merely experiencing the other by way of analogy (in much the same way as he argues against any kind of picture-theory of knowing). But I never have anything like an experience of the other that is exactly like that I have of myself. Instead, to experience the other "as other" is to have an experience of the limits of my own experience. Early, we noted that intentionality is always limited and this all the more so in our intending human others. For human subjects have a kind of "transcendence" that objects do not have.

As we shall see, the new phenomenologists take up this question of "otherness" in different ways and, even when not explicitly the subject under discussion, it is often in the background. Yet, having considered some of the basic aspects of Husserlian phenomenology, we need to see how Martin Heidegger both continues and develops these aspects.

Phenomenology revised: Heidegger and the "phenomenology of the unapparent"

In many important ways, Heidegger carries on the phenomeno-logical tradition as inaugurated by Husserl. To be sure, Husserl would have preferred a "follower" who would have carried out his project just as he had laid it out. However, Heidegger provides an excellent example of how most phenomenologists—including the new phenomenologists—have both appropriated Husserl (and are so indebted to him that it would be impossible to imagine their thought apart from his) and yet gone their own ways. As we shall see, either to interpret the new phenomenologists as simply a continuation of the Husserlian project or as something altogether different (as some commentators have done) would be a serious mistake.

In *Being and Time* (German original in 1927; cited as Heidegger 2010), Heidegger turns to the question of "being," claiming that it is a basic philosophical question that has been generally forgotten or not appropriately addressed by past philosophers. While the question of being remains the central question for Heidegger in his later thought, our focus here will be on how Heidegger carries on the phenomenological project. In order to see this, we need to turn to the aspects of his thought dealing with (1) intentionality, (2) horizonality or interpretation, and (3) the question/problem of the unapparent.

In redefining the phenomenological method, Heidegger once again restates the formula of *"zu den Sachen selbst"*—to the things themselves. The goal of phenomenology, then, is to get at the phe-nomena themselves. But Heidegger asks: what is a phenomenon? Classically, the term "φαινόμενον" denotes simply that which appears. Yet Heidegger very carefully sorts through various senses of "appearing" and "appearance." A phenomenon, says Heidegger, is not a "seeming" or a "semblance" (in which something only appears to appear); rather it is *"das Sich-an-ihm-selbst-zeigen"*—the showing-itself in itself—or "to let what shows itself be seen from itself, just as it shows itself from itself" (Heidegger 2010, 32). As wordy as that seems, Heidegger is simply trying to empha-size that we actually intend the actual thing that shows itself, not merely some representation of it. Here Heidegger is almost copying

Husserl, who back in 1907, in *The Idea of Phenomenology*, had said: "The meaning of the word 'phenomenon' is twofold because of the essential correlation between *appearing* and *that which appears*" (Husserl 1999b, 69). The alternative to a "phenomenon," then, is "covered-up-ness," which Heidegger calls "*Verdecktheit*."

Once again, then, the goal is to experience the object "just as it is." All of this sounds very good, but then we get to §32 of *Being and Time*, which is all about interpretation. Heidegger tells us that Dasein is the being who *interprets*—in other words, that's just what we *do* as the beings we are. In fact, Heidegger says that "as understanding, Dasein projects its Being upon possibilities" (Heidegger 2010, 144). That means that we always look at things as somehow related to us, as being useful or not useful for our being-in-the-world. Not surprisingly, this raises a kind of question: if the meaning or identity of the thing encountered has much to do (perhaps everything to do?) with our own goals and purposes, then to what extent do we experience it "as it really is"? Whenever we understand or make sense of a thing, says Heidegger, that thing has "the structure of *something as something*": this is the "*als Struktur*" or, simply put, the "as such." Whether it is the identification/interpretation of something *as* a cabbage, *as* a Volkswagen, or *as* a poem by T. S. Eliot, we perceive something "*as*" something. Here we have the notion of the horizon showing up in Heidegger. Moreover, Heidegger makes it clear that we perceive that thing— and interact with it—as it is applicable to our lives. In other words, we don't have anything like hermeneutical neutrality. We know the world in a certain way and it is a way that relates to our interests.

Much like Husserl, Heidegger makes it clear that the world, the other, and oneself (whom he terms "Dasein") go together. Indeed, Dasein is such that it can be described as "being-in-the world" (*Sein-in-der-Welt*). The idea of being-in-the-world can be viewed as a very practical extension of the notions of intentionality and lifeworld. As Heidegger puts it: "Self and world are not two beings, like subject and object, or like I and thou, but self and world are the basic determination of the Dasein itself" (1982, 297). Yet he likewise insists that this very state of being-in-the-world means that "Dasein is essentially *being-with* others *as being-among* intraworldly beings" (1982, 278). So Heidegger likewise sees the three ideas—self, world, other—as essentially going together.[8]

However, it is particularly Heidegger's later philosophy that becomes important for the new phenomenologists. And here it is helpful to turn to Dominique Janicaud's account of the "theological turn" in French phenomenology, which we will consider in detail in Chapter Three. Because new phenomenology has rarely been considered as a coherent philosophical trajectory (and almost never as one continuing classic phenomenology), asking into its origins is not as straightforward as it might seem. Yet Janicaud sees that, while the "turn" begins in the work of Emmanuel Levinas and Michel Henry, it does not have its source there. In order to make sense of the "theological turn," he claims that we need to go back to a different "turn." "Without Heidegger's *Kehre*, there would be no theological turn," says Janicaud (2000, 31). Here Janicaud is referring to the shift in focus that occurs in Heidegger's thought after the publication of *Being and Time* (in 1927) in which Heidegger moves from a consideration of "fundamental ontology" to a focus on language, poetry, and different ways of inhabiting the world and engaging in philosophy (which Heidegger will now term "thinking" [*Denken*]).[9] Heidegger first speaks of this turning or reversal in the "Letter on Humanism" (German original in 1947; cited as in Heidegger 1993), though he affirms that such a turning had already taken place in his thought much earlier (Heidegger 1974, xvi). The result is that *Being and Time* and with various lecture courses that he gave at the time are often classified as "Heidegger I," with texts from roughly the mid-1930s onward being grouped together as "Heidegger II." Despite pointing to Heidegger's *Kehre* as offering the central gestures that give rise to the "theological turn," Janicaud continues, "this affirmation is not a legitimation" (2000, 31). For Janicaud, Heidegger clears the ground upon which Levinas and Henry begin to build the new (and for Janicaud, *non-*) phenomenological edifice. The central move that Heidegger makes in this regard is his embrace of the notion of a "phenomenology of the unapparent" (*Phänomenologie des Unscheinbaren*).[10]

This specific phrasing shows up quite late in Heidegger's work—namely, in the 1973 Zähringen seminars—and, given that this is a full decade after the publication of Michel Henry's *L'essence de la manifestation* (French original in 1963) and Emmanuel Levinas's *Totalité et infini* (French original in 1961), it might seem odd to suggest that it is the idea that undergirds both books. Janicaud's attribution of such influence arises from his contention that the

Phenomenology of unapparent

philosophical gesture that the specific phrase, "phenomenology of the unapparent," attempts to name, goes back much further to Heidegger's *Kehre* itself as begun in the 1930s. "Can it be denied," Janicaud rhetorically asks, "that Heidegger's 'turn' was conditioned by his quest for the Sacred, through his reinterpretation of Hölderlin?" (2000, 31). While we do think that such a "condition" could be challenged, what is important is to see that, for Janicaud, there is an essential connection between the "unapparent" and the "Sacred" as it gets worked out in Heidegger's philosophy. It is the "quest for the Sacred," which Janicaud takes to be definitive of the *Kehre*, that he views as the central component of the Heideggerian notion of the "phenomenology of the unapparent" and, as such, it is this link that allows Janicaud to claim that without the Heideggerian *Kehre* there would be no "theological turn" in Levinas and Henry. This is a strong claim and worth considering in detail. Accordingly, let's look at Heidegger's 1973 seminar as a way of moving backward to the thought that conditioned it in order to then move forward to the thought that Janicaud claims it to have so decidedly influenced.

The opening questions of the Zähringen seminar are raised by Jean Beaufret:

1 To what extent can it be said that there is no question of Being in Husserl?[11]

2 In what sense is Heidegger able to call his analysis of environment an "essential gain" and yet claim elsewhere that it "remains of subordinate significance"? (Heidegger 2003, 64)

Heidegger deals with the second question in order to then move on to the first. His explanation of this seeming paradox in his thought hinges on the important distinction between means and ends. He explains that, although his conception of "being-in-the-world" is "discovered as the primary and irreducible fact, always already given, and thus radically 'prior' to any conception of consciousness" (Heidegger 2003, 64), it is only offered as a way of getting at the "guiding aim" of *Being and Time*: to "work out the question of the meaning of being and *to do so concretely*" (Heidegger 2010, xxix, emphasis added). In other words, while the goal of *Being and*

Time is an understanding the (question of the) meaning of being itself, the means to this goal is an analysis of Dasein. In response to Beaufret's question, then, Heidegger makes clear that the project in *Being and Time* "is only the 'concrete' way of approaching the project itself. As such, the project includes this analysis as nothing more than a means, which remains subordinate in relation to the project," more broadly construed (2003, 64). The central concern for the "question of Being" pushes against concretion when understood as an end in itself. It is important to remember that Heidegger originally planned an all-important part 3 of *Being and Time*, which was supposed to stand as the "end" toward which the "means" of part 1 and part 2 were aiming.[12] Accordingly, Heidegger uses this explanation to pivot from the notion of environment in his own thinking to Beaufret's first question about Husserl's apparent disregard for the "question of being." In order to understand the context in which Heidegger's reference to a "phenomenology of the unapparent" occurs, it is important to engage in a short excursus dealing with Heidegger's reading of Husserl offered in that seminar as a response to Beaufret's question.

The interpretation that Heidegger offers of Husserl in this seminar is quite revealing of both how Heidegger took Husserl's thought to run into problematic limits that needed to be superseded and also how Heidegger viewed the task of phenomenology more generally (at least within his later thought). It is in light of these two conceptions that we can begin to understand Heidegger's *Kehre* more broadly and, more importantly for our purposes here, the possible link between it and the new phenomenology as concerns the limits and possibilities of phenomenology itself. For Heidegger, Husserl's consideration of "the question of being" is answered differently depending on what one takes the "question of being" to mean. If it is understood, quite technically, according to Heidegger's own rubric—namely, as "the question concerning the truth of being," which entails that the "question of being" itself "can no longer be taken as a metaphysical question"—then "there is no question of being in Husserl" (Heidegger 2003, 64–5). Heidegger's explains that, for Husserl, the central questions and problems of phenomenology are "more strictly metaphysical" than ontological (2003, 65), and as an example of this metaphysical focus, Heidegger offers Husserl's *Logical Investigations VI*. Thus, on Heidegger's account, Husserl is not really interested in being per se. Despite Husserl's failure to consider the "truth of being" in the sense understood by Heidegger, Heidegger suggests that Husserl "touches upon or struggles" with the question of being in the second section of *Logical Investigations VI* when he works through the idea of a "categorial intuition" (2003, 65). A brief consideration of Husserl's complicated discussion of this idea is warranted, here, because it will bear heavily on what follows.

Husserlian "categorial intuitions"

In chapter 6 of *Investigation VI*, titled "Sensuous and Categorial Intuitions," Husserl begins by asking how it is possible to understand meaning when applied to a total perceptual statement. As Husserl explains:

> If a man thinks the fulfillment of nominal meanings clear enough, we shall ask him how we are to understand the fulfillment of total statements, especially as regards that side of them that stretches beyond their "matter," in this case beyond their nominal terms. What may and can furnish fulfillment for those aspects of meaning which make up propositional form as such, the aspects of *"categorial form"* to which, e.g., the copula belongs? (Husserl 2001 v.2, 271)

Notice, here, that Husserl is questioning into the way meaning shows up in total statements "beyond their nominal terms." Husserl's way of expressing this "beyond" is quite telling. His concern is with "that side of them that stretches beyond their 'matter.'" Attempting to dislodge those accounts of meaning that suggest meaning "has its seat in perception" (2001 v.2, 272), Husserl suggests that when considering predication, universals, and being, we find that a "mirror-like" relationship between perception and meaning fails to be adequate (2001 v.2, 273–5). "We need only earnestly ponder what things can be possible matter for perception," Husserl writes, "and what things possible matter for meaning, to become aware that, *in the mere form of a judgment, only certain antecedently specifiable parts of our statement can have something which corresponds to them in intuition, while to other parts of the statement nothing intuitive possibly can correspond"* (2001 v.2, 275, emphasis in original). Attempting to explain this gap between form and matter, Husserl turns to being. Allow us to quote from him at length here in order to get the full shape of his argument:

> The form-giving flexion *Being*, whether in its attributive or predicative function, is not fulfilled, as we said, in any percept. We here remember Kant's dictum: *Being is no real predicate.* This dictum refers to being *qua* existence, or to what Herbart called the being of "absolute position," but it can be taken to be no less applicable to predicative and attributive being. In any case it precisely refers to what we are here trying to make clear. I can see colour, but not *being*-coloured. I can feel smoothness, but not *being*-smooth. I can hear a sound, but not that something *is* sounding. Being is nothing *in* the object, no part of it, no moment tenanting it, no quality or intensity of it, no figure of it or no internal form whatsoever, no constitutive feature of it however conceived. But being is also nothing attaching *to* an object: as it is no real (*reales*) internal feature, so also it is no real external feature, and therefore not, in the *real* sense, a "feature" at all. For it has nothing to do with the *real* forms of unity which bind objects into more comprehensive objects, tones into harmonies, things into more comprehensive things or arrangements of things (gardens, streets, the phenomenal external world). On these real forms of unity the external features of objects, the right and the left, the high and the low, the loud and the soft etc., are founded. Among these anything like an "is" is naturally not to be found. (Husserl 2001 v.2, 277)

In light of being's going "beyond" matter, sensuous intuition, and percept, Husserl concludes that "we are at once saying and maintaining *that being is absolutely imperceptible*" (2001 v.2, 277). And yet, even though being does not appear such that intentional consciousness could take it up as an object as such, it still *means* something and we understand its meaning such that we express it in our language. Accordingly, Husserl suggests that we need to expand our conceptions of perception and intuition in order to try and make sense of how this meaning is possible. Hence,

Husserl differentiates between a "narrow" and a "wide" notion of sense-perception.

According to a "very narrow concept of perception," we perceive as objective only that which we see with our eyes and hear with our ears, etc. But, if we widen our notion so that it is "suitable, so as to include 'inner perception',," then we allow for the sphere of objectivity to include not only external objects, but also "inner objects, the ego and its internal experiences" (2001 v.2, 277–8). On the other side of the *epoché*, the focus is simply on that which is immanent to conscious experience. As such, it is entirely possible to experience oneself thinking about one's experience as the object of experience itself. Said a bit more simply, we can think about our thinking about something. Nonetheless, even on such a widened conception of sense-perception, we can clearly see that "a meaning like that of the word 'being' can find no possible *objective correlate*, and so no possible fulfillment in the acts of such perception" (2001 v.2, 278). In other words, even if we, following John Locke, begin to look to an "inner sense" for the "surplus of meaning" inherent in the form that "remains over" (2001 v.2, 273) and above the appearance available "in the sphere of real objects" (2001 v.2, 278), we will continue to search in vain. There is no thing in outer sense or inner sense that corresponds to being. It is for this reason that Husserl claims that "being is not a judgment nor a constituent of a judgment" (2001 v.2, 278). "Being is as little a real constituent of some inner object as it is of some outer object," he continues (2001 v.2, 278). Yet, if Husserl is right to say that the only objects in which the phenomenologist is interested are those that, in some sense, appear to consciousness, and the only meaning available within a phenomenological framework is that which is rooted in lived experience, then what are we to make of being, especially as expressed in the copula ("x *is* y")? To what does the "is" refer here such that it could be available for phenomenological inquiry?

It might be tempting, thereby, to conclude that the copula is either simply meaningless or somehow mystical due to the lack of a straightforward intentional objective correlate. Similar to his resistance to skeptical and sophistic worries elsewhere, Husserl does not give into either a nihilistic or mystical temptation here. Rather, he suggests that the key to understanding states of affairs expressed in predicative statements (e.g. "The car is red," "This book is too long," etc.) is to realize that they are "self-given" in the fulfillments of judgments themselves. But what does that mean? Here, Husserl's argument is offered by analogy: *"As the sensible object stands to sense-perception so the state of affairs stands to the 'becoming aware' in which it is . . . given"* (2001 v.2, 279, emphasis in original). In both cases, givenness is the crucial aspect and it is in this respect that Husserl goes beyond Immanuel Kant's account in the *Critique of Pure Reason*, which rejects self-givenness in favor of deduction. Yet Husserl recognizes that, just as with any other concept or idea, the concept of being "can arise only when some being, actual or imaginary, is set before" us (2001 v.2, 279). In other words, Husserl remains true to his phenomenological convictions: it is only as presented/given that something can become available for phenomenological study and explanation. Accordingly, if being "is taken to mean predicative being, some state of affairs must be given to us, and this by way of an act which gives it, an analogue of common sensuous intuition" (2001 v.2, 279–80). However, we are now in need of a way of distinguishing between that which is presented in sensuous intuition and those intuitions that are "supersensuous" (as would be the case in states of affairs expressed in copulas that lack objective correlates in even a wide conception of sense-perception). In response, Husserl says that we must be able to "draw a quite general distinction between sensuous and categorial intuition" (2001, 281). It is only if the latter is possible that we could account for the meaning expressed in the fulfillment of total statements (rather than merely nominal ones).

At this point, Husserl again introduces a narrow/wide distinction, but this time it is not offered *internal to* sense-perception, but as a way of *distinguishing between* sensuous percepts on the one hand and supersensuous (or categorial) percepts on the other hand. This allows Husserl to describe the difference between these two types of perceptual objects as a difference between reality and ideality: "Sensuous or real objects can . . . be characterized as *objects of the lowest level of possible intuition,* categorial or ideal objects *as objects of higher levels*" (2001 v.2, 282, emphasis in original). Whereas real objects are "perceived in a straightforward *(schlichter)* manner" as immediately given, ideal objects are relational insofar as they are "founded" on "other acts" that allow for the givenness of a higher level objectivity (2001 v.2, 282). These new, higher level, objects are *"related to what appears in the basic acts"* and, as such, *"can only show themselves 'in person' in such founded acts"* (2001, 283, emphasis in original). However, they show themselves as the condition of the very appearance of the basic acts themselves. We might say, then, that although the order of discovery locates higher objects as derivative of, or built upon, the lower level objects, at the level of being, the higher objects allow for the lower objects to show themselves. Hence, from start to finish, Husserl's commitment to the centrality of the self-showing of that which shows itself to consciousness remains in place.

Heidegger on Husserl in 1973

At this point, let's return to Heidegger's reading of Husserl's account of categorial intuitions. It is easy to see why Heidegger would turn to this section of the *Logical Investigations* in order to respond to the question of whether Husserl was concerned with the "question of being." Husserl's account of that which emerges as self-given only as in relation to that which is immediately given in sensuous perception bears a striking resemblance to Heidegger's own suggestion of the ontological difference: namely, that "the being of being 'is' itself not a being" (Heidegger 2010, 5). Heidegger admits of such a resemblance, but in a way that still allows him to distinguish his thought from that of Husserl. Claiming that Husserl's "decisive discovery" is located in the categorial intuition, Heidegger also locates therein Husserl's "fundamental difficulty" (Heidegger 2003, 66). By distinguishing between the sensuous percept and the supersensuous percept, or as Heidegger will say, between the "substantiality" of what appears and simply the appearance itself, or, in language more appropriate to new phenomenologists such as Henry and Marion, between the phenomenality of that which appears as phenomena, Husserl allows for the "non-appearance" of substantiality to "enable what appears to appear" (Heidegger 2003, 67). Upon recognizing this relationship of the unapparent to appearance, Heidegger then claims the following: "In this sense, one can even say that [the non-appearance of substantiality] is more apparent than what itself appears" (2003, 67). On Heidegger's reading of Husserl, the notion of categorial intuitions demonstrates that the givenness of the unapparent is what conditions the givenness of that which appears.

According to Heidegger, the radicality of Husserl's thought shows up in this realization. When Husserl goes beyond Kant by freeing "being from its attachment to judgment," Heidegger claims that "the entire field of investigation is re-oriented" (2003, 67). This is a big deal and it is important to clearly understand what is going on here. Echoing Husserl's own references to going "beyond nominal terms," Heidegger formulates the key upshot of categorial intuition as a conditional claim: "*If* I pose the question of the meaning of being . . . [*then*] I must already be beyond being, understood as the being of beings. More precisely still: in the question concerning the meaning of being, what I ask about is being" (2003, 67, emphasis added). "Husserl's achievement," says Heidegger, "consists in just this making present of being, which is phenomenally present in the category" (2003, 67). Husserl's "decisive discovery," then, is that "being is no mere concept, no pure abstraction arising by way of deduction" (2003, 67). Heidegger's point is that Husserl understood that being is not an empty transcendental category that was achieved through asking into the conditions of possibility of experience, but instead is the ontological substrate for all that "is" insofar as being is always the being *of* a being. It is for this reason that Husserl avoids the Kantian conclusion that "being is not a real predicate." Husserl understood that being changes everything, as it were, *not* as a conceptual overlay, but rather as a constitutive dimension.

Unfortunately, however, according to Heidegger, Husserl does not go any further than to arrive at this realization. Husserl does not subsequently inquire into the meaning of being itself as would be required in order to lay out the ontological stakes of phenomenality. Indeed, says Heidegger, "there was not the slightest possibility of a question" of the meaning of being, "since for [Husserl] it goes without saying that 'being' means being-object" (2003, 67). In other words, on Heidegger's reading, Husserl was content to understand being as simply the supersensuous objectivity, as it were, of what gives itself to consciousness. So, although Husserl clears the space for an overcoming of the metaphysically formulated history of ontology, he remains firmly situated internal to this history *as metaphysical* because he does not inquire into the *meaning* of being (Heidegger 2003, 68). Heidegger takes his own key advance over Husserl to occur in his movement away from consciousness and toward Dasein such that "being-there" is now situated "in-the-world" as an ontological constitution of Dasein's ontic existence. Yet this seems to imply that Heidegger was not absolutely committed to the centrality of the *epoché* to phenomenology itself. In fact, in an honest admission, Heidegger claims that in *Being and Time* "consciousness is plain and simply set aside," and he notes that "for Husserl this was a pure scandal!" (2003, 68).

Heidegger sees *Being and Time* as scandalous to Husserlian phenomenology because therein he goes beyond the limitations of consciousness, which amounts to going beyond the sphere of pure immanence. Now, one might suppose that the Husserlian focus on intentionality already takes a significant step in the direction of rupturing the confines of consciousness in such ways. However, since the intentional object is still one located in consciousness, "Husserl remains trapped in immanence" (Heidegger 2003, 70). Alternatively, "in *Being and Time*," Heidegger notes, "the 'thing' has its place no longer in consciousness, but in the world (which again is itself not immanent to consciousness)" (2003, 70). Here we can again see the two guiding questions of the Zähringen seminars to be intimately connected: it is by going through (i.e. understanding it as a means) the notion of environment, of being-in-the-world, that we arrive at a way of renewing the meaning of the question of being in a way that Husserl was unable to achieve because of his unwavering commitment to the singular concern for consciousness and, thereby, his decidedly metaphysical entrapment in immanence. Heidegger says that, like a Leibnizian monad, the Husserlian *ego cogito* is "an enclosed space" and, thus, without exit from itself (2003, 70). Heidegger suggests that by focusing singularly on the phenomenological residuum as the only proper focus of phenomenological inquiry, Husserl forgets the contextuality and historicity of existing individuals. An alternative starting point is required and, for Heidegger, this alternative is, again, what Heidegger names "Dasein." Unlike the meaning of being internal to the *ego cogito*— that is, *being-in-consciousness (Bewusst-sein)*—Dasein expresses a *"being-outside-of"* (2003, 71). Hence, Heidegger explains that in his early thought, Dasein is described as having the mode of being of *ek-stasis* (i.e. a standing out from). And, in this way, he overcomes ruptures the purity of immanence by asserting the transcendence of Dasein itself. Or, in the vocabulary of Heidegger's later work: Dasein is in the mode of "instancy in the clearing

[*Inständigkeit in der Lichtung*]" (2003, 71). "Immanence, here, is broken through and through," Heidegger explains (2003, 71).

Questions remain, however: What exactly is this "clearing"? And how are we to gain entry to it? Heidegger's answer is that we must return to the beginning—that is, we must "*turn towards Parmenides*" (2003, 77). Reflecting on Parmenides's answer to the question, "what is?" with the statement, "Being namely is" (ἐστι γάρ εἶναι), Heidegger claims to have been "ensnared" in this passage "for a long time," which is certainly understandable given that it might seem to demonstrate why philosophers are often considered a bit strange (2003, 79). In Heidegger's characteristic, even if occasionally problematic, mode of interpreting Greek philosophy, he says that the Greek phrase is better understood as "presencing namely presences" [*anwest nämlich Anwesen*] (2003, 79). Of course, one might quickly protest that surely a long ensnarment in Parmenides's claim could yield a more understandable philosophical explanation. Nonetheless, while noting the tautological dimension of this way of rendering the passage, Heidegger makes the rather odd claim: "We are here in the domain of the inapparent: presencing itself presences" (2003, 79). It is appropriate to ask, here, why this tautological thought opens us onto the inapparent and not simply onto linguistic incoherence.

It seems at least plausible, in light of Rudolf Carnap's understandable frustration with Heidegger's phrase "the nothing itself nothings" (*Das Nichts selbst nichtet*), to suggest that Heidegger's alternative translation of this Parmenidean fragment simply makes it either meaningless or nonsensical. However, to be charitable to Heidegger, we propose that Heidegger's interpretation of this phrase is best understood as an expression of his belief that truth is not a correspondence between a sentence and a mind-independent reality, or a coherence of a sentence with the set of sentences affirmed to be true by a community, etc., but instead is a *revealing*, or *disclosure*, or *unconcealing* of that which shows itself (*aletheia*). Accordingly, the truth of being is the very unconcealment of what is revealed. But, drawing on Heidegger's consideration of "eventuation" (*das Ereignis*) in his book, *Contributions to Philosophy* (Heidegger 1999), this unconcealment is not simply a noun, but more of a verbal happening. As a happening, this truth is not a thing that occurs internal to being, but instead being happens in truth: *presencing presences.*

Here, then, we find Heidegger's alternative to Husserl's categorial intuition. Whereas Husserl turned to the beyond being in order to explain that which "is," he did so according to the categories of the being of being—that is, metaphysics. Alternatively, Heidegger's late thought is a sustained attempt to talk about the beyond in a way that is not pulled back into the vocabulary and, hence, conceptuality, that is anathema to its very excessiveness. In other words, Heidegger (re)turns to Parmenides in order to think differently about the truth of being by making different decisions than those made in the metaphysical history of philosophy. Rather than making being an object (whether intentional or not) grasped by the *ego cogito*, Heidegger attempts to think things differently by forcing the copula into a tautology ("x is x"). Yet this "tautological thinking" (2003, 80) does not lead to triviality, but rather to the *depth* of being itself as unconcealment. Rather than starting to think by looking at appearance, Heidegger says that we should tarry with that which doesn't appear—namely, the *presencing* of what is presented, rather than that which is presented. In this way, as we saw earlier in Husserl, we shift registers from a "what" to a "how," but now the shift is one from a metaphysical to ontological framework as distinguished from Husserl's shift from the natural attitude to the phenomenological attitude. As such, Heidegger's Parmenides is a thinker who thinks prior to metaphysics rather than inaugurating metaphysical thinking. Dasein's mode of being as standing in the clearing is now understandable as a being-receptive to the happening of the truth of being. This mode is a dispositional openness-to rather than a concept derived taking-possession-of. It is the willingness to "allow" being to provide its own meaning in a deeply phenomenological sense. For Heidegger, this announces a distinction between Husserl's scientific "method" (even if distinguished from other positive sciences) and the philosophical "path" that Husserl opened, but did not adequately follow (2003, 80).

All of this has significant implications for the very conception of phenomenology. Heidegger seeks to overcome the Husserlian supposition that phenomenology should be understood as a presuppositionless "rigorous science." Instead, Heidegger's wants to go beyond the conscious, intentional sphere of phenomenological immanence. He does this first with *being-in-the-world,* in which Dasein goes together with a world in a way that goes beyond intentionality. Then, with the notions of *the clearing* and *the event* accessed by tautological thinking, he announces a different approach to phenomenology itself. It is here that we arrive at Heidegger's all-important claim: "phenomenology is a path that leads away to come before . . ., and it lets that before which it is led show itself. *This phenomenology is a phenomenology of the inapparent*" (2003, 80, emphasis added). Phenomenology, at its root, is for Heidegger an inquiry into appearance in such a radical way that it begins with a receptivity to the inapparent insofar as it allows for the apparent to then be considered according to the categories of being. *Phenomenology is not merely about phenomena, but ultimately about phenomenality itself.* Although Husserl opened the door for such a claim, Heidegger's concern is then to try to walk through it. Yet it is the new phenomenologists, in particular, who fully follow the phenomenological path in order to see where it might lead in this regard. Developing on Heidegger's attempt to find the unthought in the history of thought, the new phenomenologists, albeit controversially, attempt to make visible that which might otherwise have simply been ignored or passed over as invisible. As Marion explains:

> In its movement of expansion . . . phenomenology does not cease to give rise to new fields of research for phenomenality, so as to place phenomena within it permanently that no eye has yet constituted, let alone seen. Its legitimacy consists entirely in this work of bringing into visibility what would have remained unseen and considered invisible without it and its effort. (Marion 2012, 19)

In the next chapter, we will look at the new phenomenologists who all walk through this door in a variety of ways as they inherent both Husserl's account of phenomenology and Heidegger's critical radicalization of it.

CHAPTER TWO

How to be a phenomenological heretic: The origins and development of new phenomenology

Introduction

Let us begin our consideration of the new phenomenologists by recounting an event that took place at Villanova University in 1997. It is a brief exchange between two of the new phenomenologists, Jacques Derrida and Jean-Luc Marion. Despite its brevity, it reveals something important about how new phenomenology, at least potentially, differs from classical phenomenology.

Jacques Derrida: Then you would dissociate what you call phenomenology from the authority of the as such? If you do that, it would be the first heresy in phenomenology. Phenomenology without as such!

Jean-Luc Marion: Not my first, no! I said to Levinas some years ago that in fact the last step for a real phenomenology would be to give up the concept of horizon. Levinas answered me immediately: "Without horizon there is no phenomenology." And I boldly assume he was wrong.

Derrida: I am also for the suspension of the horizon, but, for that very reason, by saying so, I am not a phenomenologist anymore. I am very true to phenomenology, but when I agree on the necessity of suspending the horizon, then I am no longer a phenomenologist. So the problem remains if you give up the as such, what is the use that you can make of the word phenomenology? That is the problem for me. (Derrida et al. 1999, 66)

In Chapter One, we considered the notion of horizon and the role it plays in phenomenology. We saw that, when we experience something, we always do so in a particular way, from a certain perspective. To be sure, we can change our perspectives to greater or lesser degrees, at least in many cases. Indeed, Husserl thinks that multiplicity of perspectives is what helps us get at truth: we can see things from different angles and put these perspectives together to form a more coherent whole. Yet what else might be at stake in the phenomenological "as such" such that the "suspension" of the horizon would seem to count as phenomenological "heresy"? Although we will be discussing this "as such" quite at length in this chapter, we have seen in Chapter One that it is something like a "point of view" or "the way in which something is seen or interpreted" or "how something or someone appears."

If you know anything about the two persons in this dialogue, then you might know that both of them are more than a little unorthodox in terms of their views regarding phenomenology—or, at least, such is how they have often been interpreted. For instance, Derrida has often been seen as doing everything *but* phenomenology—and even in this passage he admits that often he seems to go beyond phenomenology in specific ways at various points in his authorship. Accordingly, some might take what he does to be a kind of counter-phenomenology or even anti-phenomenology. Of course, Derrida has also often been accused of being a nihilist or a relativist or some other bad sort of thing. Yet, if one reads Derrida carefully, it becomes clear that such charges are ungrounded and that Derrida specifically denies them.[1] Alternatively, to be sure, Jean-Luc Marion is considered to be much more "traditional" in many ways, but his phenomenological views are significantly different from those of Husserl and, in this sense, his views would certainly not be considered "orthodox." Note that we get the term "orthodox" from the Greek term "*orthos*," meaning straight, right, or true, and "*doxa*," meaning belief or opinion. Someone who is orthodox holds to the "true" belief. More originally, orthodoxy had to do with praise or worship, so it designated right worship or proper praise. With this in mind, its opposite was taken to be "heterodoxy," a word composed of "*heter*" (i.e. "other") and "*doxa*." Thus, to be a "heretic" means to have an "untrue" belief.

For the new phenomenologists, it is this very question of phenomenological orthodoxy that needs to be put into question *itself*. Neither Derrida nor Marion is willing simply to write himself off as a phenomenological "heretic" such that he fails to be a phenomenologist. Indeed, they would insist on seeing themselves as—in important respects—*more* true to phenomenology than Husserl or Heidegger. As we will see throughout this book, the new phenomenologists generally "innovate" in the name of orthodoxy: they claim that *their* ways of reframing phenomenology are really more "orthodox" (true belief) than the "orthodoxy" assumed to be authoritative in the phenomenological tradition. So the fundamental question for any student of new phenomenology is: who really has the "right" version of phenomenology and who is really the "heretic"? Could it be possible that Derrida is *wrong* when he accuses Marion of being a phenomenological heretic? Or, alternatively, is Husserl the real heretic? The new phenomenologists are themselves frequently at odds, both with Husserl and with one another, on the question of the specific ways this orthodoxy should be worked out. As mentioned in the introduction to this book, our suggestion is that there are important points of resonance among all of the new phenomenologists concerning the question of the areas in which phenomenology should rightly be pushed up against traditional limits. However, inquiring into how exactly those limits are articulated, questioned, and occasionally trespassed by the various new phenomenologists reveals a complex discussion rather than a monolithic homogeneity. It is for this reason that we have defined new phenomenology as a particular philosophical trajectory, rather than a school or movement from which one might expect doctrinal purity.

Ultimately, the question about orthodoxy in phenomenology comes down to the question of whether there could be anything like phenomenology—let alone thought in general—*without the "as such."* Put even more pointedly: can such a version of phenomenology be formulated or even thought? The new phenomenologists think, albeit in different ways, that it can. Questions of orthodoxy, of course, are not new. Dominique Janicaud's text *The Theological Turn in French Phenomenology*, which we will consider at length in the next chapter, criticizes people like Marion for "hijacking" phenomenology by turning it into something like a covert theology and thus "distorting" phenomenology. What Janicaud assumes is that phenomenology is properly characterized by a kind of objective neutrality and that, consequently, these various folks like Emmanuel Levinas, Marion, Michel Henry, and Jean-Louis Chrétien have departed from phenomenological orthodoxy (Janicaud 2000). Yet Janicaud's assumption that phenomenology is a stable designator for a very specific (Husserlian) methodology that yields a very determinate (theologically neutral) content is itself open to question, as will soon become evident.

Phenomenological orthodoxy: Immanuel Kant (1724–1804)

Given what we have seen regarding Husserl in Chapter One, it would seem that he would be the logical place to start in order to determine what counts as phenomenological orthodoxy. Of course, Husserl himself sees even such philosophers as René Descartes and David Hume as anticipating phenomenology. More specifically, Husserl sees Kant as having discovered the notion of the phenomenon, at least in modern philosophy. We have already seen that the term "phenomenon" [φαινόμενον] is an ancient Greek term. Still, Husserl sees Kant as being the first to employ this as a distinctly philosophical term. Moreover, Husserl contends that "the transcendental deduction in the first edition of the *Kritik der reinen Vernunft* [*Critique of Pure Reason*] was actually operating inside the realm of phenomenology" (Husserl 1982, §61, 118–19).

According to Husserl, Kant goes wrong by interpreting the realm of the phenomenon in a psychologistic way, in the sense that Kant only sees the phenomenon as an object of a psychological act and not an object in its own right.[2] While the early Husserl embraced such "psychologism" (see Husserl 2003), by the time of the *Logical Investigations* (published in 1900–1; cited as Husserl 1970b), he no longer does, and, in response to Gottlob Frege, he even provides a substantial refutation of all such views.

In light of this genealogy claimed by Husserl, it should come as no surprise that Marion goes back to Kant's *Critique of Pure Reason* as a fundamental wellspring for phenomenology, in which Kant actually speaks of "phenomena" (which, for a rough and ready definition, is anything that appears). Yet Marion thinks that Kant sets things up so that the subject is in absolute control of how exactly the phenomenon *can* appear. Consider what Kant says: "What agrees (in terms of intuition and concepts) with the formal conditions of experience is *possible*" (Kant 1996, 283; A218/B265). At issue here is "phenomenality": what does it mean for an object to appear or what is the status of such appearance? In effect, Kant says that the subject to whom a phenomenon appears makes something possible or impossible. Thus, Kant's claim is quite strong: something that does not appear not only *is not* but is likewise not *possible*. Unless it appears to *me* (or else to Kant or anyone reading this book) something is not and is not possible. Suddenly the *I* becomes very important in constituting the world. To put this point another way, the *I* is the *source* of the "as such," since the *I* is a necessary condition of appearance.

One way of working out what it means for the *I* to be the source of the "as such" is accomplished by examining Kant's notion of *judgment*. For Kant, there are two sorts of judgments—determinant and reflective. A determinant judgment is the subsumption of a particular under a universal (such as a rule or principle); this is simply the movement of applying something that already exists. For instance, I see an orange and I see it *as* an orange, which means that I see it *as* something to eat and *as* something sweet, among other things. We make these kinds of judgments all the time simply by perceiving things "as" *this* sort of thing, as opposed to some other sort of thing. In other words, we always perceive things *as such*. But what makes such judgments possible? As it turns out, determinant judgment requires there to be a prior reflective judgment: the finding of the universal under which the particular may be subsumed (Kant 1987, 19). According to Kant, what this requires is a grasp of the purposiveness of things and, ultimately, nature in general (1987, 20). To make a reflective judgment about an orange, for instance, could involve perceiving that it is a sweet thing to eat. And it is not just human beings that make that kind of judgment: so do other beings. Reflective judgments are clearly the most important of the two sorts of judgments. Indeed, according to Kant, this purposiveness is *not in things themselves* but only in a principle gained by reflective judgment. We are only able to see the orange *as* something sweet to eat by way of such a judgment. Moreover, this type of judgment allows us not merely to make sense of the world (which is necessary even for the lowest level of perception) but to place values on it: reflective judgments are always *evaluative* in nature.

In considering the subject as the maker of determinant and reflective judgments, Kant does at least two things at once. First, he clearly privileges the subject: the subject is central to how the world gets constituted and how objects are described. In effect, Descartes's *ego cogito* becomes the transcendental *I*—in practice, this means that an object is defined in terms of time and space, Kant's famous "categories" that allow us to determine objects as particular sorts of objects, and even in terms of causality, the notion of which resides—once again—in the subject (and not somewhere in the world as understood as a domain beyond, or over and against, the self). Put bluntly: there is no time, space, or causality "out there" in the world; instead, they are in our minds—we see the world *as* caused, temporal, and spatial. Second, in effect Kant creates the idea of the "object" as object to my subject: the object cannot *be* without me as subject. It's not hard to see that the object ends up playing second fiddle to the subject, since all objects are "subject" to the subject.

Beyond phenomenological orthodoxy: Hans-Georg Gadamer (1900–2002)

It is partly in response to such a Kantian view that both Husserl and Heidegger emphasize going back to the things themselves and allowing the *logos* for a phenomenon to come from the phenomenon itself rather than from the subject. We have seen in Chapter One that each of these thinkers continually attempts to have a kind of access to these things without something interfering and "affecting" that access. Here it is helpful to pause to consider a phenomenologist and a student of both Husserl and Heidegger, Hans-Georg Gadamer, who is primarily known for his work in philosophical hermeneutics, but who does quite a bit of work thinking through the stakes of mediated experience. For Gadamer has some helpful things to say about "preconceptions" [*Vorurteilen*]—or, to use an ugly word, "prejudices." Gadamer begins with the idea that our relation to experience is mediated hermeneutically. In other words, we know the world in a mediated way—mediated by language, concepts, and culture. Indeed, how would it be possible to have an experience of anything *without* it being hermeneutically mediated? We can get at this point by quoting Paul Ricoeur, who writes:

> The most serious difficulties are not those that could be associated with the theme of intentionality. . . . The biggest difficulty according to which a phenomenology of religion must be assessed lies elsewhere. It concerns the status of *immediacy* that could be claimed by the dispositions and feelings allied with the call-and-response structure in a religious order. If it were only a matter of taking into account the *linguistic* mediation without which feelings and dispositions, left in silence, would remain unformed, the difficulty would be minor, and not much of a rebuttal would be required. . . . to the *linguistic* mediation a *cultural* and *historical* mediation is added, of which the former is a mere reflection. (Ricoeur 2000, 127, 129, 130)

Gadamer reminds us of what the Enlightenment tries to deny: that we *are* prejudiced with all kinds of ideas about what and whom we encounter. We might hear "prejudice" here in its resonance with the idea of *prejudgment*. For Gadamer, as for Ricoeur, we never encounter the world free of ideas about it, but instead always only as such an encounter can occur: internal to our social, cultural, historical, and biographical contexts. For example, it is precisely because I have the concept "unicorn" that I would be able to perceive a unicorn were I to happen across one. When I pick up a book to read it, it is my assumption—"this is a book"—that causes me to read it, rather than to put it in the blender in the attempt to make a smoothie. Yet the fact that one *needs* prejudices does not in any way absolve one from the responsibility of examining them and questioning their validity. Gadamer speaks of encountering something (in this case, also a book) and being "pulled up short." One finds that one's ideas are simply inadequate. When that is the case, it becomes clear that "we cannot stick blindly to our own fore-meaning about the thing if we want to understand the meaning of another" (Gadamer 1989, 268). In thus coming to understand the meaning of another, we also come to understand the limits of our own understanding, that is the limits of our prejudices. So prejudices (prejudgments) are necessary—we can't simply get rid of them by trying to be "objective." But what is necessary likewise needs to be questioned. Prejudgments that occur through interpretive categories are what allow for experience even as those categories create problems within experience. This is easily seen if we consider the notion of prejudging persons because of their race, gender, or religion. While such judgments might seem straightaway problematic, it seems just as problematic *not* to take seriously that a particular person must be perceived "as" raced, gendered, and religious in determinate ways if we are to presume the distinctiveness of individual persons that exists through such categories. Moreover, although Gadamer seeks to write a phenomenology of interpretation (hermeneutics) and not an ethics, there is a sense of "responsibility" to the other that is clearly felt in Gadamer's seminal book *Truth and Method,* and even more clearly articulated in a seldom-referenced autobiographical reflection. "According to Kierkegaard," Gadamer writes, "it is the other who breaks into my ego-centeredness and gives me something to understand. This Kierkegaardian motif guided me from the beginning" (Gadamer 1997, 46). As will become clear once we turn to Levinas's phenomenological ethics, this sounds remarkably "Levinasian" in character.

For Gadamer, as for Levinas, and as we will see for Marion, Chrétien, Derrida, and Henry as well, we don't start life by making the first statement. Instead, we are first spoken to and our first word is always already a response. One can argue that, in addition to the Kierkegaardian influence, this is Gadamer's Hegelianism showing through. In Hegel's master-slave dialectic, both the master and slave discover that, much to their disappointment, their identities each require the existence of the other: the master cannot be a master without the slave's existence, so there is a sense in which the slave "masters" the master (Hegel 1977, 111–18, B/IV/A). This *concern* for an other who "breaks into my ego-centeredness" makes Gadamer an important bridge figure, one who is in many ways thoroughly phenomenologically orthodox and yet close to heresy. More precisely, the "as such" is fully in place in Gadamer, but, if "my ego-centeredness" is now threatened, then the intentional structure we find in Husserl is at least contested and the balance is open to being shifted.[3] One could also make the case for Gadamer as the bridge figure in that, for him, a genuine experience (*Erfahrung*) puts the subject into question. A genuine experience *changes us*, says Gadamer, so that we are no longer the people we were: "The experiencer has become aware of his experience; he is 'experienced'. He has acquired a new horizon within which something can become an experience for him" (1989, 354). This idea of having a *new* horizon—one effectively *given to* the experiencer—opens up the possibility for what we might term a phenomenological *reversal*. A real experience, and here Gadamer is again following Hegel, is always *negative*. To put this differently: when I experience something either for the first time or in a new way, I am in some sense *surprised*. Things don't go exactly as I had expected. Yet that would definitely mean that the subject is *not* in control, at least to whatever extent my experience doesn't meet my expectations. Both of these aspects present in Gadamer's philosophy nicely set the scene for looking to the development of new phenomenology.

Briefly put, we could summarize the development of phenomenology as follows. Even though Husserl is not the "originator" of phenomenology in an absolute sense (the word is first used in 1764 and appears in the title of G. W. F. Hegel's *Phenomenology of Spirit* [originally published in 1807]), he is credited as the "founder" of the phenomenological *movement* that becomes prominent beginning at the turn of the twentieth century. Early phenomenologists include such figures as Alexander Pfänder, Adolf Reinach, Moritz Geiger, Max Scheler—all of whom were more or less contemporaneous with Husserl. In the 1920s, Heidegger rises to prominence. In the wake of Heidegger, Gabriel Marcel, Jean-Paul Sartre, and Maurice Merleau-Ponty become influential French philosophers. Hans-Georg Gadamer and Paul Ricoeur both become known for their work on hermeneutics, which is deeply phenomenologically inspired. As Gadamer and Ricoeur become prominent in the 1960s, Jacques Derrida begins to be noticed as an up-and-coming philosopher working largely on Husserl. Although Levinas was part of the philosophical scene as an important translator and interpreter of Husserl in the 1930s, his work from this period is not as well known as his more recent work. Meanwhile, Michel Henry becomes known both as a philosopher and a writer. Levinas reaches prominence in the 1970s (though it is about a decade later that he begins to be read in the United States). Marion's early texts appear in the 1980s, when he becomes known both as a Descartes scholar and as a phenomenologist. Jean-Louis Chrétien first publishes his texts in the 1990s. Levinas dies in 1995, Henry in 2002, Derrida in 2004, and (as of the publication of this book) only Marion and Chrétien remain alive. In the remainder of this chapter, we will look in turn at these last five figures in particular as forming the core of new phenomenology.

Varieties of phenomenological heterodoxy: The new phenomenologists

Jacques Derrida (1930–2004)

Of all the new phenomenologists, Derrida is unquestionably the best known, so we will start with him, since his wide influence (at least outside of France) occurred earlier than, say, Levinas and Henry, even though Levinas and Henry were writing important new phenomenological texts earlier than Derrida. Despite his fame, or perhaps partly because of it, Derrida's ideas have been often misinterpreted, in some cases quite bizarrely. He has been accused of being a relativist, a nihilist, and a skeptic, and deconstruction has been denounced in various ways as undermining truth, goodness, and meaning. His (in)famous claim that "there is nothing outside of the text" (Derrida 1997a, 158) has been read as a claim that everything is somehow encased in words. As it turns out, and as we will see in our later discussions of moral and political philosophy, Derrida *isn't* a relativist, a nihilist, or a skeptic. Some of the misreadings of Derrida might be chalked up to the difficulty of his texts. To be sure, as will become quite clear in the chapters that follow, Derrida can be hard to read. Stylistically, his texts are often beautiful, yet they need to be read very closely and carefully (an effort that is usually amply repaid) in order to avoid confusing his attempt to problematize a particular category, term, or idea with a straight-out rejection of it. Yet there are still places in his texts that are simply difficult, and one longs for more clarity about the claims being made. Given this state of confusion about Derrida, we need a little deconstruction of Derrida and deconstruction itself in order to understand Derrida's approach to phenomenology and its limits.

Perhaps the best place to begin to situate Derrida is with his early essay on Husserl, "'Genesis and Structure' and Phenomenology" (in Derrida 1978). Consider what he says at the beginning of that essay.

> Husserl has always indicated his aversion for debate, dilemma, and aporia, that is, for reflection in the alternative mode whereby the philosopher, at the end of his deliberations, seeks to reach a conclusion, that is, to close the question, to enclose his expectations or his concern in an option, a decision, a solution. . . . The phenomenologist, on the contrary, is the "true positivist" who returns to the things themselves, and who is self-effacing before the originality and primordiality of meanings. . . . Thus one might say, and in an entirely prejudicial fashion, that Husserl, by his rejection of system and speculative closure, and by virtue of the style of his thought, is attuned to the historicity of meaning and to the possibility of its becoming, and is also respectful of that which remains open within structure. (Derrida 1978, 154–5)

It is this essential phenomenological openness that Derrida so admires in Husserl. Whereas some read Husserl as trying to find scientific closure, Derrida thinks that it is exactly the opposite—or at least in an important sense. True, Husserl seeks to find a kind of structure and so does not reject structure per se.[4] Yet the structures he constructs still leave room for novelty and surprise. We might say that Derrida understands Husserlian phenomenology not to circumscribe phenomena, but truly to be open to phenomena "as" they appear, present themselves, or are given. Although Derrida says here that Husserl is averse to "aporia" (questions that arise that seem to have no easy answers), we might better say that Husserl is deeply attuned to such questions. Indeed, this is one of the reasons why Husserl is so difficult to summarize: his conclusions do not fit into a neat and tidy "system." Husserl is constantly re-asking questions and problematizing his own conclusions. He refers to himself as a "perpetual beginner" in the sense of feeling that he is ever starting anew and looking at issues as if for the "first time." In a preface written for the first English edition of *Ideas I*, written toward the end of his life, he says that his philosophical work has caused him "on practical grounds, to lower the ideal of the philosopher to that of a downright beginner" and that he might hope one day "to still be able to become a philosopher." He continues:

> The far horizons of a phenomenological philosophy, the chief structural formations, to speak geographically, have disclosed themselves; the essential groups of problems and the methods of approach on essential lines have been made clear. The author sees the infinite open country of the true philosophy, the "promised land" on which he himself will never set foot. . . . Gladly would he hope that those who come after will take up these first ventures, carry them steadily forward, yes, and improve also their great deficiencies, defects of incompleteness which cannot indeed be avoided in the beginnings of scientific work. (Husserl 1931, 28–9)

It is hard to imagine a more modest statement of one's own project and its completion. Husserl lays out phenomenological philosophy as a kind of infinite task.[5] For Derrida, the notion of phenomenology as an infinite task resonates well with his own deconstructive project. Deconstruction is not something that one does at a particular time and place while reading philosophy, but rather an outlook, an approach, a way of doing whatever philosophy one does. Deconstruction is also appropriately understood as an infinite phenomenological task—which we might summarize as the attempt to be absolutely hospitable to the Other (put more phenomenologically: the attempt to receive that which gives itself in its very mode of givenness)—though it is a task with explicit ethical overtones that are hard to discern in Husserl's project.

Yet this expansive phenomenological openness needs some qualification, for Husserl was actually rather closed in some important ways. Consider simply how he describes the vista looking toward the "promised land": the basic lines of phenomenology have been set and so now it is just a matter of following the blueprint (to mix metaphors). As much as Husserl was open to rethinking his philosophy, he thought that he had set the boundaries for where phenomenology needed to go. Derrida is not similarly prescriptive. Deconstructive openness involves even being open to the termination, occlusion, and overcoming of deconstruction itself. However, Husserl increasingly found that his "followers" ended up going in their own ways, albeit ways that he had to some extent charted. For instance, as explained in the previous chapter, Heidegger continues the phenomenological enterprise and describes his own work in Husserlian terms. Yet, even though Husserl and Heidegger had planned to write a joint article on phenomenology for the fourteenth edition of the *Encyclopedia Britannica*, eventually Husserl decided that he needed to write it on his own, since he no longer saw Heidegger's phenomenology as being enough "like" his own. While Husserl had high hopes that other phenomenologists working at the time might inherit his "mantle," his hopes were ultimately unrealized.

It is precisely this tension between openness and structure that both allows for and problematizes phenomenology after Husserl. Indeed, it is this tension that allows for us to invoke a sense of phenomenological "orthodoxy," while at the same time calling it into question. On the one hand, Husserl opens up a field that allows for infinite possibilities in terms of further development. On the other hand, Husserl's own conception of how that development should go turns out to be somewhat narrow. Husserl expects that his followers will take up *his* projects in *his* manner. What happens is that his followers take up their own projects in their own respective ways. And the result is that phenomenology continues to blossom and flourish, even if in ways not envisioned by Husserl. The result is not simply that there are new phenomenological projects but also that there are new ways of formulating the phenomenological enterprise.

Derrida's specific contribution to such (re)formulations occurs in roughly two ways. On the one hand, his early work in the 1960s and the 1970s on language, textuality, signification, and meaning helps to destabilize philosophical practice, the act of reading, and the notion of identity—see such books as *Of Grammatology* (French original in 1967; cited as Derrida 1997a), *Writing and Difference* (French original in 1967; cited as Derrida 1978), *Margins of Philosophy* (French original in 1972; cited as Derrida 1982), and *Speech and Phenomena* (French original in 1967; cited as Derrida 1973). On the other hand, Derrida's later work on religion, ethics, and politics helps to articulate the stakes involved in living in a destabilized world—see such books as *Given Time* (French original in 1991; cited as Derrida 1992a), *Specters of Marx* (French original in 1993; cited as Derrida 1994), *The Politics of Friendship* (French original in 1994; cited as Derrida 1997b), and *Of Hospitality* (French original in 1997; cited as Derrida 2000). Even though we would challenge a hard and fast split between Derrida's early and late authorship, we might say, generally, that his early work attempts to think about the implications of phenomenological openness as it affects philosophy, and that his later work attempts to think about the implications of phenomenological openness as it affects social existence.

Throughout his prolific authorship, Derrida consistently attempts to think what remains unthought in what we think, what we say, and what we do. In his essay *"Différance,"* for example, he claims that he "will speak, therefore, of a letter" (1982, 3). In a long and complicated discussion of the way in which "difference" (with an "e") sounds the same as "differance" (with an "a"), he shows that such sonic identity masks linguistic (and maybe even conceptual) difference. For Derrida, the "a" in differance really makes a difference! Derrida uses this seemingly mundane example to make the case that the notion of "presence," which has been so central to the history of western philosophy, is something that should be challenged as we attempt to understand what Derrida will sometimes term "the play" that occurs, despite our best intentions, in our speech, writing, and thinking. Indeed, such presence is already challenged in our speech, writing, and thinking whether we attend to it or not. In light of our continuing discussion of the phenomenological "as such," we should be able to see that Derrida's discussion of difference certainly would put the stability of the "as such" in question, inasmuch as the "play" that he discusses challenges the notion of stable presence and structure. Although the phenomena under discussion shift slightly as his thinking progresses, Derrida's later discussions of hospitality, invitation, faith, gift, and promise, for example, can all be appropriately understood as maintaining his interrogation of the "as such" as itself being as central as Husserl had thought. Despite the fact that, in his discussion with Marion, we saw Derrida claim no longer to be a phenomenologist when he operates beyond the "as such," it is important to ask whether such gestures, which put Derrida squarely in the new phenomenological philosophical trajectory, are the moments when Derrida is at his most phenomenological. In a decidedly Derridean fashion, we might say that Derrida's phenomenology is orthodox heresy, or heretically orthodox.

Emmanuel Levinas (1906–95)

While all philosophy is personal in some sense—think of Augustine's *Confessions* and Descartes's *Meditations*—it is particularly difficult to speak about Levinas without saying something about his life. Levinas first made his mark by publishing the first major work on Husserl in French in 1930 (*The Theory of Intuition in the Phenomeonology of Hussserl*), which received a prize from the French Academy. Yet, for much of the next 40 years, he was virtually ignored. Much of his career was spent in small positions at inauspicious places and his publications—which were relatively few—were not widely read. More important for the development of his thought, though, is the fact that he lost most of his family in the Nazi death camps. "My critique of the totality," Levinas says in an interview, "has come in fact after a political experience that we have not yet forgotten" (1985, 78–9). Moreover, Levinas also took his Judaism seriously and his writings on Talmudic commentary are just as important in understanding his thought as his philosophical works.

Probably the easiest way of getting to the heart of Levinas's early philosophy is by way of the following rather common example: you're going through life trying to enjoy yourself and suddenly it dawns on you that there are other people with other agendas. Whereas the new phenomenologists tend to think that the very goal of an adequation between the mind and the thing it thinks is problematic because it is *unreachable*, Levinas comes along and says that it's also *immoral* (so unreachable and immoral at the same time). The problem with this whole project—which one can call metaphysics or ontology—is that it always "succeeds" precisely by "universalizing the immanence of the Same [*le Méme*] or of Freedom, in effacing the boundaries" of the other (Levinas 1996, 11).[6] The *problem* with intentionality (as Husserl defines it) for Levinas is as follows: "Intentionality is the way for thought to *contain ideally something other than itself*. . . . *It is essentially the act of bestowing a meaning* (the *Sinngebung*)" (1998b, 59). Of course, Levinas realizes that metaphysics has always *claimed* to be a desire "toward *something else entirely*, toward *absolutely other*" (1969, 33). But when he claims that we are actually attempting to place everything—including God—within "being's move" [*gest d'être*], he is clearly criticizing both phenomenology and the entire tradition of metaphysics for not really wanting the truly other and certainly for settling for the same (1996, 130).

Of course, this leaves Levinas with a serious problem: if the other is never reducible to anything that fits within the "as such" of the horizon, then how do we speak of the other in the first place? One strategy is to deploy metaphors that announce the linguistic and conceptual difficulty of such discourse. Most famously, Levinas speaks of the "face" that "is present in its refusal to be contained" (1969, 194). Call this what you like—the call of the other or the call of revelation—but it comes down to the same thing. There is the other (whether as *autre*, a thing or a person, or *autrui*, the Other who is always a person) that either has a kind of claim on me or, at the very least, is not such that I have an ultimate claim on *it*. The human other's "primordial *expression*" is the first word: "you shall not commit murder" (1969, 199). Levinas's point, though, grows increasingly stronger. In *Otherwise Than Being or Beyond Essence*, he speaks of being held hostage and being traumatized by the Other (1997, 111).

So, with this all-too-brief sketch of Levinas's thought in place, in what ways does Levinas "change" phenomenology? First, with Levinas comes the focus on the human other. Famously, Levinas insists that *ethics is truly* "first philosophy." In order to see the force of this claim, we need to remember that, historically, philosophers have thought that philosophy begins either with metaphysics or epistemology. The metaphysical question was for centuries at the heart of western philosophy—what *is* everything. Yet, with Descartes, the focus shifts to the question of how we *know*—really the question of "how do we know that we know?" That becomes the quintessential question of modernity. Levinas thinks that both of these projects do not get at what philosophy should truly be about. In saying that ethics should be "first," Levinas is not claiming that we should get our ethics correct first and then move on to other areas. Instead, he is making the much more radical claim that philosophy is first and foremost about the human other. Whereas phenomenology was conceived of by Kant or Husserl or even Heidegger in terms of the interaction of the subject and object in general, the focus of Levinas's phenomenology shifts toward the question of how we relate to human others. This shift is one that is picked up directly by Derrida such that in light of Levinas and Derrida it is plausible to ask about the content of a phenomenological ethics and even a phenomenological political philosophy. We will return to these topics in Chapter Eight.

For now, we ought to ask what brings about such an ethical shift? One explanation is that, if you think about it, how you relate to things in the world ends up being very closely connected with how you connect with other people. Think, for a moment, about the products you buy: they all come from somewhere and someone (or many someones) who has had a hand in their manufacture. Practically, that means that everything we buy is connected to a very concrete set of labor conditions. We may not know exactly how a particular item was manufactured or by whom. But we can't pretend as if these products come from nowhere. In fact, it's not all that hard to get some idea of what kinds of labor conditions are likely for many of the products we buy. Yet this means that we are connected in some way to the living conditions of others around the world, simply by purchasing goods. One doesn't have to think long before it becomes clear that there is some sort of *ethical* dimension to that relationship. It is something like that recognition that animates Levinas' philosophy. Fundamentally, for Levinas, the world in which we find ourselves is always already a social, shared world. Subjectivity is conditioned by a prior sociality. In the case of Levinas, this sociality is not merely a matter of logical relation: it is an instantiation of ethical obligation. For Levinas, such an idea is inspired heavily by his Jewish tradition: a major teaching of Judaism is that the moral barometer for how Jews are doing comes down to how they treat the least of their neighbors—the stranger, the widow, the orphan. So it is hardly a surprise that Levinas takes the quintessential "Other who dominates me in his transcendence [to be] thus the stranger, the widow, and the orphan, to whom I am obligated" (Levinas 1969, 215). This is Levinas in *Totality and Infinity*, a work of *philosophy* rather than Talmudic commentary. This essentially Jewish concern becomes a major source of Levinas's philosophical thought.

In subsequent chapters, we will discuss whether phenomenology can legitimately draw upon theological archives in such ways, which we think it can. Yet, regardless of how one comes down on that issue, what we get in Levinas is a kind of "reverse phenomenology" (to use his own terminology). Instead of the subject being in control, the subject is now "subject" to what was formerly the object. This fundamentally shifts the whole framework of phenomenology. Although classical phenomenology (particularly Husserl) has seen itself as "transcendental" (and it certainly has functioned in this way), Levinas speaks of a "rupture of immanence" (Levinas 1998a, 14–15). What we have in Levinas that we don't have in the "orthodox" phenomenologists is the breaking-through of the infinite into the finite (that Dasein, for instance, actually is infinite according to Heidegger also complicates this orthodoxy, but we'll leave this discussion aside). At this point, it might seem that this is no longer phenomenology, for the "as such" has been shattered. Yet Levinas claims (in a relatively late interview), "I remain to this day a phenomenologist," and phenomenology means for him "a way of becoming aware of where we are in the world" (1986, 14–15). Earlier, he had spoken of "manifestation *kath' auto* in a being telling itself to us independently of every position we would have taken in its regard, *expressing itself*" (Levinas 1969, 65). While this sounds *exactly* like something Husserl would say, it is meant as a repudiation of Husserlian phenomenology. Here it is clear what Levinas seeks instead: a challenge to self-sufficiency. As Levinas will say, "the notion of the face . . . opens other perspectives: it brings us to a notion of meaning prior to my *Sinngebung* and thus independent of my initiative and my power" (1969, 51). If we can say that there *is* an "as such" here, the subject is no longer in control of it—that is, it has truly shifted away from the subject.

Yet make no mistake here: Levinas is not presenting this as a "contra-phenomenology" but more as something along the lines of a "fulfilled phenomenology," a phenomenology that is finally true to *itself* insofar as it is true to alterity (otherness). In a way analogous to Derrida's appreciation of Husserlian "openness," we might say that Levinas, too, saw this openness to be the strength of phenomenology, even if the classical phenomenologists failed to appreciate its true importance. Already here, then, we should have serious questions about who is really the orthodox phenomenologist and who is the heterodox phenomenologist: before deconstruction ever was, Levinas *already* is reading Husserl against himself, arguing that *he*, not Husserl, is giving us the "true" phenomenology. To be sure, Levinas's phenomenology is a phenomenology without the traditional "as such," but his point is that *this is the truly orthodox philosophy*; moreover, it is the orthodox philosophy because it allows the truly "hetero" nature of the Other to show itself. In this way, Levinas is properly understood to be the first of the new phenomenologists.

Michel Henry (1922–2002)

In many ways, Michel Henry's move is similar to that of Levinas. In *The Essence of Manifestation* (French original in 1963; cited as Henry 1973), Henry explores a very phenomenological theme: what it is for something to be *made manifest*. Or, as Marion will later put it, building upon Henry's work, what it is for something to be *given*. By criticizing the privileging of the subject in both Husserl and Heidegger, Henry clearly champions the phenomenality of the phenomenon. His focus is the very phenomenon of "manifestation," which, in effect, is the revelation of life itself, as he will come to term it in his later work. For Henry, manifestation is fully immanent, so much so that *"there is nothing transcendent"* (1973, 283). In *this* respect, Henry goes the exactly opposite direction of Levinas. Whereas Levinas emphasizes transcendence—the transcendence of the phenomenon—Henry emphasizes its immanence. But then the question is: manifestation of *what*? Ultimately, the answer turns out to be manifestation of manifestation itself, which turns out to be alternatively referenced as "Life" and/or "God." It is no accident that Meister Eckhart makes more than a short appearance in *The Essence of Manifestation*, nor that the search for the absolute leads us to a version of God that is inspired by Eckhart (see 1973, 309–35, 683).

Henry goes beyond Eckhart, however, for God is life itself and, because we are alive, God is fully present to us. It is in his later writings that this theme of *God as life* is developed: there, Henry works out what it means to say that "living is possible only outside the world, where another Truth reigns" (2003, 30). Within Christianity, Henry claims, the very meaning of the word "truth" means something quite different than it does within the realm of empirical sciences. Whereas scientific truth alienates,[7] Christianity provides a radical phenomenology that reveals the ultimate; the result, though, is not *theology* but *phenomenology*. Henry's conception of God is considerably different from that of Levinas or Marion, who would both emphasize the transcendence or "otherness" of God. In contrast, Henry stresses God's immanence to us—said otherwise, there is nothing closer to us than our own life as lived. But, in making God and revelation central to phenomenology, Henry remains nevertheless strongly linked with Levinas and Marion insofar as he also challenges the "as such" by attending to that which remains invisible so long as we only concern ourselves with visibility. Henry's deeper concern for the affectivity of living as the condition for any particular phenomenon's visibility is not something that Husserl's approach seems to admit, though given a reading as careful as Henry's, Husserl's approach might seem to allow for such an admission.

Like Levinas, Henry would consider himself to be one of the "true" phenomenologists. Yet, while Henry accepts most of the basic principles of Husserlian phenomenology, he reverses intentionality. This is why Henry speaks of breaking with "historical" phenomenology in favor of what he calls a "radical" phenomenology. In effect, intentionality is suspended in order to allow the object to be manifest in total immanence—thus, without any "as such." What Henry thus explains is the very givenness of the phenomenological appearance, since here the focus is on the object that is given, rather than on the subject that intends the object. In this regard, it is no accident that Marion clearly acknowledges his indebtedness to Henry for the latter's earlier work on givenness (2002a, 330n14).[8] In his later work, Henry makes a claim that is very similar to that of Chrétien: that the structure of Christianity ultimately teaches us about the structure of phenomenology. Thus the question arises of whether phenomenology is most itself when it is thoroughly secular and naturalistic or whether it is only truly phenomenological when placed into a decidedly Christian (or at least religious) context. Of course, as we will see in Chapter Three, Janicaud is going to side with the former option.

Jean-Luc Marion (1946–)

Although in many ways Marion continues the projects of Levinas and Henry by paying close attention to that which would seem to remain excessive to classical phenomenological inquiry, he is much clearer in terms of what he is doing regarding his relation to the classical phenomenological project. In terms of what he wants to accomplish, he wants to dissolve any conditions of possibility for the appearing of an object to appear. We could also say that he is concerned with establishing that givenness—the fact that an object is *given* to consciousness—is the *primary* aspect of phenomenology. He writes that "the phenomenological breakthrough consists neither in the broadening of intuition, nor in the autonomy of signification, but solely in the unconditional primacy of the givenness of the phenomenon" (Marion 1998, 32). Marion clarifies and punctuates this claim even more strongly:

> Can the givenness in presence of each thing be realized without any condition or restriction? The question marks Nietzsche's last advance and Husserl's first point of arrival. . . . In undertaking to free presence from any condition or precondition for receiving what gives itself as it gives itself, phenomenology therefore attempts to complete metaphysics and, indissolubly, to bring it to an end. (Marion 1998, 1)

All of this means that Marion is not just trying to change phenomenology but also metaphysics. From his point of view, the problem with Husserl is as follows: "A phenomenality of givenness can permit the phenomenon to show *itself*, but a phenomenality of objectness [i.e. Husserl] can only constitute the phenomenon on the basis of the *ego* of a consciousness that intends it as its noema" (Marion 2002a, 32). With an emphasis on the ego, the phenomenality of givenness is passed over. Thus, Marion moves from "the things themselves" and the "principle of principles" to another principle found in both Husserl and Heidegger: "So much appearing, so much Being." As it turns out, this principle [*Soviel Schein, soviel Hindeutung aufs Seyn*] actually goes back to J. F. Herbart (1776–1841). This is Herbart's answer to the question "what is given?" It is picked up by Husserl in *Erste Philosophie* II, §33 and the *Cartesian Meditations* §46, and then by Heidegger in *Being and Time* §7. The goal of this principle for Marion is moving from "mere appearance" to genuine and immediate appearance: here the idea is that to the degree that there is genuine appearing, to that same degree there is being.

Earlier in Chapter One, when we considered Husserl's phenomenological reduction, we noted that the reduction is to that which is actually given. Marion infers from this that arriving at pure givenness is actually the whole point of the reduction. With this in mind, Marion concludes that "the givenness of any reduced phenomenon is an absolute and indubitable givenness" (Marion 2002a, 40). Whereas Husserl establishes that the limits of givenness are exactly those of intuition, Marion thinks that givenness is more fundamental and thus also more worthy of setting any limits, if they are to be set. Accordingly, Marion calls for a "third reduction" (with Husserl's phenomenological reduction as the first and Heidegger's reduction to being as the second). "Reducing givenness," Marion explains, "means freeing it from the limits of every other authority, including those of intuition" (Marion 2002a, 17). So why is this third reduction known as the reduction of givenness? Here we come back to givenness as a kind of *call*: "The third reduction . . . has tended toward nothing other than to render the recognition of it inevitable—properly speaking *is* not, because the call that exercises it nevertheless rigorously no longer issues from the horizon of Being (nor of objectity), but from the pure form of the call" (Marion 1998, 204).

Since the call *precedes* the subject, the *I* or Dasein becomes the *interloqué*, which we might translate as both "the questioned" and "the one who is put in question," whose very identity is possible because of being called; once again, we have the same reversal of subject and object. The call may take on a variety of forms: that of the Christian God as found in Marion and Chrétien, that of the claim on us by being as found in Heidegger, that of the ethical call of the Other as found in Levinas, or that of Henry's call to life from the pathos of auto-affection. Regardless of the specific form, this general idea of the phenomenological call goes back to Heidegger, who writes in "Letter on Humanism": "Alone among all beings, man, claimed by the voice of Being [*angerufen von der Stimme des Seins*] experiences the wonder of wonders: *that* being is" (Heidegger 1993, 238). So already here in Heidegger we have a kind of heterodoxy. We are called to actualize ourselves; being calls us to understand the essence of existents; being calls us to understand ourselves in terms of the essence of existents. Although Heidegger believes in the priority of the call of being [*Anspruch des Seins*], Marion argues for the priority of the call that is both Christian and Jewish (though admitting that there are distinctly Jewish and Christian calls). The locus classicus is: "Hear, O Israel: The Lord is our God, the Lord alone" (Deut. 6:4). For Marion, here we have "the call to render oneself to the call itself" (1998, 197). The one who is called, the *interloqué*, finds itself displaced from the nominative to the acusative case: it is now the object of a "counter-intentionality." The *interloqué* now becomes the gifted and finds itself grounded in a relation that precedes it.

Yet how can Marion call this a "pure call" when it is clearly drawn from specifically Jewish and Christian sources and cultural traditions? As seemed to be the case in Levinas's appropriation of Jewish wisdom, haven't we slipped into a pure theology? Marion recognizes that the situation is, at the end, the following: "Between these two interpretations of a single phenomenological situation [i.e. the subject according to Husserl and Heidegger versus Marion], interpretations that define the two irreconcilable tendencies cutting across the entire history of philosophy (either constitute the object poor in intuition or receive the excess of givenness without objectifying it), no reason could decide" (Marion 2002a, 306). In other words, Marion may not have any ultimate argument for saying that his "Hear, O Israel" is the pure call, but Heidegger is in the same position. Of course, for that matter, so is Janicaud when he calls for phenomenological neutrality. The exact nature of the call is precisely what is at issue. And even calls for "neutrality" are themselves *motivated* rather than being neutral.

Jean-Louis Chrétien (1952–)

Jean-Louis Chrétien's "phenomenology" is difficult to characterize. That he subtitles one of his books "Phenomenology of the Promise" might lead one to the conclusion that his thought is linked to Derrida's *l'avenir*—the idea that the future is radically unknown and unpredictable. Yet Chrétien maintains that "the promise always already surrounds us" (1990, 60). In other words, the promise is both to come and yet also already here. That kind of paradoxical formulation is at the heart of Chrétien's philosophy, which often evokes that Heideggerian phrase "always already [*immer schon*]." Although Janicaud admits that Chrétien writes with care and nuance, he insists that Chrétien is writing against the theological backdrop of Christ's incarnation (Janicaud 2000, 67). Chrétien does nothing to hide his influences: he cites both philosophers and theologians abundantly and frequently centers his meditations around passages from both Hebrew and Christian scriptures. Although he writes on such topics as the body, the presence of the voice, and testimony, his take on them, like Marion's, relies on distinctly theological resources, which leads Janicaud to wonder how it could be *phenomenological*. Yet, where Marion would insist that his phenomenology of the "givenness" of the saturated phenomenon is "strictly phenomenological" (even though, strangely enough, it leads to a "theophany"), Chrétien—in an analogous way—would say that including theological voices actually *illuminates* the phenomena, resulting in what he, like Marion, would insist is something that is "strictly phenomenological" (Marion 2000, 215; Chrétien 2004, 33). The result is a clash between a minimal, naturalistic phenomenology and a radical phenomenology that is either somewhat secretly or quite explicitly motivated by religious concerns.

While Chrétien writes on a wide variety of topics, the theme of a call that "wounds" is one that appears in multiple texts and can be considered a dominant motif in his thought. One might even argue that it is the heart of the theological turn not just in Chrétien but French phenomenology in general. Chrétien insists that the call that comes to us always already precedes us and has both the effect of decentering us and constituting us; it is yet another example of the usual phenomenological paradigm being turned on its head. "We speak only for having been called," says Chrétien, who also claims "we are entangled in speech as soon as we exist" (2004, 1, 28). In place of a privileged, autonomous subject, he sees us as intersubjectively constituted, so that our voice is never fully our own. Chrétien pushes this intersubjectivity to a point where the idea of the "self" as discrete is seriously challenged—and that challenge is clearly presented within a distinctly theological context. Chrétien says that "each new encounter shatters us and reconfigures us" (2000, 156). And it is not incidental that the phrase appears in an essay on prayer. Yet what is remarkable about that essay is how Chrétien uses prayer—a specifically religious phenomenon—to illuminate speech and conversation in general. Whether in prayer or in conversation with a human other, one is both touched by the other and touches in return. This movement is further complicated by Chrétien's claim that any response to a call "also calls out in turn and appeals to other calls" (2004, 24). So the structure of the call is not merely two-way but multidirectional: it reaches out in many directions at once.

Speech comes to us *as* gift and so we both give back and give away. Whereas the gift has been a subject of much discussion in Derrida, due to what he considers to be its impossibility, for Chrétien, the problem of the gift (and thus economic exchange) simply isn't a "problem," precisely because of a fundamental "inequality" of gifts. As he puts it, "no response will ever correspond. The perfection of the answer will lie forever in its deficiency, since what calls us in the call is from the start its very lack of measure, its incommensurability" (2004, 23). That gifts cannot be measured means that there can be no reciprocity involving measurement. Since no "even exchange" is possible, the gift remains possible. All of this exchange is deeply connected to wounding: it is not just that anyone who speaks "opens himself to more than himself and to others," but that every "opening up" is like a kind of wound. Chrétien is speaking particularly of prayer when he writes that it "exposes [the one praying] in every sense of the word *expose* and with nothing held back" (2000, 150). Prayer in particular is "always agonic," for it opens us up to God and in a way that involves a kind of "suffering." Here it is helpful to remember that many encounters with God in the Hebrew Bible are ones in which the one called by God is opened up. For example, in one of the earliest, Moses hears God speaking to him from the burning bush and replies, "Here I am" (Exod. 3:4), which signifies that he is willing to be at God's disposal. When we think of "suffering," we tend to forget that its original meaning—and its French equivalent "*souffrir*"—is "to submit to." Although Chrétien also has in mind the idea of being in pain, that notion of submitting is first and foremost: we become a "subject" before God, since "all prayer confesses God as giver by dispossessing us of our egocentrism" (2000, 153).[9] So the same reversal that we found in Levinas and Marion is likewise found in Chrétien.

Yet this is a *painful* reversal and it is decentering, precisely because we so want to be in the center. It should be no surprise, then, that Chrétien sees prayer as an agonic struggle. He points to the somewhat strange and troubling story of Jacob's wrestling with a man or an angel or God in the book of Genesis as paradigmatic for prayer. What takes place is a *violent* and prolonged encounter in which there is *both* a wound (Jacob's hip is displaced) *and* a blessing (Jacob becomes Israel). Although not all such encounters with God (or with human others, for that matter) are so agonic in nature, Chrétien sees at least something agonic in prayer per se, since even the act of submitting to God is a struggle. Unlike Levinas—and particularly unlike Derrida—Chrétien does not simply want to eliminate all violence or suffering. So he has a very different response to the problem of violence (especially as posed by Hegel).

In one sense, Chrétien can be viewed as simply more realistic than either Levinas or Derrida, for he thinks that struggles in which there is suffering or violence are a necessary part of the human condition. Although some might be willing to level the charge of falling into an all too easy justification of evil, Chrétien has a highly nuanced account of suffering and violence in which he maintains that "the benediction can wound" (2002, 122). Here the reference is again to Jacob's struggle. Chrétien points out that it is hard to see in the narrative who is the victor or who is the vanquished. Jacob is *both* blessed and wounded. We could say that Chrétien does not provide a theodicy—an attempt to *explain* evil—but a *phenomenology* that attempts to think "loss, wound, and passivity, as well as forgetting and fatigue" from the point of view in which "there is no philosophical *parousia*" (2002, 126). Precisely *because* there is no such *parousia*, thinking of loss, wound, and suffering *either* as wholly gratuitous *or* as ultimately good—or at least offset by good—is simply impossible. For Chrétien, one is left in the phenomenological middle in which good and evil commingle, a world in which evil often masquerades as good and good is often less good than we take it to be. Chrétien is no wide-eyed optimist, but he is too nuanced as a phenomenologist to reduce the phenomena to any simple categories. The result is that the reader is left with a particular sort of unease, for there is no real resolution or clear conclusion—just a meditation on the phenomena that leaves them in all of their complexity and paradox.

Yet Chrétien *does* envision a kind of *parousia*: in much the same way as he affirms a kind of memory beyond that remembered, so he speaks of a future that cannot be anticipated, one that "exceeds all expectation, and thereby founds anticipation" (1989, 75). Here Chrétien's "anticipation" and a future exceeding expectation sounds like Derrida's "messianic" and *l'avenir*. Chrétien himself says that "the *unhoped for* is what transcends all our expectations"; yet, unlike Derrida, Chrétien sets this within a decidedly Christian context, saying "at the point where Revelation permits hope to become hope in God and confidence in God's promise, the unhoped for is charged with a new meaning" (2002, 105–7).

Conclusion

Phenomenology has traditionally been constituted by an intentionality that consists of both subject and object. However, what we have seen is that this relation looks somewhat different depending upon the phenomenologist in question. The instability of this relation means that, even in phenomenology, there is a shifting balance of the object and the subject. Those of us who have taken the hermeneutical turn will likely still put more of an emphasis on the subject, though Gadamer's emphasis on "the other who breaks into my ego-centeredness" should keep that emphasis in check. On the other hand, my hermeneutical grasp of an object (the "as such") that is given to me does *not* have to function purely as a limit. Instead, that grasp, aided by prejudices, is subject to change; and it is subject to change through the sheer force of the object which does *not* to conform to my interpretation of it. True, I may be resistant to that lack of conformity or be willing to overlook it, but repeated lack of conformity often (though, we must admit, not always) does have a tendency to break my inadequate interpretation. Further, if true experience is the experience of the *negative* (or the reversal), I may not necessarily have a choice. My experience may be such that, unless I'm simply willfully blind or stubborn, I am forced to see or hear differently. In other words, the Other is always surprising (Levinas) and requires essential openness

(Derrida) such that being put in question by the Other's call serves to rupture my assumptions of self-sufficiency (Marion) insofar as my being wounded (Chrétien) and/or being affected (Henry) opens up new possibilities for moving forward.

It is even more important that one of the most radically innovative of the new phenomenologists (Chrétien) and the most "orthodox" of the classical phenomenologists (Husserl) end up being much closer than one would expect. We have seen in Chrétien that the call and the response are mutually constitutive. There is a sense in which we can say that the "as such" is double sided—it comes from both the other and the self; that is to say that it is "intersubjective." Indeed, the very self that Chrétien presents is one that is highly intersubjective: if our voice is comingled with others, then clearly our very selves are similarly comingled. One of the problems with the way in which the different phenomenological accounts play off of one another is that they often seem as if what is at issue is the intentionality of *one person*. On this reading, it becomes a contest of "the one subject" versus the "other subject" or "object" as to who is "in charge" of the horizon. On this front, it might seem that phenomenology gives way to a matter of power play. But this is too simple an account of the horizon that operates in these accounts. True, if one simply reads *Ideas I*—with its emphasis on the transcendental ego—then one might come to the conclusion that it is the individual ego who "controls" the horizon. Yet, if we take what Husserl says in the *Crisis* about the horizon or the "as such," we get a very *intersubjective* "as such." Husserl says, for instance, that "the pregiven world is the horizon which includes all our goals, all our ends, whether fleeting or lasting, in a flowing but constant manner, just as an intentional horizon-consciousness implicitly 'encompasses' [everything] in advance" (Husserl 1970a, 144).

Turning to Husserl's work on intersubjectivity provides us a way of altering the very terms of this debate. This debate tends to presuppose that there is something like a discrete subject that is self-enclosed. The appearance of the Levinasian Other, then, brings about a shakeup of that self-enclosed subject. Levinas asks: what follows if we start with a subject that is a *porous* subject that does not merely constitute itself but is always already constituted by the other? With such a conception of the self, we may still have "self" and "Other," but neither have truly discrete identities. That is, the Other is always already *within* me and I in the Other. This is exactly what we noted in Chrétien as it concerns the call and response. Alternatively, if we follow Heidegger's account of the Other, we find the following: "The world of Dasein is a *with-world* [*Mitwelt*]. Being-in is *being-with* [*Mitsein*] others" (Heidegger 2010, 116). For Heidegger, a problematic aspect of this proximity is that our own identities can be threatened by the other, so that we are not able to be truly ourselves. At this point, of course, we are starting at a different place than either Kant or Levinas, since there is not really a choice between autonomy and heteronomy. Whereas Kant chooses the former and Levinas the latter, perhaps no choice is really necessary—there can be no "pure" autonomy and no pure heteronomy. Instead, there is mutual constitution, in which no one is the true possessor of the "as such."

My experience of the world is always one in which there are others. In effect, this "objectifies" the world by revealing it to be something that precedes me and also supercedes me as a *non-enclosed* subject. Consequently, I am put in my place. Moreover, since there are Others who experience the world from *their* perspective, *my* perspective is decentered and becomes simply another perspective—one among many. But note what does *not* happen: there is no simple reversal of self and other. Rather, there is a complex of self and other that even blurs the differences between "self" and "Other." So now we see that *both* subjectivity *and* intersubjectivity constitute the world. I am not simply out there constituting the world on my own; I am accompanied by others in this infinite task. But we can also say—and this is a very Hegelian and very *non-Kantian* point—that my own subjectivity finds its full self in intersubjectivity. Husserl writes in the *Crisis* that "subjectivity is what it is—an ego functioning constitutively—only within inter-subjectivity" (Husserl 1970a, 172). The result is that we no longer have the centrality of the self, but neither do we have the centrality of the Other: instead, we have moved on to a different way of conceiving the relation. This means that the "as such" is communal, intersubjective, and constantly open to change. Rather than any of us being the one who "masters" the phenomenon, it is something that none of us control—it is not mine or yours; rather, it is common property that can never be made into private property. And, from this perspective, the terms of the debate shift.

New phenomenology takes this implicit suggestion and makes it an explicit hallmark of phenomenological inquiry itself. The new phenomenologists disagree on important points, but they all recognize the excessiveness of phenomenality in any particular phenomenon. This excessiveness not only puts us in question, but it also simultaneously calls us to ourselves. That new phenomenological discussions of phenomenality, excess, invisibility, etc., tend quickly to draw on seemingly "religious" expression and conceptuality in the attempt to speak about that which "overflows," "saturates," and "ruptures" expression has spawned significant critical debate. It is to that debate that we now turn.

CHAPTER THREE

Phenomenology and onto-theology

In the introduction to this book, we expressed our agreement with François-David Sebbah's claim that "we must not allow the question of the 'theological turn' to be our investigation's foundation, yet we must equally attempt not to evade its problematic charge" (2012, 3). In this chapter and the next, we will directly confront this "problematic charge" and consider why it is rightly understood as "problematic." We will do so in the attempt to demonstrate the important resources that lie within new phenomenology for contemporary philosophy of religion, while not shying away from articulating the limits of new phenomenology in relation to the current debates in this area.

This chapter will unfold as follows. First, we will provide a brief overview of Janicaud's notion of a "theological turn" in French phenomenology. Importantly, this look at Janicaud's account is not meant to be a sustained consideration of all the complicated moves in his argument, but merely a summary of the basic charge that he lays out. Following this summary, we will lay out the conceptual and historical background required for a consideration of Janicaud's charge in light of new phenomenology. In order to do this, we will look at the various reasons offered by Husserl and Heidegger for why discussions of "God" are problematic within phenomenological inquiry. Specifically, we will give a close reading of Husserl's "exclusion" of God from phenomenology in section 58 of *Ideas I*. Then we will turn to Heidegger's critique of "onto-theology." In our discussion of Heidegger, we will pay special attention to his account of phenomenological method in *The Phenomenology of Religious Life*.

In the next chapter, we will look at the ways in which new phenomenologists have quite explicitly engaged in quite a bit of "God-talk." We will argue that this God-talk should not be understood as *a turn to theology* but merely as a *deepening of the phenomenological impulse in the direction of the philosophy of religion.* Specifically, our suggestion is that the new phenomenologists have not been interested in God or religion *as such* but have instead been interested in exploring the ways in which non-intentional intuition might be possible such that there might be things given to consciousness that do not "appear" in any straightforward way. This is what leads Levinas to consider alterity, Marion to consider givenness, Henry to consider the auto-affection of life, Derrida to consider the trace and *différance*, and Chrétien to consider the call and promise. None of these notions are *necessarily* religious, but the inquiry into these various modes of excess and the exploration of the limits of phenomenology does open onto discussions that can quite legitimately be confused with a theological turn.

Finally, with a basic framework for how new phenomenological philosophy of religion tends to operate in place, we will suggest some ways in which it might be productively brought into dialogue with "analytic" philosophy of religion, which tends to be more prominent in philosophy of religion discussions. Namely, we will consider the relationship of apophatic and kataphatic discourse as a way of considering the relationship between faith and reason, and the fate of apologetics in a postmodern world.

Dominique Janicaud's "problematic charge": Theology in phenomenological clothes?

Originally published in French in 1991 (English translation in 2000), Janicaud's *The Theological Turn of French Phenomenology* inaugurated a significant debate within contemporary continental philosophy. The vigorous reaction to Janicaud's essay is likely due as much to the polemical tone in which the essay is written as to the

actual thesis it defends. According to Janicaud, the new phenomenologists, in particular Levinas, Henry, Marion, and Chrétien, are
guilty of having abandoned the specific phenomenological methodology laid out by Husserl. Instead of the presuppositionless "rigorous science" of phenomenal description called for by Husserl, the
new phenomenologists all swim in the waters of biased, normative,
confessional, and revealed theology. Referring to the shift from
classical phenomenology to new phenomenology as a theological swerving (*embardée théologique*) that eventually "veers" off
course, Janicaud metaphorically presents new phenomenology as
a "vehicle going out of control" (Greisch 1998, 65). It is as if the
young, new phenomenologists have stolen the keys to the phenomenological car from their father Husserl and have taken it out for a
theological joyride!

Janicaud locates several moments in which the theological turn
began to show itself in French phenomenology. The first indication can be found in Paul Ricoeur's 1950 French translation of
Husserl's *Ideas* (see Husserl 1950). Janicaud notes that, as a result
of Ricoeur's work on the *Ideas*, "in a short sentence, full of underlying meaning, and impossible to pass over indifferently, [Ricoeur]
lets this slip out: 'Is the most radical subject God?'" (Janicaud 2000,
23; for the quote from Ricoeur, see Ricoeur 1967, 28). Placing significant emphasis on this short question, Janicaud claims that "the
theological turn is obviously contained *in ovo* in this genre of interrogation" (2000, 23). Yet, unlike the new phenomenologists to
come, Ricoeur "restrained himself from taking the next step. His
methodological scruples led him to multiply the hermeneutical pre-
cautions prior to any passage from phenomenology to theology"
(2000, 23). While admitting Ricoeur's question does announce
"difficulties handed down by Husserl" (2000, 23), Janicaud resists
considering the question to be itself phenomenologically legitimate, since that would require entertaining the very sort of radical
critique of Husserl engaged in by new phenomenology.

For Janicaud, the really key moment in the theological turn is
the year 1961. During that year, Maurice Merleau-Ponty dies and
Levinas publishes his seminal work *Totality and Infinity*. Making
quite a bit of the dual events of that year, Janicaud suggests that
between these two thinkers there opens a gap that spans from strict
phenomenology to revealed theology. Janicaud proposes that we
understand the difference between Merleau-Ponty and Levinas to

be a difference between the strategy of "intertwining" and that of "aplomb" (2000, 24–7). Whereas both thinkers offer discussions of invisibility, and in that sense do originally develop their own philosophy in ways that expand upon the specifics of Husserlian phenomenology and the centrality of intentionality, Merleau-Ponty does so in a way that never allows the invisible to become disjoined from the visible. So, even though "the visible is never pure, but always palpitating with invisibility," it is nonetheless a *corporeal* invisibility. In this way, Merleau-Ponty "intertwines" the visible and the invisible. Alternatively, Levinas suggests a "philosophical attitude every way different and even antithetical" to that of Merleau-Ponty and Husserl (2000, 25). Instead of bringing together the visible with the invisible that troubles it, Janicaud understands Levinas to offer a "categorical affirmation of the primacy of the idea of infinity" rather than a constant engagement with the depth and invisible dimensions of visibility itself (2000, 25). The problem is that Levinas seems to admit into phenomenology an *absolute* invisibility.

Though Janicaud rightly notes that Merleau-Ponty and Levinas share the goal of "overcoming the intentional horizon" laid down by Husserl, he worries that they do not do so in equally legitimate ways (2000, 26). "Between the unconditional affirmation of Transcendence" (i.e. the strategy of Levinas) and "the patient interrogation of the visible" (i.e. the strategy of Merleau-Ponty), Janicaud claims that an "incompatibility cries out; we must choose" (2000, 26). Yet this choice is not a simple matter of deciding between two alternative inheritors of phenomenology—the choice is between phenomenology and non-phenomenology. In light of our discussion of orthodoxy in the previous chapter, we might say that, for Janicaud, the new phenomenologists are straightaway heretical, since phenomenological orthodoxy is already a settled matter. Janicaud's account of the two alternatives presented by Merleau-Ponty and Levinas is extremely revealing and so we will quote him at some length here:

> The task, insofar as it remains philosophical and phenomenological, is to follow the sole guide that does not buy itself off with fine words: interrogation of method. It then appears clearly that Merleau-Ponty's way has a most heuristic

fragility: it is a moving quest, searching for the very words to approximate the richness of an experience each and everyone can undergo. His is a minimalist method, shunning hasty reductions and the idealist temptation, but not at all attention to the other. . . . Intertwining excludes nothing, but opens our regard to the depth of the world.

On the contrary, the direct dispossessing aplomb of alterity supposes a nonphenomenological, metaphysical desire. . . . It supposes a metaphysico-theological montage, prior to philosophical writing. The dice are loaded and choices made; faith rises majestically in the background. The reader, confronted by the blade of the absolute, finds him- or herself in the position of a catechumen who has no other choice than to penetrate the holy words and lofty dogmas. (Janicaud 2000, 26–7)

And, just in case anyone missed his not-so-subtle point, Janicaud continues:

All is acquired and imposed from the outset, and this is no little thing: nothing less than the God of the biblical tradition. Strict treason of the reduction that handed over the transcendental I to its nudity, here theology is restored with its parade of capital letters. But this theology, which dispenses with giving itself the least title, installs itself at the most intimate dwelling of consciousness, as if that were as natural as could be. (2000, 27)

Janicaud closes this description of the strict dichotomy between Merleau-Ponty and Levinas with the following pointed questions: "Must philosophy let itself be thus intimidated? Is this not but incantation, initiation?" (2000, 27). In the work of Levinas, says Janicaud, "phenomenology has been taken hostage by a theology that does not want to say its name" (2000, 43).

In light of Janicaud's account, we might find ourselves tempted to respond as Heidegger did to a passage from Hegel: "We stop, baffled" (Heidegger 1969, 44). Indeed, we think that there are multiple reasons that one might be "baffled" by Janicaud's account here: (1) Why is the opposition between phenomenology and theology so stark? It is as if Janicaud takes it as obvious that phenomenology should discard *all* theological questioning (or, we might even say, all "God-talk"), but isn't that precisely what Janicaud admits that Ricoeur rightly hits on as a "difficulty" left open by Husserl? (2) Does Janicaud mean to suggest that philosophy and theology ought to be rigidly distinguished, as such? Or does he mean to suggest that only phenomenology ought to refuse to let itself be "intimidated" by theology? If the former is the case, then Janicaud certainly has a long way to go if he hopes to refute the very notion of philosophical theology in toto. Janicaud does give an indication as to his views on this front when he claims that "the polemical part of this little book is not at all directed against the theological as such," but rather at trying to maintain "phenomenology in [its] methodological limits" (2000, 34). For Janicaud, Merleau-Ponty lays out an "incontestably" phenomenological limit that must not be transgressed when he claims that phenomenologists must not pursue "an absolute invisible . . . but the invisible of this world" (Janicaud 2000, 34).

Janicaud's claim here requires a very specific understanding of both phenomenology and Levinasian philosophy if his thesis is even to be plausible at all. Namely, he must assume that phenomenology requires very specific limits (which Merleau-Ponty respects, but Levinas does not) regarding contact with visibility, and he also must assme that Levinas is not simply *drawing upon theological vocabulary* to enrich his phenomenological account, but *appealing to theology as authoritative* in his philosophical texts. Neither claim is obvious. On the one hand, as we have already discussed, Husserl himself opens the door for discussions of invisibility in various ways: the co-presented adumbrated perspectives that remain constitutively unavailable and yet are somehow "given" to consciousness, the idea of "categorial intuitions," the various implications of the "lifeworld," and even the infinite task of inquiry invited in his late work as a result of the phenomenological openness that Derrida so appreciated about it. On the other hand, Levinas goes to great lengths to distinguish between his philosophical works and his more theologically inclined "Talmudic" lectures and essays. Although Levinas himself recognizes that his thought might push beyond Husserlian phenomenology in important ways, it is not clear that phenomenology must be so rigidly demarcated. As we have seen, part of what is at stake in the questions being asked by Levinas and the other new phenomenologists is what ought to count as phenomenological orthodoxy.

After claiming that 1961 was the key moment in the theological turn, Janicaud goes on to suggest that the turn receives further support in 1963 with the publication of Michel Henry's *The Essence of Manifestation* (cited as 1973), which Janicaud claims displays a "theological orientation" (Janicaud 2000, 33). Given that Henry chastises Husserl and Heidegger for being too willing to linger with transcendence as expressed in an ontologically monist perspective, rather than focusing on the radical immanence of self-affecting life, it might seem odd that Janicaud would choose to characterize Henry as so influential on the origins of the theological turn. Indeed, although Janicaud is worried about going beyond intentionality, he admits that even Merleau-Ponty pushes forward into new ground on that front. The real crux of Janicaud's frustration with new phenomenology, then, results from new phenomenology's willingness to allow transcendence back into the phenomenological method—thus threatening the reduction. But we might ask whether Henry's account is best understood as being precisely a more radical commitment to the reduction itself. Janicaud is doubtful here because he worries that a move from "manifestation" to "the essence of manifestation" shifts the focus to that which does not directly show/give itself in the immanent mental process. Although Janicaud admits that Henry's theological trajectory leads "less to the God of a positive theology than toward the Deity in Meister Eckhart's sense," and to that extent is more supportive of Henry's project than of Levinas', Janicaud contends that Henry still abandons the methodological strictures of phenomenological inquiry by "reorienting" phenomenology away from a study of phenomena and toward a study of the phenomenality *of* phenomena (2000, 33–4).

Following on this description of the initiation of the theological turn by Levinas and Henry, Janicaud then identifies Marion and Chrétien as the primary thinkers who have continued in this heretical direction. Although Janicaud does appreciate the phenomenological sophistication of Marion's *Reduction and Givenness*, he still claims that "in Marion's work, there is no respect for the phenomenological order; it is manipulated as an ever-elastic apparatus, even when it is claimed to be 'strict'" (2000, 65). Whereas Janicaud's critique of Marion primarily concerns the way in which he sees Marion as playing fast and loose with the phenomenological method, his critique of Chrétien is focused on the way in which he perceives Chrétien as giving in to decidedly Christian biases and, in that sense, abandoning the presuppositionless rigor required of phenomenological research. "Let us be clear," Janicaud writes of Chrétien,

> It is not at all a question here of contesting the interest, for a Christian thinker, of rethinking corporeality, including in the perspective of the resurrection promised by the Scriptures. But we must observe, as a matter of fact, that in the text in question the recourse to phenomenology is constantly biased by both a "call" that is purportedly original and a reference, imposed on the reader, to religious experience. It is a question here, we might put it, of a Christian phenomenology, but whose properly phenomenological sense must fall away, for a nonbeliever, midway through the journey. (2000, 67)

Yet it is hard to see—*phenomenologically*—why Janicaud simply assumes a conception of objectivity that seems to deny the possibility of such a "call" and such an "experience." Surely these must be open questions within phenomenology.

At the closing of his consideration of the phenomenological "veerings" of Marion and Chrétien, Janicaud notes that in addition to the key methodological slippage in Marion and the Christian biases in Chrétien, they both offer "analyses that verge on edification" (2000, 69). Such a claim might seem surprising in light of the idea that, as Socrates, Kierkegaard, C. S. Peirce, and many others make clear, the search for truth should always "verge on edification." So surely Janicaud's complaint is not connected with the level of truth-seeking itself. It seems more likely that what he means by "edification" is something like "normative recommendation" or "ethico-religious encouragement." Yet, while Husserl tended to view phenomenology as a science devoted to descriptions of phenomena rather than to offering normative judgments about those phenomena, is it really so clear that phenomenology must remain *singularly* descriptive in ways that seem to assume agnostic neutrality, if not atheistic dogmatism? Though we will consider normativity in detail in Chapter Eight, for now we want to simply point out that, in light of the developments in critical theory, deconstruction, and postmodern philosophy more broadly,

there are reasons to doubt that description can stand isolated from
normativity in the first place. Put even more basically: any good
phenomenological description is going to have normative implications. When Gadamer provides a phenomenology of understanding in *Truth and Method*, it quickly becomes clear that there are
certain things we can do that hinder understanding and others that
enhance it. Gadamer doesn't need to say: "avoid the former and
strive for the latter"; it becomes simply obvious. Similarly, when
Levinas describes how we relate to others, the normative implications grow rather organically from the description. So it is hard to
see how phenomenology could or *should* remain "neutral" in this
sense.

We are not the only ones who have questions regarding Janicaud's
assumptions and entailments. Jean Greisch goes as far as to claim
that "the most serious objection" to Janicaud

> concerns the monolithic use of the word "theology." It
> remains unclear whether Janicaud opposes the possibility of a
> philosophical theology as such, or objects to the contamination
> of phenomenology by an assumed "theology of revelation." In the
> first case, it is incomprehensible why precisely phenomenology
> as such should be forbidden to elaborate a "theology," i.e., a
> philosophically based concept of God, which falls entirely
> within the competence of philosophy. . . . The polemic thus
> appears to be reduced to the second possibility. In this case,
> however, the question necessarily arises as to which concept
> of theology is applicable at all to the four authors treated [viz.
> Levinas, Marion, Henry, and Chrétien]. (1998, 71–2)

As Greisch demonstrates, problems accompany any easy identifica-
tion of any of the new phenomenologists as theologians without
significant qualification. We will consider this more in the next
chapter, but for now we want to simply point out that Janicaud's
view has elicited responses that are as stark as Janicaud's own
account of the difference between phenomenology and theology.

On the one hand, some have suggested that Janicaud's notion
of a theological turn misses the deeply philosophical motivations of new phenomenology. For example, Peter Jonkers claims
that "Janicaud's reproach of a metaphysico-theological montage

fails to recognize that these thinkers really try to renew philosophy. This renewal consists in asking, from a *philosophical* perspective, whether there can be a givenness which goes *beyond* onto-theology, transcending our (power of) thinking, but which at the same time moves us most profoundly and throws us out of balance" (Jonkers 2005, 10). Alternatively, some have claimed that the basic thesis that new phenomenology has begun to be deeply interested in the specifics of revealed theology is largely on target. For example, although worried about some of the equivocation in Janicaud's essay, Greisch boldly proclaims that "there is no doubt that Janicaud's diagnosis is basically correct. Even if not all the work of the new generation of phenomenologists in France can be classified under the rubric theological turn, this turn is undoubtedly one of the descriptive characteristics of this movement most strongly manifested. At least in this regard, the author cannot be accused of crying wolf" (1998, 69).

In light of such contrasting scholarly voices, what ought we to conclude? Though we are substantively more sympathetic to Jonkers's assessment than we are to Greisch's, much depends on what is meant by the fundamental notions of "phenomenology" and "theology." While it is possible to define "phenomenology" in such a way as to exclude the new phenomenological "trajectory," as we have called it, from the phenomenological ranks, it is also possible to define *theology* in such a way as to mean that *any* God-talk whatsoever would amount to theological discourse. However, such quick and rigid definitions are questionable at best. Instead, it is important to understand that there are ways in which both Jonkers and Greisch are on to something important about the relationship between phenomenology and theology in light of Janicaud's problematic account of that relationship.

While there are significant and various ways in which new phenomenologists walk a fine line between a radicalized phenomenology and phenomenological heresy, as we suggested in the previous chapter, there are also significant and various ways in which new phenomenologists are willing to explore the paths opened by classical phenomenology that were not necessarily explored by Husserl, the early Heidegger, or the first generation of French phenomenologists that included Sartre and Merleau-Ponty, who were all exploring phenomenological paths in their own different directions. In the case of Sartre, these phenomenological paths opened onto existential themes such as freedom, anxiety, decision, and the encounter with others in a social world. Alternatively, Merleau-Ponty followed such paths in the direction of the experiences of embodiment, intersubjectivity, and enfleshed existence. Yet Janicaud claims that "whatever liberties [Sartre and Merleau-Ponty] had taken in regard to the Husserlian methodological prescriptions, at least [they] remained faithful to this fundamental Husserlian inspiration: the essence of intentionality is to be sought, by the phenomenological reduction, in phenomenal immanence" (2000, 35). However, a statement like this simply presumes what the "fundamental Husserlian inspiration" *is*. Yet that is precisely what is questioned by the new phenomenologists. To put this another way: it seems odd to assume that these earlier phenomenologists were "simply carrying on" the work of phenomenology, whereas the new phenomenologists somehow either abandon it or take it in a wholly different direction. So, although there are certainly ways to read these earlier phenomenologists as more directly in line with some aspects of Husserlian thought, we want to stress that they too were willing to depart from Husserlian orthodoxy in order to "renew philosophy" in key ways that, on a different view of phenomenology, might themselves be seen as problematic. Again, *what counts as heresy depends on what counts as orthodoxy—and both are thoroughly constructed and contingent categories internal to historical communities of discourse.* In this context, we think that, even for those who are tempted to conclude that new phenomenology is really just theology in phenomenological clothing, there is reason to attempt to delay such a conclusion as long as possible in order to more charitably consider the claims offered within new phenomenology. Moreover, as Greisch, Sebbah, and Jonkers all recognize, suggesting that new phenomenology is merely a turn to theology can miss the nuance and complexity of the thinkers associated with this general trajectory.

In the end, we remain skeptical of Janicaud's claim that his "critical inquiry means . . . to make room for all phenomenological and philosophical possibilities" (2000, 51). It seems only to make room for those possibilities that lie on the *horizontal axis* of relationality—thereby allowing for the invisible of *this* world—while absolutely precluding the possibilities that might lie on the *vertical axis*, even if such an axis is always intersectionally related to the horizontal axis, as is the case according to the new phenomenologists. Hence, though there is much in Janicaud's essay that stands as an important challenge to new phenomenology, the notion that Levinas, Henry, Marion, and Chrétien are playing with "loaded dice" continues to assume a very particular, and potentially problematic, account of phenomenology, which presumes notions of objectivity and neutrality *that are themselves* phenomenologically contested by the new phenomenologists as they, themselves, attempt genuinely "to make room for all phenomenological and philosophical possibilities."

Philosophy, theology, and phenomenology

For readers uninitiated in continental philosophy, it might seem odd that the charge of a theological turn in French phenomenology carries the significance that it does. As we already asked in reference to Janicaud's own account of theological "intimidation," we might now ask more generally: *What is so bad about philosophical theology after all?* Alternatively, to other readers who are familiar with continental philosophy, it also might seem odd that anyone even questions why a theological turn would be inappropriate, since the continental tradition has a long history of quite famous atheistic proponents—including Nietzsche, Heidegger, and Sartre.[1] For example, Jean Greisch notes that even if "derogatory assessments will lose acceptance, assessments such as Alain's much-quoted quip to the effect that theology is but 'a short-sighted philosophy', or worse, Nietzsche's suspicion that German metaphysics was, for the most part, no more than a theology in disguise because the blood of too many theologians flowed in the veins of its practitioners" are troubling indeed (1998, 53). Moreover, haven't non-continental philosophers also often worried about slides toward theology?[2]

Why, then, would it be so obviously inappropriate for French phenomenology to take a theological turn? Well, first we want to say that it is not *obviously* problematic at all. Rather, the problematic dimensions of this turn are only seen within a quite particular understanding of both theology and also of phenomenology. Janicaud's charge does not occur within a vacuum, however. As we have said, it comes from the context of a very particular way of reading classical phenomenology. Let's get a better grasp on the history of this way of reading before moving on to consider new phenomenological responses to it in the chapters that follow.

As we discussed in the last two chapters, new phenomenology attempts to rethink some of the basic claims of classical phenomenology regarding the *epoché*, intentionality, appearance, and in particular the "as such." The new phenomenologists also take issue when it comes to the philosophy of religion, and here they attempt radically to rethink some of the basic phenomenological claims of Husserl and Heidegger regarding the limits of phenomenological inquiry. For Husserl, the phenomenological reduction eliminates "God" as a possible concern for phenomenology because, as transcendent, God would face the same fate as everything else that is phenomenologically bracketed. It is important to note that, for Husserl, God is not rejected (as in logical positivism), denied (as in atheism), or even questioned (as in agnosticism). Rather, God is suspended, bracketed, or, as the title of section 58 of Husserl's *Ideas I* states, "excluded" from phenomenology. However, Husserl does not say that the transcendence of God and the transcendence of the world are identical such that to exclude one necessitates excluding the other. Instead, these two modes of transcendence stand "in polar contrast": God is transcendent "*in a sense totally different* from that in which the world is something transcendent" (Husserl 1982, 133–4, emphasis in original).

Regrettably, Husserl does not go into significant detail in this section of *Ideas I* as to exactly how the two transcendences are different, which might give us a sense of his own positive conception of God and religion.[3] He does give some important hints in this direction that are quite instructive, however. First, Husserl claims that the transcendence of God is not given in the same way that the transcendence of the "pure Ego," which is given "immediately in union with reduced consciousness." In contrast, the transcendence of God is only presented and "cognized in a highly mediated fashion" (1982, 133). What Husserl means here is that, upon enacting the reduction, the pure Ego shows itself as immediately present to consciousness as its conditioning subjective aspect. For example, when I consider my intentional consciousness of the phone sitting on the table, the givenness of the pure Ego as the requirement for all "intentional acts" is necessarily presented. After the reduction, Husserl explains, "we shall not encounter the pure Ego anywhere in the flux of manifold mental process which remains as a transcendental residuum—neither as one mental process among others, nor as strictly a part of a mental process, arising and then disappearing with the mental process of which it is part" (1982, 132). In other words, the pure Ego is not itself the object of intentional consciousness as would be an object like a cup or hat, a fictional object like Hamlet or a unicorn, an idea such as freedom or justice, or even the empirical subject as a thing in the world. Dan Zahavi nicely explains the difference between the transcendental subject and the empirical subject:

> The relation between the transcendental subject and the empirical subject is not a relation between two different subjects, but between two different self-apprehensions, a primary and a secondary. The transcendental subject is the subject in its primary constitutive function. The empirical subject is the same subject, but now apprehended and interpreted as an object in the world, that is, as a constituted and mundanized entity. (Zahavi 2003a, 49)

Husserl explains that, rather than coming and going, "the Ego seems to be there continually, indeed, necessarily, and this continualness is obviously not that of a stupidly persistent mental process, a 'fixed idea'. Instead, the Ego belongs to each coming and going mental process; its 'regard' is directed 'through' each actional cogito to the objective something" (1982, 132). The pure Ego would thus be both immediately present and constantly identical. It does not undergo change as the intentional ray moves to and fro from one object to the next. When it comes to the pure Ego, we find a *"transcendency within immediacy"* such that the transcendence "is not constituted" but rather plays an "essential role" in constituting "any cogitation" (1982, 133). When it comes to God, however, Husserl finds no such immediacy. Rather, it seems that one only cognizes God as the result of a long string of mediated presentations. In some sense, Husserl's account is quite straightforward: God is never immediately the object of intentional consciousness because God does not "appear" as a thing in the world upon which my intentional gaze might rest, but instead appears as precisely other than the world and transcendent to it. Consequently, when I bracket everything that is not immediately presented to intentional consciousness, God gets excluded as a transcendence that does not belong to the immediate, immanent mental process, which is exclusively the object of phenomenological focus after the reduction.

Husserl then turns his attention to a particular way in which phenomenology considers the notion of "grounds" and how this excludes God from phenomenology. Consider what he writes:

> The transition to pure consciousness by the method of transcendental reduction leads necessarily to the question about the ground for the now-emerging factualness of the corresponding constitutive consciousness. Not the fact as such, but the fact as source of endlessly increasing value-possibilities and value-actualities forces the question into one about the "ground"—which naturally does not have the sense of a physical-causal reason. We pass over whatever else, from the point of view of religious consciousness, is able, as a rationally grounding motive, to lead to the same principle. What concerns us here, after merely indicating different groups of such rational grounds for (believing in) the existence of an extra-worldly "divine" being is that this being would obviously transcend not merely the world but "absolute" consciousness. (Husserl 1982, 134)

There is a lot going on in this passage and Husserl uses quite a bit of technical terminology. We shouldn't be too quickly intimidated by this complicated vocabulary, however. Husserl is merely attempting to show that, once one engages in the phenomenological reduction, a new set of questions emerge. Fundamentally, one should inquire into the condition, source, inspiration, or impetus that underlies the way in which the phenomenologically reduced self (i.e. the self that remains after the reduction—which is not identical to the empirical individual) now serves to give rise to (or be the "source" of) an ever-expanding set of evaluative judgments ("endlessly increasing value-possibilities"). We might say that Husserl is drawing our attention to the importance of inquiring into the conditions in and through which consciousness is not merely a passive recipient of the givenness of the things themselves (as objects of intentionality), but actively constitutes the things *as mattering* in various ways (ethically, aesthetically, religiously, etc.).

To ask how it is that consciousness can be understood to work this way—that is, to ask about its "grounds"—is not to investigate into empirical explanations ("physical-causal reasons"), such as those that provided could be explained by Newton's laws of motion, but rather to inquire into the phenomenological background that underlies that which is presented or given to consciousness in the ways exposed by the reduction.

If one then considers such questions from the point of view of "religious consciousness," it might seem that God would serve as the "rationally grounding motive" for arriving at a self who values and evaluates in the ways to which Husserl wants to draw our attention. Yet making such a move would require going beyond what is given to consciousness itself as immanent and integral to the subjective mental process. At the risk of oversimplifying things a bit, we might say that Husserl is worried about the way in which the transition from constituting consciousness as the source of value-possibilities to God as the ground of such a source would lack the requisite phenomenological *evidence*. Husserl is quick to point out that it is phenomenologically appropriate to "indicate" different ways of offering rational justification for belief in God. Such indications are mere descriptions of how consciousness sometimes operates, but they are not normative assessments about the legitimacy of such belief.

Moreover, the "divine being" would *necessarily*, Husserl suggests, transcend what could be given to consciousness itself. It would not be too far off the mark to summarize Husserl's position here as a methodological wariness of any "leaps of faith," as it were. For Husserl, the qualifier added to the principle of all principles regarding the limits of presentation would require such hesitancy and, given the stringent requirements of the reduction, we would thereby be better off "excluding" God as an object of phenomenological inquiry. Of course, Husserl does not claim that belief in God is irrational, but simply that it is *phenomenologically* problematic because the object of the belief itself would lie beyond the domain of consciousness (as required by the model of God with which Husserl operates—namely, as one who is distant and non-relational). Put in slightly more technical terminology, Husserl remains suspicious of any claim to a non-intentional intuition, which would seem to be required if God were to be available for phenomenological consideration, which is exclusively concerned with that which is immanent and immediate to consciousness itself. As we will see later, such a non-intentional intuition is precisely what new phenomenologists such as Marion and Levinas consider to be important possibilities in their philosophical accounts.

In sum, then, an attentive reader of Husserl should not be surprised in seeing God-talk as likely being out of bounds for phenomenology. One such attentive reader was Martin Heidegger, who extends (while transforming the specifics of) Husserl's consideration of the limits of phenomenology when it comes to theology.

Heidegger's critique of onto-theology

As we have already seen in Chapter One, Heidegger's early phenomenology shifts from a concern for consciousness to a concern for fundamental ontology. In the process, Heidegger offers a sustained polemic against what he terms the "onto-theological constitution of metaphysics" (see Heidegger 1969).[4] While "onto-theology" can sound a bit strange,[5] Heidegger appropriates it from Kant and uses it as a general term to refer to the "presupposition that there is an analogy of being between our philosophical ideas about (the structures of) the world as such" and the notion of God as the highest, and most perfect, being who stands as the absolute ground of the world (Jonkers 2005, 6). Or as Heidegger says:

> The question "What is an entity?" [or "What is that which is?"] simultaneously asks: Which entity is the highest [or supreme, *höchste*] entity, and in what sense is it? This is the question of God and of the divine. We call the domain of this question theology. This duality in the question of the being of entities can be united under the title ontotheology. (Heidegger 1998, 340)

Onto-theology has both metaphysical and epistemic ramifications.[6] *Epistemically*, the idea of God serves as the standard and condition by which we could appropriately think about anything else—it is God as the highest being that allows any thought of being to be judged and understood in relation to being. *Metaphysically*, the being of God is the ground or source for all else that "is"—in this sense, God as *causa sui* is a key aspect of the "sense" in which the highest being "is." Heidegger brings both of these aspects together when he writes: "When metaphysics thinks of beings with respect to the ground that is common to all begins as such, then it is logic as onto-logic. When metaphysics thinks of beings as such as a whole, that is, with respect to the highest being which accounts for everything, then it is logic as theo-logic" (1969, 70–1).[7] In a way that is coordinated with his attempt to "destruct the history of western ontology" (see *Being and Time* section 6), Heidegger calls for a rethinking of the onto-theology that underlies it (see Heidegger 1969). In an onto-theological framework, Matheson Russell explains, theism occurs "in its metaphysical mode" (2011, 644).

If Heidegger is right in his affirmation of the "ontological difference" whereby "the being of being 'is' itself not a being," but rather "always the being of a being" (Heidegger 2010, 5, 8), then God can no longer serve the epistemic and metaphysical role that God has traditionally served. By rethinking the onto-theological framework according to which western thought has operated, Heidegger hopes to "step back" (see Heidegger 1969, 49–52) to the original inspiration of pre-Socratic philosophers who were not yet operating within the implicit Platonism that has subsequently shaped western philosophy, in order then to move forward into a philosophical future in which the "question of being" is no longer "forgotten" (Heidegger 2010, 1). Heidegger's strategy is similar to that of a mountain hiker who realizes that she is going in the wrong direction. Rather than charging ahead while continuing to hope that she will eventually get back on the right path, the hiker is best served by turning around and going back to where she last knew herself to be properly directed. Having obtained a secure footing and direction, she can now begin to move forward once more while avoiding her previous missteps. Similarly, Heidegger hopes to get philosophy back on the right track by going back to a point where we might begin anew and avoid the problems and confusions that plagued previous generations. Yet the hiker does not get back the time she lost by going in the wrong direction. Moving forward correctly will now involve taking into account the ways in which one has previously moved sideways, as it were. The same is true for Heidegger: the hope he has in a new future for philosophy is not for one achieved by ignoring the missteps of the tradition but by working through them and appropriating them *as missteps*.

Overcoming onto-theology is necessary, says Heidegger, in order that we avoid moving in the wrong direction while still thinking we are moving properly toward our final goal.

In the context of twentieth-century continental philosophy, the influence of Heidegger's critique of onto-theology is difficult to overestimate. Greisch has even claimed that the "debate around the onto-theological situation of Western metaphysics," which Heidegger inaugurated, has in the past few decades "become almost limitless" (1998, 60). It is important to realize that Heidegger's resistance to onto-theology is not an opposition to theology as such, but to the way in which philosophy has understood theism as simply a particular sort of metaphysical and epistemic thesis. Indeed, most postmodern philosophers of religion agree that onto-theology is something that should be avoided. Such avoidance is not an impetus to atheism, however, but to a conception of religious existence that is not first and foremost articulated according to the assumptions that underlie the model of God found in "classical theism"—whether those assumptions be metaphysical (God as the highest being, who is self-caused, and the transcendent standard of all value judgments), or epistemic (God as the source of "objective" truth and absolute certainty). As we will see, the new phenomenologists all challenge onto-theology, but none of them understand this challenge to entail atheism.[8] And, contra Janicaud, such a position does not force them out of the phenomenological domain into that of theology.

Although Heidegger began his academic career as a student of theology, he eventually moved away from theology toward the phenomenological methodology and philosophical concerns offered by Husserl. While Heidegger's relationship to theology is anything but simple, his early phenomenological understanding of theology is not as complicated as it might seem.[9] In a lecture course titled "Introduction to the Phenomenology of Religion," which he delivered in 1920–1 and which is published in English as *The Phenomenology of Religious Life* (Heidegger 2004), Heidegger claims that he is not interested in a "dogmatic or theological-exegetical interpretation" of religion (specifically as it concerns Pauline letters), nor does he want to offer "a historical study or a religious meditation," but instead his singular interest is in offering "guidance for phenomenological understanding" (2004, 47). In such a phenomenological undertaking, "the theological method falls out of the framework of our study," claims Heidegger (2004, 47). Not dismissing theology outright, Heidegger instead describes phenomenology as being the distinctive way in which "a new way for theology is opened up" (2004, 47) such that "genuine religious-philosophical understanding" is itself articulated in terms of a "phenomenological understanding" (2004, 53). What Heidegger claims to be searching for in his reading of Paul is "the grounding phenomena of primordial Christian life" (2004, 47). "Primordial Christian life" should not be confused with the metaphysics that onto-theology displays (2004, 52–5).[10] Even getting clear on such a distinction requires, according to Heidegger, a careful phenomenological analysis of what is going on in Galatians, which Heidegger sees as presenting the phenomena of Christian life itself.

It is tempting to think that Heidegger's discussion of "grounding phenomena" might be similar to the searches for some account of the sui generis aspects of religious experience by other "phenomenologists of religion"—especially Rudolph Otto (1969–37), who published his seminal *Das Heilige: Über das Irrationale in der Idee des Göttlichen und sein Verhältnis zum Rationalen* [*The Idea of the Holy: An Inquiry into the Non-Rational Factor in the Idea of the Divine and Its Relation to the Rational*] in 1917, but also Gerardus van der Leeuw (1890–1950), whose *Phänomenologie der Religion* [*Religion in Essence and Manifestation: A Study in Phenomenology*] was published in 1933, and Mircea Eliade (1907–86), who published *The Sacred and Profane: The Nature of Religion* in 1957. For the phenomenologists of religion such as Otto, van der Leeuw, and Eliade, the goal was to find the essential dimension of religious experience that unites all such experiences *as religious*. Yet Heidegger explicitly challenges such a conception of phenomenology as misguided in his direct critique of Otto:

Today's philosophy of religion [Heidegger provides a footnote to Otto here] is proud of its category of the irrational and, with it, considers the access to religiosity secured. But with these two concepts [rational and irrational] nothing is said, as long as one does not know the meaning of rational. The concept of the irrational, after all, is supposed to be determined from out of the opposition to the concept of the rational, which, however, finds itself in notorious indetermination. This pair of concepts is thus to be eliminated entirely. Phenomenological understanding, according to its basic meaning, lies entirely outside of this opposition, which has only a very limited authority, if at all. *Everything that is said of the—for reason—indissoluble residue that supposedly remains in all religions, is merely an aesthetic play with things that are not understood.* (Heidegger 2004, 54–5, emphasis added)

This passage is important not only because it concludes with a statement that might be mistaken for the work of such contemporary religious studies scholars as Jonathan Z. Smith (1982), Russell McCutcheon (1997), and Timothy Fitzgerald (2000), who all vigorously challenge that there is a sui generis essence of religion, but also because it necessitates a distinction between what is often referenced as the "phenomenology of religion" and the philosophy of religion that one finds occurring in the phenomenology of Heidegger. This is crucial for understanding new phenomenology's approach to the philosophy of religion, because it comes closer to Heidegger's inquiry into what Matheson Russell (2011) terms "faith in the primitive Christian mode" than it does to the essentialist discourse of Otto, van der Leeuw, and Eliade.[11] Unfortunately, it is difficult to use the appropriately descriptive phrase "phenomenology of religion" to describe the philosophy of religion occurring in new phenomenology, because it is unavoidably linked to these essential thinkers who ultimately share less than might be expected with classical phenomenology and, especially, the radicalization of such phenomenology that occurs in new phenomenology.

In Heidegger's early analysis of the phenomenology of religious life, his concern is with the lived "enactment of the observer," rather than with some sort of historico-sociological account of the essence of religion. In this way, we might say that Heidegger follows Husserl's (and in a different way, Kierkegaard's) attempt to articulate objectivity *in* subjectivity, rather than attempting to find the objective account of the subjective, as the phenomenologists of religion seem to do. Stressing the subjective quality and defeasible nature of phenomenological inquiry, Heidegger claims that "phenomenological understanding" consists in two things:

First, not in the projecting of what is to be understood, which, after all, is no kind of object, in a material complex. It has, *secondly*, never the tendency of determining such a realm with finality, but rather is subordinated to the historical situation—insofar as the foreconception is even more decisive for phenomenological understanding than object-historical understanding. Thus, one has to begin at the starting point (the foreconception) of the phenomenological understanding. (2004, 57)

Here we can see that, unlike Husserl, Heidegger's worry about theology does not concern the transcendence of God beyond the immanent mental process, but instead the problematic nature of theological discourse itself. Simply put, theology seems to start with answers to the questions that phenomenological philosophy attempts genuinely to ask. Heidegger stresses the lack of "finality" that exists due to the historical situatedness of the inquiry itself. Here we can see his resistance to the epistemic aspects of onto-theology. Elsewhere, Heidegger will claim that all philosophy must be methodologically atheistic, because only then can it engage in serious questions without particular theological foreconceptions (or presuppositions) serving to shut down paths where inquiry might otherwise travel. As Laurence Paul Hemming notes: "Martin Heidegger says that 'philosophical research is and remains atheism'. Even before this he said that only when philosophy is properly atheistic, 'only then is it honest . . . before God'" (2002, 1).

Heidegger then offers two "hypothetical" starting points for a phenomenological investigation into primordial Christian religiosity that would allow for both a methodologically atheist starting point and a robustly historical contextualism for such inquiry:

1 Primordial Christian religiosity is in factical life experience . . .

2 Factical life experience is historical. (Heidegger 2004, 57)

The way in which one investigates the hypothetical starting points, Heidegger notes, is by claiming "if they are valid, then such and such results for the phenomenon," and then testing such results "in phenomenological experience itself" (2004, 57). This hypothetical qualifier is important here, because it allows Heidegger to remain solidly descriptive rather than normative when it comes to his consideration of the basic phenomena of primordial Christian religiosity. That is, he does not make claims about what religion *should* be, but simply about what it *is*. Yet he is not concerned here with religion as conceived in some essentialist or historicist way, but with religion *as experienced, lived, and engaged.*

In a later essay on Hegel titled "The Onto-theo-logical Constitution of Metaphysics," Heidegger turns to history as a source for phenomenological thinking as it attempts the task of "entering into the force of earlier thinking." Phenomenological thinking is interested here not so much in what has been claimed or thought in that history, but instead in that "which has not been thought, and from which what has been thought receives its essential space" (1969, 48). Here we can, again, see a way in which Heidegger's thought is differentiated from the thought of the traditional phenomenologists of religion, who search for the essence or fundamental quality in historical thought as a metaphysical reality on display in history. As already noted, Heidegger's turn to history is meant as a "step back" in a very particular way, as opposed to a search for historical foundations for ontological truth. It is in this way that Heidegger sees his own thought (at least as presented in the 1950s) to be non-metaphysical: "The step back thus moves out of metaphysics into the essential nature of metaphysics" (1969, 51). Heidegger is thus able to join his earlier phenomenological account of "primitive Christian religiosity" to his critique of onto-theology developed in his later thought, insofar as overcoming onto-theology might be the best way to step back to the risky faith expressed in the determinate ways of life of primitive Christian religiosity.

At the end of "The Onto-theo-logical Constitution of Metaphysics," Heidegger more explicitly makes the connection between the critique of onto-theology, the limits of philosophy (read: phenomenology), and the possibilities of genuine religious faith and practice. In a complicated, though oft-cited, passage, Heidegger states:

> The deity enters into philosophy through the perdurance of which we think at first as the approach to the active nature of the difference between Being and beings. The difference constitutes the ground plan in the structure of the essence of metaphysics. The perdurance results in and gives Being as the generative ground. This ground itself needs to be properly accounted for by that for which it accounts, that is, by the causation through the supremely original matter—and that is the cause as *causa*

sui. This is the right name for the god of philosophy. Man can neither pray nor sacrifice to this god. Before the *causa sui*, man can neither fall to his knees in awe nor can he play music and dance before this god.

The god-less thinking which must abandon the god of philosophy, god as *causa sui*, is thus perhaps closer to the divine God. Here this means only: god-less thinking is more open to Him than onto-theo-logic would like to admit. (1969, 71–2)

Notice that Heidegger comes close to saying that the problem with onto-theology is itself *theological*! Namely, onto-theology fails to open us to the depth and risky significance of lived religious existence. By seeing the "enactment of life" as decisive, as Heidegger puts it in 1920–1 (see 2004, 56), phenomenology helps us to see that classical western metaphysics assumes a model of God that seems quite far from "the divine God," who is worshiped, praised, celebrated, and feared in religious existence as historically lived. It is for this reason that Merold Westphal rightly notes that Heidegger's critique of onto-theology is

> not directed toward the God of the Bible or the Koran, before whom people do fall on their knees in awe, pray, sacrifice, sing, and dance. It is a critique of a metaphysical tradition that extends from Anaximander to Nietzsche and includes Aristotle and Hegel as high points. (Westphal 2001, 4)

So where does this realization get us? Heidegger admits that "no one can know whether and when and where and how this step of thinking will develop into a proper . . . path and way and road-building" (1969, 72). Even worrying about the possibility that metaphysics will simply "absorb" this new future opened by the "step back," Heidegger warns that it is very possible that "the step back [will] itself remain unaccomplished, and the path which it opens and points out [will] remain untrod" (1969, 73).

Despite the worries about a theological turn in new phenomenology, we actually see the new phenomenologists as some of the main inheritors of this Heideggerian invitation to explore where such new "paths" might lead. In this sense, we remain convinced that their phenomenology, while possibly heterodox, is not heretical.

For Heidegger, such explorations were not un-phenomenological, but simply an extension of phenomenological inquiry in directions that require attending not only to the unthought in the history of thought, but also, as we saw in Chapter One, to that which might *appear as invisible*, or even *give itself as unapparent*.

Although Heidegger's critique of onto-theology has been widely influential on continental philosophy of religion, it is often understood to be more philosophically sweeping than it truly is. As we have argued above, even for Heidegger, onto-theology should not be understood as a synonym for the determinate beliefs and practices of religious traditions conceived with the God of faith (as opposed to the God of philosophical speculation). Accordingly, overcoming onto-theology does not mean overcoming determinate religious belief and practice, but merely overcoming a conception of such belief and practice that is problematically wedded to speculative abstraction and epistemic arrogance. Perhaps no one has done a better job in making this case than Westphal, who rightly notes that Heidegger's critique of onto-theology is quite close to Søren Kierekgaard's critique of speculative philosophy. According to Westphal,

> Kierkegaard helps us to see that the onto-theological gesture consists not in positing a God who differs radically from us by satisfying the requirements of Hegel's Logic and Philosophy of World History, who sees the world synchronically as system and diachronically in terms of a grand metanarrative. It consists in positing such a God as an excuse for making the claim that we can occupy the divine perspective on the world, or at least peek over God's shoulder. (2001, 6)

We agree with Westphal's assessment that onto-theology is not so much about a particular model of God as "omnipotent, omniscient, and benevolent" (de Vries 1995, 218) as about the way in which one assumes to be in relation with that God. So saying, for instance, that God is self-caused is not, *by itself*, a problem. The problem arises when we think that God *must* be this way, not because this is how a religious tradition appropriates its revealed text, but because the conceptual requirements of our metaphysical system *need* God to be this way in order to allow for certainty and adequacy between thought and being. Hence, with Westphal—and we believe with Heidegger as well—overcoming onto-theology is more a matter of avoiding epistemic arrogance than of denying metaphysical realism.[12]

In line with Heidegger's own hopes for the new path opened by the step back, Greisch rightly reminds us:

> One should look at the everlasting talk about the "end of metaphysics" just as critically as one considers the content of this metaphysics. I am well aware how difficult it is to attend to those thinkers who are in search of a thought that begins differently, such as Heidegger's, and yet at the same time, take into account that even apparently quite outmoded models of thought still hold enough critical potential to generate new impetus. (Greisch 1998, 61)[13]

Although Greish is not directly thinking of new phenomenologists, the suggestion that old ways of thinking might still possess "critical potential to generate new impetus" is one with which new phenomenologists would be likely to agree. However, the new phenomenologists appear willing, when they consider old ways of thinking, to draw on theological archives in ways that cause Dominique Janicaud to argue that they should no longer be understood as doing phenomenology at all. In the next chapter, we will look at such willingness as we consider a positive account of what new phenomenological philosophy of religion involves by rethinking the relationship between phenomenology and theology.

CHAPTER FOUR

Phenomenology and theology reconsidered

In this chapter, we will work through the distinction between phenomenology and theology as affirmed by all of the new phenomenologists (in slightly different ways). In the process, we look at quite a bit of new phenomenological God-talk and we will quote a lot from new phenomenological texts in order to convey the tone and style of the God-talk that shows up in them. While granting that the suspicions about a "theological turn" are not entirely without textual support, we aim to show that new phenomenological philosophy of religion deserves to be weighed and considered *as* philosophy of religion.

New phenomenological philosophy of religion

In the previous chapter, we demonstrated that there is at least some support in Husserlian and Heideggerian texts for Janicaud's suggestion that new phenomenology amounts to a non-phenomenological turn to revealed theology insofar as it is willing to allow significantly more God-talk into phenomenological research. Yet, in Chapter One, we considered in some detail why Heidegger's "phenomenology of the unapparent" is named by Janicaud as a key source for the turn. It might legitimately seem odd that the same thinker can be understood as both laying out reasons for why God-talk in phenomenology is problematic and also for why phenomenology ought to follow the "path" toward the "unapparent" that might be closer to the "divine" than traditional onto-theology. There are a variety of plausible explanations that can make sense of this seeming tension in Heidegger's thought. Most obviously, it could be all chalked up to a change of mind, hence the importance of Heidegger's "*Kehre*" to Janicaud's account. Nonetheless, we should realize that, as evidenced by Heidegger's reading of Husserl in 1973, the development of Heidegger's philosophy was not a rejection of his former defense of phenomenology, but reflected a profound reconsideration of the project of fundamental ontology. Accordingly, we should attend to Heidegger's continued loyalty to the basic commitments of phenomenology as he becomes attuned to the depths of phenomena that might otherwise get ignored or overlooked by classical phenomenological formulations. In this respect, Janicaud is right to locate Heidegger as one of the sources of new phenomenology, *regardless of whether there has been a theological turn*.

At least part of Heidegger's later concerns with the event, art, poetry, language, thinking, and such strange notions as "the fourfold," and "the unapparent," can be read as a deepening of phenomenological attention itself in new directions.[1] In this way, Heidegger himself challenges the methodological straightjacket imposed by Janicaud (and perhaps even by the early Heidegger himself) upon phenomenological inquiry as being too limiting on the receptivity to the givenness of phenomena in all its variety. Although "there is no doubt that, for Janicaud, every horizontal broadening of the phenomenological domain of operations is not only justified but also to be welcomed," as Jean Greisch says, "as soon as phenomenology addresses itself to the vertical, it is in for a fall: thus all raising in this area (of heads, of eyes to the heavens, of questions) leads only to self-elevation" (1998, 71). While Heidegger is certainly worried about such self-elevation (and the onto-theological underpinnings that might accompany it), he comes to realize that a prima facie exclusion of openness to the "unapparent," as Husserl seems occasionally implicitly to encourage and Janicaud explicitly endorses, is not to be scientifically rigorous, but phenomenologically limited.

While it is clear that phenomenological inquiry will face some sort of limitation (i.e. all philosophical inquiry is not necessarily phenomenological, and all inquiry is not necessarily philosophical), it is not *obvious* that *these* horizontal limits are the right ones to impose from the outset. Such a commitment amounts to a very determinate decision about what in Husserl's philosophy ought to remain phenomenological *orthodoxy* and what ought to be seen as merely *important first steps* that open up new "paths," as Heidegger says.[2] Indeed, as we have already suggested, the very question about the limits of phenomenology (i.e. what counts as orthodoxy) is part of phenomenological inquiry itself. Just as Heidegger worries about positive theology potentially shutting down genuine questioning because it presupposes quite particular answers to questions that then don't get asked, his later thought seems to worry that classical phenomenology does not live up to its full potential and, hence, needs to follow the new paths that might open up before it.[3]

Long ago, Socrates encouraged the lover of inquiry to "follow the beloved wherever it may lead" (*Euthyphro* 14c–d). We take the later Heidegger, and the new phenomenologists working in his wake, to continue to adhere to this Socratic imperative. Just as Plato's attempt to follow Socrates, and Aristotle's attempt to follow Plato, eventually led both Plato and Aristotle radically to challenge and to move beyond the thoughts of their mentors, Heidegger attempts to follow Husserl and the new phenomenologists attempt to follow Heidegger by offering serious objections and eventually moving in different directions than those previously laid out by their forerunners. As David Wood (2002, 3) appropriately explains, what it means to follow someone in the sense of "thinking after" her is decidedly ambiguous. It can mean that one consciously attempts to continue the prior intellectual project—in the sense of "following after the master." But it can also mean that one uses that project as a starting point and a sounding board, though not as a goal—in the sense of "following after someone by beginning where they left off and seeing what new horizons might begin to open up." It is this latter sense that we take to be characteristic of most of the really important philosophical trajectories: for example, Socrates/Plato/Aristotle, Kant/Hegel/Kierkegaard, and Husserl/Heidegger/the new phenomenologists.

The proposal of a theological turn, we believe, ignores the deeply phenomenological motivations of the new phenomenologists. Even though many of the new phenomenologists are personally religious, and although the tone and focus is slightly different in each case, the new phenomenologists are all guided by primarily *philosophical* motivations, as opposed to religious ones. They remain phenom-enologically attentive even when they push beyond Husserl's and Heidegger's phenomenological formulations. Now, Christians such as Jean-Luc Marion and Jean-Louis Chrétien operate with a con-cern for (the possibility of) religious phenomena at the very center of their philosophical project such that they are largely (though not exclusively) occupied with questions of relevance to the philosophy of religion. While this has led some to refer to new phenomenology as simply "Christian phenomenology,"[4] this moniker is mislead-ing for two reasons. First, it would mean that new phenomenology would exclude both Emmanuel Levinas and Jacques Derrida, who were both Jewish. Second, it misunderstands the way in which the new phenomenologists understand the relationship between phe-nomenology and theology, which is strikingly unified given that new phenomenology includes a diverse set of Christians (Marion, Chrétien, and Henry), an explicitly religious Jew (Levinas), and a Jew who "rightly passes as an atheist" (Derrida).

Despite this important meta-philosophical unity, the degree to which questions in the philosophy of religion are taken to be central to phenomenology varies quite a bit among the new phenomenolo-gists. So, while Marion and Chrétien tend to start with philoso-phy of religion and move outward to other topics and questions (aesthetics and ethics in particular), Henry begins with questions about the conditions of phenomenality and the problems faced by the "ontological monism" of western philosophy. As we will see, though, even though Henry's starting point might seem more obviously phenomenologically oriented, it does not take long for him to turn to the philosophy of religion. And, although writing widely on ethics, psychoanalysis, and Marxist political philoso-phy, Henry devotes a series of books to the philosophy of religion. Similarly, while Levinas's philosophy is best understood to begin with questions about the possibility of transcendence in light of worries about ontological totality, and his thought is primarily affiliated with continental ethics, Levinas's mature philosophy is never far from the philosophy of religion as part and parcel of any inquiry into ethics or transcendence. Indeed, Levinas even claims that "every philosophical thought rests on pre-philosophical experiences, and because for me reading the Bible as belonged to these founding experiences," it is not a wonder that his philosophy would be occupied with such issues (1985, 24). Understandably, then, Levinas will eventually claim that his authorship is a sustained attempt to translate Hebrew wisdom into Greek philosophical language. Finally, the new phenomenologist who is plausibly read as the least *directly* concerned with the philosophy of religion, Jacques Derrida, writes several essays and books that deal directly with religion, and he ends up ironically being the one most influential on contemporary debates in continental philosophy of religion, which is a subdiscipline even sometimes referred to as "deconstructive" philosophy of religion.

We want to be clear that it would be a mistake to reduce new phenomenology to the philosophy of religion, and even more of a mistake to collapse the diverse perspectives of new phenomenological philosophy of religion into a hegemonic account. However, all of the new phenomenologists are deeply invested in the phenomenological legitimacy of the philosophy of religion even while resisting the phenomenological slide into revealed theology about which Janicaud worries. Accordingly, we agree with Anne A. Davenport's claim that "there is no 'theological turn' of phenomenology: rather, phenomenology becomes the extreme plenitude of philosophy. Radical phenomenology is not, and could never be, 'theological'" (2004, xxvi). Jonkers makes a similar claim when he suggests:

> Generally speaking, [the new phenomenologists'] use of religious ideas and concepts is not so much for the sake of religion as such, but is primarily motivated by their philosophical interest. For all these reasons, it seems to me incorrect to interpret the attention of contemporary (French) philosophy for God and religion as a turn to religion or theology, as some do. (2005, 8)

Jonkers appropriately challenges those who would suggest that "the reasons for numerous French . . . philosophers to be interested in religious issues can be interpreted as a *turn to religion*" (2005, 11). Referring to de Vries (1999) as well as to Janicaud (2000), Jonkers rightly points out that in order to sustain the claim that there has been a theological turn, or a turn to religion, one has to equivocate on the meanings of such terms as "theology" and "religion." For

example, Jonkers takes de Vries to "unif[y] all kinds of heteroge-
neous movements in contemporary (French) philosophy under the
heading of a turn to religion. In this way, he seems to deny the
crucial differences" among the French phenomenologists (Jonkers
2005, 11). Moreover, Jonkers rightly notes,

> De Vries can only maintain his argument that in contemporary
> (French) philosophy there is a turn to religion because he explicitly
> detaches the concept of religion from any personal engagement
> in a religious conviction, and reduces religious traditions to a
> semantic and symbolic archive, which can be, to a great extent,
> formalized and transposed into concepts and philosophemes. If
> one agrees with De Vries's argument, what, then, is left of the
> religious character of this kind of religion? (2005, 11)

Jonkers's question here is crucial. What, indeed, is left of religion
in new phenomenology?

Is the only option now merely a "religion *without* religion," as
Derrida will term the postmodern religiosity that he sees as remaining available within deconstruction?[5] Can new phenomenologists
engage in God-talk only if such talk is stripped of its location in
determinate religious traditions? Is the God-talk that is viable in
postmodern phenomenology that which eliminates all determinate religious content? Does new phenomenology even allow for
something like the "Christian philosophy" advocated by Alvin
Plantinga? Moreover, if we are right to suggest that new phenomenology is not a turn to religion, but a deepening of the phenomenological impulse in the direction of the philosophy of religion, how
does new phenomenology stand in relation to classical philosophy
of religion as well as contemporary analytic philosophy of religion?
These are difficult questions. We will only be able to go so far in
addressing them in this book, but we will do our best to at least
start a conversation that might help to illuminate possible ways to
further consider such issues elsewhere.

Phenomenology and theology: Take two

As is usual when reading sophisticated thinkers, answers to complicated questions are rarely immediately made clear and offered
without nuance and numerous qualifications. Attempting to get

clear on the relationship between phenomenology and theology as understood by the new phenomenologists is, thus, not as straightforward as it might seem. There is evidence that could be presented as supporting different conclusions on the matter. In this way, we want, again, to stress that Janicaud's reading is not thoroughly misguided. Although his proposal of a theological turn is not a sustainable interpretation of their thought as a whole, nonetheless, the new phenomenologists do agree with his fundamental claim that "phenomenology and theology *make two*." Let's consider how this gets worked out by Levinas, Chrétien, and Marion.

First and foremost, the new phenomenologists are wary of allowing the theological authority structures to operate in their philosophy. For example, Emmanuel Levinas was careful to distinguish between his philosophical work (*Totality and Infinity* and *Otherwise than Being*, say) from his more theological work (as contained in a series of "Talmudic Readings and Lectures"— see Levinas 1990a; 1990b; and 1994). Levinas even repeatedly notes that he used different publishers for these different authorships so that there would not be any confusion between them. "I separate very clearly these two types of work," he says, and then continues on to note that "I even have two publishers: the one publishes my confessional texts, the other my texts which are called purely philosophical" (2001, 62). Although Levinas's claim here might seem a bit naïve regarding the suspicions that critics might have concerning the way in which one's religious commitments can influence and affect one's professional life, his rationale for such a separation very sensibly rests on the way he understands authority structures to operate in inquiry. For Levinas, theology can legitimately appeal to a sacred text, say, as authoritative in ways that philosophy cannot. Levinas addresses this issue explicitly in an interview, when he is asked whether he objected to being termed a "Jewish thinker":

> To be considered a Jewish thinker is not in itself something that shocks me. I am Jewish and certainly I have readings, contacts, and traditions which are specifically Jewish and which I do not deny. But I protest against this formula when by it one understands something that dares to establish between concepts relations which are based uniquely in religious traditions and texts, without bothering to pass through the philosophical critique. There are two ways of reading a biblical verse. One

consists in appealing to the tradition, in giving it the value of the premise in one's conclusions, without distrusting and without even taking account of the presuppositions of that tradition. . . . The second reading consists not in contesting straightaway, philosophically, but rather in translating and accepting the suggestions of a thinking which, once translated, can be justified by what manifests itself. For me, the relation to phenomenology has been extremely important. . . . *A philosophical truth cannot be based on the authority of a verse. The verse must be phenomenologically justified.* But the verse can allow for the search for a reason. . . . It irritates me when one insinuates that I prove by means of the verse, when sometimes I search by way of the old ancient wisdom. I illustrate with the verse, yes, but I do not prove by means of the verse. (2001, 61–2, emphasis added)

Apparently not satisfied with such an answer, the interviewer again asks, "Would you say that you are a religious thinker?" to which Levinas responds:

Here again, that can mean: are you a believer? Do you practice a religion? But this is not as thinker in any case. Because your question asks: in your thinking, do the truths acquired once and for all by revelation intervene as the truths which constitute the basis of your philosophical life? I don't think so. But "religious" can also mean—I am repeating myself—suggestions, calls to analysis or research in religious texts, that is to say, in the Bible. (2001, 63)

Despite affirming such a clear demarcation between theology and philosophy, Levinas is similarly clear in both of these passages that religion has much to offer to philosophy. Even going so far as saying that the Bible is "essential to thinking" (2001, 63), Levinas's view is, contra the early Heidegger, not that philosophers ought to be atheistic in their thinking (and even less that they ought to be atheists in their personal lives), but that phenomenological philosophy is unable to appeal to *theological* authorities as immediately *philosophically* authoritative.

When asked how he "harmonized these two modes of thought, the Biblical and philosophical," Levinas responds:

> Were they supposed to harmonize? The religious sentiment such as I had received it consisted much more in respect for books— the Bible and its traditional commentaries going back to the thought of ancient rabbis—than in determinate beliefs. . . . The texts of the great philosophers . . . seem to me closer to the Bible than opposed to it, even if the concreteness of Biblical themes was not immediately reflected in the philosophical pages. But I did not have the impression, early on, that philosophy was essentially atheist, and I still do not think it today. (1985, 23)

Though there have been numerous scholars who have questioned whether such a division in Levinas's authorship is as thoroughgoing as he claims (and whether the authority structures operating variously therein are as neatly separated as he suggests),[6] it is important that Levinas himself understood his work to remain faithful to an important distinction between philosophy and theology.

We can see a distinction between phenomenology and theology also affirmed by Jean-Louis Chrétien when he suggests that such a demarcation is crucial for both disciplines:

> Concerning . . . the relations of philosophy and theology, simple good sense suffices for one to see that the only act calling for critique would be the one that confuses the two (and in two senses! There are theologians who are in fact only philosophers). There is nothing at all contentious in what the same author writes of philosophy *and* theology, which is the case here [i.e. in Chrétien's own work]. The criterion of theology is to be expressly under the *lumen fidei*, in the light of faith, and thus in obedience to the Word of God—a trying obedience, since it is one that will always fall short of the excess of what it must hear. This criterion suffices to discriminate which among the diverse works evoked here belong to philosophy and which to theology. As for the internal articulation, it resides in the fact that it is possible, as many philosophers have thought, that philosophy poses questions to which it cannot respond in ultimate fashion,

and that philosophy cannot close on itself. One is certainly at liberty to say (but one must also demonstrate this) that such questions are badly posed, or that they have no response. It is also possible (and indeed, by saying this one does it) to seek the response in another source, and to examine what light harks back to it. (2002, 128–9)

Three things are especially worth noting here. First, Chrétien articulates the boundary between theology and philosophy as a matter of authoritative appeals as made available by particular criteria: namely, "the light of faith" and "obedience to the Word of God." Accordingly, he concurs with Levinas regarding the fact that theology can appeal to authorities that are not available to philosophy.

Second, the final sentence in this passage suggests that phenomenology might eventually have legitimate cause to look elsewhere (especially to theology) for answers to its questions. The claim that philosophy might end up inviting theological inquiry in such ways stands in contrast to Levinas's suggestion that "at no moment did the Western philosophical tradition in my eyes lose its right to the last word; everything must, indeed, be expressed in its tongue; but perhaps it is not the place of the first meaning of beings, the place where meaning begins" (1985, 24–5). Whether theology will be a source for philosophical reflection (Levinas) or the terminus toward which philosophy ultimately is understood potentially to tend (Chrétien) is very much a debate for the new phenomenologists. The difference between Levinas and Chrétien in this regard, we believe, is best understood as a matter of divergent philosophical practice: while Levinas attempts rigidly to demarcate between his writings on philosophy and his writings on theology, Chrétien claims to write "of philosophy *and* theology" in the same works. As such, for Chrétien, the border between the two is deployed at the same time as it is itself being phenomenologically considered *as* a border. For Levinas, alternatively, the border is in place as a prima facie criterion for thought. Not surprisingly, then, while Levinas seems to guard against illegitimate border-crossing, as it were, Chrétien understands the border to be a necessity if one wants intentionally to explore what would even count as an illegitimate crossing (as opposed to a legitimate one) in the first place.

Third, Chrétien rightly emphasizes the important hermeneutic tasks that accompany appeals to theological archives, whether as authoritative and evidential or merely as heuristic and inspirational (and perhaps leading to what Janicaud terms "edification"). In this way, he admits that, although the distinction between philosophy and theology is necessary, it is not always one that is easily identified in ways that allow for subsequent easy classifications of a particular text as being an instance of exclusively one or the other. Again, the disagreement between Levinas and Chrétien is not about whether there is (or should be) a distinction between phenomenology and theology, but about how such a distinction should be cashed out and then understood to operate in the way in which one *writes*, *thinks*, and even *thinks about writing*.

In light of Janicaud's worry about Levinas's theologically "loaded dice," Chrétien's complicated and multifaceted authorship might indicate to some that he is engaged in some sort of *theological* apologetics.[7] Yet, given the hermeneutic difficulties that accompany reading thinkers who draw on both philosophical and theological archives, Chrétien pushes back against such apologetic worries by pointing out that the very distinction between philosophy and theology raises legitimate philosophical questions about the limits of philosophy. Moreover, asking such questions is not an infrequent occupation in the history of philosophy. "What philosophy, since the end of antiquity," wonders Chrétien, "has not openly or secretly struggled with revealed theology, if nothing else for the purpose of fighting against it?" (2004, 2). Chrétien then continues on to ask, "what area of thought has not experienced the incursions of revealed theology and been penetrated by its questions and its language?" (2004, 2). Answering his own question in a manner that affirms the importance of the ubiquitous presence of questions about theology's relationship to philosophy, Chrétien claims that "philosophy cannot autocratically decide for itself what figures of the divine it must debate" (2004, 2). In other words, the very distinction between philosophy and theology, and the particular focus of anything that would count as philosophy *of religion*, would rest on determinate *decisions* about such things. Importantly, though, such decisions would be made by particular communities of discourse (as historically articulated and understood). Such decisions would be made *by philosophers* or *by theologians*, say. As Chrétien explains:

> Is it for purely philosophical reasons that astral theology and cosmic religion, so important to Plato and Aristotle, have been discarded by us irrevocably to the past? Why do we no longer call "atheist" someone who denies the divinity of stars, but rather someone who denies the existence of a single living God? We cannot simply appoint ourselves to police the presumed clear-cut border between philosophy and theology; we must first, as philosophers, call into question where the border is drawn. (2004, 2)

For Chrétien, one of the important things that philosophers do, *as philosophers*, is to question what philosophers *ought to do*. While philosophers would always start to ask such questions from within historical locations and socio-cultural contexts, being attentive to the ways in which previous conceptions might blind us to new ways of moving forward is crucial. Just as Heidegger worried about the "obviousness" of tradition, Chrétien worries about the problems that can emerge if one fails to revisit the presumptions that one has received as part of one's own intellectual heritage. Chrétien can then plausibly be understood as displaying Husserlian openness while challenging Janicaud's methodological rigidity (consider that *The Call and Response* was published just one year after Janicaud's essay on the theological turn) when he asks: "What philosopher would ever elect ignorance as the best counsel and imitate the ostrich as his most advantageous strategy?" (2004, 3). Instead of prohibiting vertical horizonality and all possible indications of revealed theology from phenomenological inquiry, Chrétien concludes that "no one therefore will be surprised to find that biblical theology has been given an integral place among the traditions of thought that we propose to study and to critically examine from a phenomenological perspective" (2004, 3). As we have seen, such a claim might just as easily have been offered by Levinas. Neither thinker allows biblical theology to operate authoritatively in their phenomenology, but both affirm the importance of understanding religious traditions and theological archives to be objects of phenomenological inquiry as well as potential inspiration for such phenomenological inquiry itself.

No new phenomenologist has more explicitly and thoroughly considered the relationship between phenomenology and theology than Jean-Luc Marion who, like Levinas, divides his authorship between books and essays that are rightly considered philosophical (e.g. *Reduction and Givenness* and *Being Given*) and those that are "written at the border between philosophy and theology" (1991, xix) (viz. *God without Being, The Visible and the Revealed, Prolegomena to Charity*, etc.). Nonetheless, as in Levinas and Chrétien, Marion also resists any understanding of this distinction between phenomenology and theology to entail a hard-and-fast separation between the two disciplines. Indeed, perhaps even more than the other new phenomenologists, Marion sees theology as a productive resource for philosophical inquiry. For example, Marion cites, with seeming approval, Husserl's suggestion that phenomenology is likely to make significant contributions to theological research[8] and then claims that although "the distinction between the domains, objects, and methods remains absolute," it is likely that they will benefit from mutual engagement (2002c, 28).

Just as with Levinas, some scholars have challenged Marion's division and suggest that he frequently crosses the very lines between philosophy and theology that he establishes for himself.[9] Nonetheless, for Marion, Levinas, and Chrétien, phenomenology and theology are distinguished regarding the methodology and task of each discourse. For Levinas and Chrétien, this distinction is primarily drawn along the lines of the respective authority structures to which one would appeal. For Marion, alternatively, the distinction is more a matter of modal ontology, which in very broad strokes can be understood as consideration of how the categories of possibility and necessity (or in Marion's case, possibility and actuality) affect the way in which things are and are thought to be. Claiming that phenomenology is only able to speculate about the possibility and not the actuality of religious phenomena, Marion understands theology necessarily to affirm the actuality of such phenomena as the basis for its own community identity. Marion suggests that, for Christianity, the incarnation of God in Christ is key, for example. In other words, phenomenologists are concerned with "revelation," Christianity is concerned with "Revelation." However, phenomenologists need not leave Revelation untouched, but must merely consider it only ever possibly the case. For Marion, Revelation would be essentially paradoxical and "saturated" with meaning such that it would overwhelm all attempts adequately to understand it:

> The border between metaphysics and phenomenology runs within phenomenology—as its highest possibility, and I stick with the phenomenological discipline only in search of the way that it opens and, sometimes, closes. But here again, possibility goes farther than actuality; the phenomenological way has not yet reached its endpoint, and I borrow it only with the hope that it will. . . . In describing saturated phenomena or paradoxes, I do not hesitate to go so far as the phenomenon of Revelation, namely Christ. Is this a blatant and perfectly unseemly theological turn? Once again, I resist this claim for at least two reasons. (i) Every phenomenon must be describable, and every exclusion must on principle be reversed, in phenomenology as elsewhere, and turned against he who effects it. This was one of the most glaring limits of classical metaphysics from Spinoza to Nietzsche: namely, to have the pretense to forbid phenomenality to what claimed it. For the very concept of Revelation belongs by right to phenomenality, and even to contest it, it is appropriate to see it. (ii) *Here*, I am not broaching revelation in its theological pretension to the truth, something faith alone can dare to do. I am outlining it as a possibility—in fact the ultimate possibility, the paradox of paradoxes—of phenomenality, such that it is carried out in a possible saturated phenomenon. The hypothesis that there was historically no such revelation would change nothing in the phenomenological task of offering an account of the fact, itself incontestable, that it has been thinkable, discussible, and even describable. This description therefore does not make an exception to the principle of the reduction to immanence. . . . What *shows itself* first *gives itself*—this is my one and only theme. (2002a, 4–5, emphasis in original)

Summarizing Marion's point, here, we might simply say that phenomenology investigates Christian Revelation as a possibility that shows up as the paradox of all paradoxes. To go further and claim that Christian Revelation *has been* given in historically determinate ways, that is, that Christ *is* the incarnate God, say, is to leave the phenomenological domain and enter the realm of faith—which is appropriately considered by theologians and not phenomenologists.[10]

Marion later repeats this central claim that phenomenology can only affirm the *possibility* of theological phenomena, but not the *actuality* of such phenomena (which would require the movement of faith):

> The phenomenon of revelation *remains a mere possibility.* I am going to describe it without presupposing its actuality, and yet all the while propose a precise figure for it. I will say only: if an actual revelation must, can, or could have been given in phenomenal apparition, it could have, can, or will be able to do so only by giving itself according to the type of the paradox par excellence—such as I will describe it. *Phenomenology cannot decide if a revelation can or should ever give itself,* but it (and it alone) can determine that, in case it does, such a phenomenon of revelation should assume the figure of the paradox of paradoxes. *If* revelation there must be (and phenomenology has no authority to decide this), *then* it will assume, assumes, or assumed the figure of paradox of paradoxes, according to an essential law of phenomenality. (2002a, 235, emphasis added)

In both of these passages, we see that Marion, like Levinas, and Chrétien, explicitly agrees with Janicaud that "phenomenology and theology make two." Similar claims can be found in Henry and Derrida. Ultimately, then, we take Janicaud's formulation to be *a fundamental characteristic* of new phenomenology as a coherent philosophical trajectory. That there is agreement between new phenomenology and Janicaud on this front, however, does not mean that they are in similar agreement about *how* phenomenology and theology, *individually*, ought to be understood. Moreover, it does not entail that Janicaud is right to say that new phenomenology is really just theology in disguise.

An apophatic theological framework, nonetheless?

As Greisch recognizes and de Vries and Janicaud both emphasize, despite the seeming clarity with which phenomenological boundaries are laid out by the new phenomenologists, there are reasons to think that the specific new phenomenological distinction between phenomenology and theology is not all that stable. In particular, given the specific sort of God-talk in new phenomenological texts, even if the new phenomenologists are not engaged in *positive* revealed theology, perhaps they are engaged in some sort of *negative* theological project? Or, minimally, perhaps they frequently operate *within* such a negative theological framework. If so, then the distinctions they draw and the borders they recognize between phenomenology and theology would be more appropriately understood as only applying to a *particular sort* of theology, but not theology *as such*. Nonetheless, while the theological traditions upon which the new phenomenologists draw are often more negative than positive, this does not support a reductive reading of their scholarship as itself merely being negative theology.

Negative theology, or *apophaticism*, is traditionally distinguished from positive theology, or *kataphaticism*.[11] In brief, and recognizing that we are oversimplifying things here a great deal, apophatic theology understands God to be so transcendent that any human conception of the divine will necessarily be inadequate. So, rather than stressing the positive claims about God (that God is all-good, or all-knowing, etc.), apophatic theology emphasizes God's excessiveness by merely speaking about what God is not. Accordingly, apophatic theology tends to display both robust, and perhaps excessive, humility (due to the fact that God is not knowable, as such), and also a profound intimacy (God is likely revealed best in some sort of mystical experience rather than in philosophical speculation).[12] It makes sense that Heidegger would draw heavily on the apophatic tradition when he attempts to overcome onto-theology because of the ways in which it seems to allow for one to dance before, sing to, pray to, and worship God without so quickly falling into anthropomorphic worries about epistemic arrogance and theological limitations (which we saw Westphal identify as the hallmarks of onto-theology). Marion, who often writes directly about the limits and possibilities of apophaticism (see 2002c, chapter 6; 2008, chapter 6), claims that "the theme of 'negative theology' has resurfaced in philosophy in recent years, at least in a vague manner" (2008, 102). "Among other indications," Marion notes,

one can cite Heidegger, who was unable to avoid "comparing" the step back of the thought of presence toward that of giving (*Geben*) "with the method of negative theology."[13] Or

Wittgenstein, who states, with a different accentuation: "There is the ineffable. It shows itself. It is the mystical."[14] It remains simpler, however, to rely on the most explicit testimony— Derrida's arguments . . . for a new pertinence for "negative theology" in the forum of contemporary philosophy.[15] As we know, Derrida revived this theme in order to subject the apophatic moment of "negative theology" to deconstruction. (2008, 102–3)

The apophatic tendencies of new phenomenology can be seen in numerous places. For example, in the "note" offered at the beginning of *Otherwise than Being*, Levinas indicates that the main goal of the book is to "hear a God not contaminated by Being," and then says that this is "a human possibility no less important and no less precarious than to bring Being out of the oblivion in which it is said to have fallen in metaphysics and in onto-theology" (1997, xlviii). Crucially, Levinas locates the task of hearing God as being just as important as Heidegger's decidedly philosophical project of fundamental ontology and even sees it as connected with the critique of onto-theology itself. Even more interestingly, though, Levinas does not say that he hopes to "understand" or "know" or "conceive" of such a God, but to "hear" that God. This might locate his text as almost being a practice in what we could term *theological receptivity*. It would not be entirely inappropriate, then, to wonder about a connection between Levinas's account in *Otherwise than Being* and those mystical theologians who ask God to guide their inquiry such that they might overcome their preconceptions of God in order truly to hear God's word and, hence, be able to speak the truth.[16]

It is worth noting, here, that an emphasis on "hearing" is found often in new phenomenology. As just two examples, consider Chrétien's discussion of an "inner voice":

The starting point from which to consider a possible inner voice is the event of an intimate call. This involves being affected: the course of my thought is suddenly modified by the feeling of having been called or hailed, of having been directly reached by an address whose object I am. . . . In calling me, the call does not leave me intact: it surges only by opening a space in me to be heard, and therefore by shattering something of what I was before I felt myself to be called. (2004, 47–8)

This passage is remarkable because of how many other new phenomenological voices can be "heard" echoing in it: Henry's notion of auto-affection, Marion's account of counter-intentionality as expressed in the notion of the *interloqué*, and Levinas's focus on the ethical content of hearing divine calls. The importance of hearing over knowing is also stressed by Marion when he discusses the practice of "de-nomination" that is characteristic of a particular kind of mystical theology:

> De-nomination, therefore, does not end up in a "metaphysics of presence" that does not call itself as such. Rather, it ends up as a pragmatic theology of absence—where the name is given as having no name, as not giving the essence, and having nothing but this absence to make it manifest; a theology where hearing happens. (2002c, 155)

Returning to Levinas, then, seemingly theological ruptures of phenomenological discourse show back up near the end of *Otherwise than Being*. There, Levinas discusses the possibility of moving from ethics (the infinite asymmetrical obligation to the Other) to politics (the necessary adjudication among multiple others) and claims that "it is only thanks to God that . . . I am another for the others. . . . The passing of God, of whom I can speak only by reference to this aid or this grace, is precisely the reverting of the incomparable subject into a member of society" (1997, 158). Moreover, in the surrounding pages, Levinas talks of "glory," "prophecy," "witness," and "transcendence," and even claims that "one is tempted to call this plot [of ethics and politics] religious," though he is quick not note that "it is not stated in terms of certainty or uncertainty, and does not rest on any positive theology" (1997, 147). That Levinas tarries at the intersection of phenomenology and theology, while exploring the boundaries of each, is not all that surprising given the distinction he draws in *Totality and Infinity* between "the extraordinary phenomenon of prophetic eschatology" (1969, 22) and "the revealed opinions of positive religions" (1969, 23).

While such passages directly counter Janicaud's claim that Levinas's thought presupposes a *positive* theological account and conception, one might still wonder if Levinas assumes some sort of *negative* theological legacy as a background for his own phenomenological work. If so, then it might seem that Janicaud is on to something, after all, regarding the "theological" directions in Levinas's philosophy. In other words, even if a theological receptivity involves being receptive to the givenness (or speech? or revelation? or command? or call?) of God, the phenomenological availability of such givenness might still appear problematic in the wake of Husserl's reduction and Heidegger's critique of theological discourse. When Levinas tries to hear a God beyond being and notes that the Other always "overflows" attempts at comprehension (as would be expected given the status of the Other as *absolutely* other), this rhetoric accords nicely with the apophatic account of knowing God only by way of "unknowing."[17] Is such resonance merely rhetorical or does it display a deeper, and more problematic, theological legacy?

While Janicaud worries about such a theology operating behind the scenes in Levinas's philosophy, one could also move in the other direction and say that *unless* such notions as prophecy, witness, eschatology, etc., keep in place the theological legacy from which such they have been drawn, they are stripped of their very meaning and significance. Nick Trakakis (2013) offers such an objection to new phenomenology and he is certainly right to worry, as did Jonkers, about what might remain of religious discourse if emptied of its theological context.[18] Additionally, even if one did allow for phenomenological consideration of such traditionally theological notions, problems would still seem to remain in the phenomenological register itself. Many years before his engagement with Marion about phenomenological heresy, Jacques Derrida (1978, chapter 4) wrote a lengthy essay on Levinas's *Totality and Infinity*, titled "Violence and Metaphysics," in which he wonders about the theological assumptions in Levinas's work alongside a phenomenological challenge to Levinas. If the Other is "absolutely other" (as opposed to merely relatively other, like the difference between this pen and book or between my wife and I), then it would be impossible to have any "encounter," since the very conditions of such an encounter would be the appearance of the Other internal to some conceptual or perceptual horizon that admits of sameness, which would thereby challenge the "absoluteness" of the alterity. In other words, if something can show itself then it seems that I would only be able to receive/intuit such a showing if it showed itself in a way that I am able to receive/intuit. Derrida's concern might be seen to echo the classical question about what a sphere would look like in a two-dimensional world.

In light of such criticisms, it can seem that Levinas just can't win. When Levinas claims that he does not allow the theological archive upon which he draws to operate as authoritative in his work, Janicaud doesn't believe him and says that Levinas is simply loading the dice. Alternatively, Trakakis does believe Levinas but claims that this empties Levinas's phenomenology of the significance it might otherwise have. Bracketing the theological worries, Derrida indicates that, even if the very motifs of "absolute alterity" and "absolute invisibility" are rightly considered phenomenological, they yield potentially disastrous consequences. What, then, are we to say to the basic suggestion that Levinas is engaged in negative theology?

Our response to this question basically repeats our above claims about Levinas's attitude toward phenomenology and theology more broadly. In brief, negative theology and positive theology are distinguished in many ways, but the ways in which authority structures operate within their discourse is not one of them. They both appeal to scriptural, ecclesial, and experiential authorities in ways that assume Revelation rather than merely revelation. As such, even if Levinas should have admitted more intersections between his confessional and his philosophical texts, which we think he should have, his dependence on negative theology is one of largely heuristic import. Although apophatic theology is certainly one way of making sense of those "pre-philosophical" influences that open particular doors through which the phenomenologist might choose to walk for decidedly phenomenological reasons, to say that Levinas is not phenomenological because he attempts to "hear a God not contaminated by being" assumes that such a "hearing" is not possible, which is, as Chrétien notes, to emulate the ostrich in one's philosophical practice.

If Levinas were to begin by saying that he *has* heard this God and now wants to tell others what God has said, then *perhaps* the theological worries would be justified—at least to someone who is worried about theology. Crucially, however, Levinas's attempt to locate God "beyond being" interrupts the assumption that God would have to "exist" in order to be even possibly "heard." For Levinas, the attempt to "hear" God is best understood as a phenomenological receptivity to the depth of phenomenality itself—even if such depths are invisible, or absolutely other. While this specific *way of being receptive* is not one that Husserl and the early Heidegger explicitly consider, *excluding it from phenomenology is something that must be demonstrated and not merely assumed.* As we have seen, the new phenomenologists are willing to argue *phenomenologically* for their positions.

Levinas is not alone in his seeming appropriation of apophatic theology as a central inspiration of new phenomenological inquiry into what Westphal (2002) terms "divine excess." Let's see how other new phenomenologists also turn to apophatic resources as they continue to radicalize phenomenological philosophy. As we briefly noted in Chapter Two, in his expansive magnum opus, *The Essence of Manifestation*, Michel Henry draws explicitly, and deeply, on Meister Eckhart in his attempt to discuss the invisibility of phenomenality itself:

> *The original revelation of the essence to itself, which is constitutive of its reality, is the invisible.* Because it constitutes the original revelation of the essence to itself and of its reality, *the invisible is not the antithetical concept of phenomenality, it is rather its first and fundamental determination.* (1973, 438, emphasis in original)

Although quoting someone does not mean that one claims that person as an authority for one's own thought, and it certainly does not mean that one necessarily agrees with all the claims offered by that person, it is striking how Henry adopts mystical language for describing the essence of manifestation. This can be seen especially well in Henry's use of Novalis's notion of the "holy, ineffable, mysterious Night" as a metaphorical description (1973, 442). According to Henry, "the Night is not merely the light of the invisible nor that which makes us see the invisible itself, it is the power which produces light; it is not merely the effectiveness of phenomenality in its original shining-forth, but its essence" (1973, 443). Further possible connections between Henry and negative theology abound. Ruud Welten (2003), for example, explores the resonance between Henry's use of the motif of "the Night" and the use of the same idea in the mystical poetry of John of the Cross. Consider John of the Cross's words in "The Dark Night" (as included in

McGreal 1996, 26–30). Of particular note is the stanza that reads: *"This guided me / more surely than the light of noon / to where he was awaiting me / -him I knew so well- / there in a place where no one appeared."* For Henry, the essence of manifestation (or the Truth of Life) is something that cannot itself be made manifest (and thereby accord with the Truth of the World). In this sense, Henry offers an extended phenomenological account of "a place where no one appeared," as it were.

One might contend, in light of such possible connections, that Henry's use of such seemingly mystical and theological rhetoric and expression is just postmodern poetic description that does not need to appropriate the theological context in which such ideas might have originally found expression. Yet Henry seems to trouble such a reading when he goes on to suggest:

> The understanding of the invisible, in its insurmountable—not dialectical opposition to that which is visible and to its element, is accomplished for the first time in Christianity wherein this understanding finds its concrete historical realization. With the appearance of Christianity there is actually discovered, as constituted by the invisible and by the effectiveness of the phenomenality which properly belongs to it, a new and infinite dimension of existence such that everything which presents itself in the world and manifests itself therein under the title of "phenomenon" henceforth is shown to be without any relationship to existence or with that which it essentially comprises. This is actually the meaning of the critique directed by Christianity against the "world" and its determinations, the meaning which fosters, in its radical heterogeneity with respect to the world first understood as a pure ontological milieu, the effectiveness and the reality of the unrepresentable essence of Being and of life. (1973, 448)

Here Henry is clear that Christianity, *in particular,* is distinctive in its understanding of the central phenomenological truth that he is attempting to proclaim. As such, connections to Meister Eckhart and John of the Cross (among others) might lead some to assume that Henry's philosophy is necessarily dependent on determinate theological traditions in ways that would again invite suspicions about a theological "swerve," as Janicaud terms it. As in Levinas, however, Henry's discussion of apophatic sources does not claim those sources as authoritative in his philosophy. Rather, Henry's point is that "the appearance of Christianity" is itself phenomenologically generative. That is, it offers ways of conceiving, approaching, and interpreting the world that attend to the phenomenality that is never properly part of that world—namely, the phenomenology of life. Henry, thereby, distinguishes between what he terms the "Word of the World" and the "Word of Life" or order to note the depth of phenomenality beyond all phenomenalization (Henry 2000a, 220–3).

Christianity both provides Henry with a model that accords with the basic phenomenological claims he makes about the philosophy of language, the philosophy of the body, as well as the philosophy of religion, and also offers him examples of religious phenomena about which he can then ask into the conditions of possibility (viz. the words of Christ as the Word of Life—see Henry 2012a). Given that much of Henry's philosophical task is to express what philosophy seems unable to express, using the language of the world is problematic when attempting to speak about that which resists worldly expression. Accordingly, as Karl Hefty writes, "Henry in no way seeks to reduce Christianity to a phenomenology of life. On the contrary, he finds of interest in the texts of Christianity precisely their power to express what philosophy cannot" (2012, xx). Does that mean that Henry has gone beyond philosophy? Not necessarily. As Hefty explains:

> The phenomenology of life is not an artificial philosophical veneer placed over the doctrinal corpus of Christianity. Nor does it understand itself in any way to supersede Christianity. [Henry's] approach is not, strictly speaking, a phenomenology of Christianity. Nor, on the other hand, does it presuppose an appropriation of Christian categories by phenomenology. Rather, it raises the bar of intelligibility to a new level, which both phenomenology and Christianity presuppose, and which Henry calls Arch-Revelation. (2012, xxii)

Hefty's point is that, although Henry's phenomenology of life is *not* simply a different way to express Christian theology, Henry

is interested in Christianity as opening genuine phenomenological possibilities. So, while there are plenty of places to which one
could turn in Henry's authorship to suggest that he is attempting to discover the "essence" of Christianity, such a project need
not abandon phenomenology. Instead, it should simply reorient
phenomenology toward a possible framework that seems to do a
good job of accounting for those questions that get raised when
one fundamentally challenges the ontological monism of western
philosophy.

As two helpful ways of making sense of Henry's philosophy in
this regard, we think that his work can be productively brought into
conversation with Søren Kierkegaard's (1985) consideration of the
conditions under which an encounter with God would be possible
in the world, as well as with Nicholas Wolterstorff's (1995) discussion of the possibility of Revelation. For Kierkegaard, encountering
God in the world would require that God bring the very conditions
under which such an encounter would occur to the encounter itself.
That is, encountering God is not simply a matter of encountering something that is then understood to be God. Rather, the very
possibility of such an encounter would have to be *presented by
God* or else the encounter would always be understood as simply
an encounter with something else (non-God)—a person, a book,
a word, a piece of bread, etc. Similarly, the Arch-Revelation that
Henry attempts to consider would likewise be inaccessible in terms
of all other revelation—that is, the condition of access would have
to be given by the Arch-Revelation itself in singular ways. Henry
describes this as an attempt to cross an "abyss" that "separates the
Word of Life from that of the world" (2000a, 237). Here one might
think of Kierkegaard's oft-used metaphor that the riskiness of faith
is like being "suspended above 70,000 fathoms" (Kierkegaard
1992, 204). For Henry and Kierkegaard, abysses are dangerous
things and the comfort and security that one might have found prior
to facing the abyss are rarely much help after such an encounter.[19]
As such, just as Kierkegaard claims that God must present both the
conditions of encounter and also the occasion for such an encounter, Henry claims that *"the Word of Life confers its classification
on what it reveals*, never disclosing it outside itself as what would
have no relation with it, as anything whatsoever, but in it as that
whose flesh it is" (2000a, 238, emphasis in original). And, resonat-
ing with Kierkegaard's resistance to natural theology and positive

apologetics, Henry claims "only the god can make us believe in him, but he inhabits our own flesh" (2000a, 241). Though operating with slightly different theological conceptions, we might say that Kierkegaard and Henry agree that there could never be a "follower at second hand" (Kierkegaard 1985, 89–110), but only an immediate, auto-affective relation with the Arch-Revelation that is variously termed God and/or the Word of Life.

Let's look at another example, this time drawn from contemporary analytic philosophy. Nicholas Wolterstorff's book-length attempt "to reflect philosophically on the claim that God speaks" (1995, 1) is an important resource for anyone wanting to study Henry's discussions of the words of Christ as considered especially in *I am the Truth* (Henry 2003) and also the appropriately titled *Words of Christ* (Henry 2012a). Although Wolterstorff does not engage Henry, he does offer fairly extended considerations of Derrida and Ricoeur, and even makes occasional mention of Levinas, who he says offers "rather haunting words [that] . . . will speak to some of us" (Wolterstorff 1995, 11). Like some of the new phenomenologists, Wolterstorff is personally deeply religiously committed. Making clear that *Divine Discourse* is not primarily motivated by religious conviction, Wolterstorff explores the topics therein in light of philosophical problems that have become of distinct interest within contemporary philosophy of religion: epistemology, philosophy of language, and philosophical hermeneutics (1995, 11–16). Though any detailed engagement between Wolterstorff and new phenomenology would require significantly more space than we are able to give it here, we simply want to use his text to highlight the ways in which the questions at issue for Henry are neither limited to an apophatic theological archive nor to a continental philosophical framework. We think that it is likely that quite productive research would result from bringing Henry's phenomenological attention to embodiment and affectivity to bear on Wolterstorff's discussions of speech-act theory and analytic epistemology, and vice versa. Wolterstorff might challenge the potentially apophatic excesses that show up in much of continental philosophy of religion and Henry might challenge the potentially kataphatic excesses that show up in much of analytic philosophy of religion. We will return to such possible engagements in Chapter Seven.

Returning to new phenomenological appropriations of apophatic theology, considerations of Novalis's account of the night and John of the Cross's mystical poetry are not limited to Henry's *The Essence of Manifestation*. The most extended new phenomenological consideration of the night is Chrétien's *L'Antiphonaire de la nuit* (1989), in which the choral dimensions of calls and responses are discussed in relation to the notion of poetic considerations of night (see also Chrétien 2004, 32). Chrétien also discusses both John of the Cross and Novalis in *The Unforgettable and the Unhoped For* (2002, 123). The consideration of John of the Cross occurs in the context of an attempt to think through the "supernatural filament of memory" (2002, 76–7), while the mention of Novalis is part of Chrétien's summary of his critique of Heidegger's conception of speech. As Chrétien explains:

> The study of nocturnal poetry would seem to show above all the responsive nature of speech, since this poetry tends always to become vocative to address itself to the night. But what is this "night"? The night is already other: a number of poetic works observe a doubling of night, affirming two distinct nights—though, of course, according to diverse distinctions. This leads one to think of words as *translation*: speech translates, it crosses from what befalls it over to what it addresses—in this case, from the night that falls on it to the night that is addressed. . . . This paradox of an originary translation belongs to the rigorous description of a phenomenology of response. (2002, 123)

In order to work out such a phenomenology of response, Chrétien stresses the importance of "religious and mystical thought and speech" due to the way in which mystics have "frequently seen and spoken higher, farther, or otherwise than metaphysics in the form that Heidegger has defined for us" (2002, 125). Accordingly, mystical religious discourse is not merely a *possible* phenomeno-logical resource for Chrétien, but instead "it is *necessary* to hear [its] promises" (2002, 125, emphasis added). Explaining the phe-nomenological necessity of apophatic theology, Chrétien claims that those in the apophatic and mystical traditions are not obsessed and blinded by the human project of total self-assurance and self-understanding as we truly are (to paraphrase St. Paul), in transparency: they are rooted at each instant in the hearing of an other Word that wounds body and soul, and which they know that, if it wounds completely, could never be completely understood—not even in eternity. (2002, 125)

For Chrétien, listening well to theological voices helps us phenomenologically to appreciate the depth of intersubjectivity, relationality, excess, and paradox that seem to accompany any serious consideration of speech and discourse as a lived reality. "This is why," Chrétien writes, "religious and mystical thought and speech are *necessary* for those who would meditate on excess and superabundance, on the force in weakness and the perfection in deficiency. They do more than speak of them; they live them and originate from them" (2002, 126, emphasis added). Given Chrétien's attempt to think though those phenomena that resist presence, or, following Henry, that show themselves in the place where nothing/no one appears (what Levinas might term a "no-place" [*non-lieu*] [Levinas 1997, 109]), it is not surprising that Chrétien draws heavily upon such thinkers as Pseudo-Dionysus (2004, 15–16; 2002, 116), John the Scott (2004, 17), John of the Cross (2004, 76–7), and Philo of Alexandria (2004, 26; 2002, 38–9, 108–12).

In addition to Levinas, Henry, Chrétien, and Marion, and even considering Derrida's own critique of Levinas's seeming apophatic tendencies regarding "absolute alterity," Derrida himself displays similar inclinations throughout his authorship. One does not have to go to Derrida's later considerations of the mystical nonbeing of "Khora" (1998, 19–22), a "messianicity without messianism" (1998, 17–18), and even references to "Nocturnal light" (1998, 16) in order to find such possible theological dimensions. As early as 1968, we can see such theological questions (or questions about theological questions) showing up in Derrida's thought. Perhaps most famously, in the much discussed essay *Différance*, Derrida wrestles with how to speak of the "a" in this term (as opposed to the normal spelling "*différence*"), since it disappears, or becomes invisible when the word is spoken. Let's consider at length what Derrida says, so we can understand the problem he faces and why it invites apophatic suspicions. The following is rather lengthy, but we want to quote this passage in its entirety because it is important to track how Derrida's argument unfolds—which is not always as clear and lucid as one might wish:

> What am I to do in order to speak of the *a* of *différance*? It goes without saying that it cannot be *exposed*. One can expose only that which at a certain moment can become *present*, manifest, that which can be shown, presented as something present, a being-present in its truth, in the truth of a present or the presence of the present. Now if *différance* ~~is~~ (and I also cross out the "~~is~~") what makes possible the presentation of the being-present, it is never presented as such. It is never offered to the present. Or to anyone. Reserving itself, not exposing itself, in regular fashion it exceeds the order of truth at a certain precise point, but without dissimulating itself as something, as a mysterious being, in the occult of a nonknowledge or in a hole with indeterminable borders. . . . In every exposition it would be exposed to disappearing as disappearance. It would risk appearing: disappearing.

> So much for the detours, locutions, and syntax in which I will often have to take recourse will resemble those of negative theology, occasionally even to the point of being indistinguishable from negative theology. Already we have had to delineate *that différance is not*, does not exist, is not a present-being (on) in any form; and we will be led to delineate also everything *that* it *is not*, that is, *everything*; and consequently that it has neither existence nor essence. It derives from no category of being, whether present or absent. And yet those aspects of *différance* which are thereby delineated are not theological, not even in the order of the most negative of negative theologies, which are always concerned with disengaging a superessentiality beyond the finite categories of essence and existence, that is, of presence, and always hastening to recall that God is refused the predicate of existence, only in order to acknowledge his superior, inconceivable, and ineffable mode of being. Such a development is not in question here, and this will be confirmed progressively. *Différance* is not only irreducible to any ontological or theological—ontotheological—reappropriation, but as the very opening of the space in which

ontotheology—philosophy—produces its system and its history it includes ontotheology, inscribing it and exceeding it without return. (Derrida 1982, 5–6)

We recognize that such passages can reinforce stereotypes about the impenetrability of continental philosophy. For example, when we asked a non-continental colleague of ours to read and respond to this Derridian passage so we could get an idea of what one might think of it upon first reading it without a significant background in this field, her response was: "This is nonsense. It displays everything that I dislike about continental philosophy and demonstrates why I choose not to read it." Though such a reaction is understandable, it is also regrettable because in this important passage, which we take to be two of the most significant paragraphs in all of his early work, Derrida forcefully displays both the reasons for worrying about a theological turn in new phenomenology and also the reasons for ultimately concluding that new phenomenology remains phenomenology, even if a heterodox version of it.

Derrida begins this passage by asking how to speak of that which cannot be expressed, presented, manifested, and even said. While this is immediately reminiscent of a negative theological attempt to say the unsayable, as Derrida himself admits when he acknowledges that his style will sometimes be "indistinguishable" from negative theology, Derrida's question is not theological, but phenomenological. This becomes at least somewhat clear when he specifies the conditions for "being-present" in directly Husserlian ways. The problem, Derrida realizes, is that *différance* can only "appear" insofar as it remains invisible. As he states, "it would risk appearing: disappearing." Yet, as an inquiry into the appearance of that which appears, phenomenology must take seriously this (dis)appearance of *différance* even if it means that phenomenology forces itself beyond its traditional mode.

Phenomenology leads Derrida to press up against the limits of phenomenology (as classically understood) and yet inquiry continues. Is such inquiry still phenomenological? This is a question asked by all of the new phenomenologists and it underlies why the negative theological sensibility and rhetoric so often find place in their writing. Derrida's specific explanation for why his thought is not negative theology depends on Heidegger's worries about the

essentialism of onto-theology. Namely, Derrida notes that negative theology remains onto-theological insofar as it continues to
name God as a being—though now an "ineffable" and "inconceiv-
able" one rather than the *omni*-God (i.e. *omni*potent, *omni*scient,
*omni*present, *omni*benevolent, etc.) so often found in kataphatic
theology. It is not that Derrida is doing theology, but that in doing
phenomenology, he finds himself unable to avoid such theological
proximity and the accompanying suspicions from some philosophical colleagues.

Derrida returns to the topic of negative theology in the essay
"How to Avoid Speaking: Denials" (Derrida 1987a).[20] Therein
Derrida reaffirms his 1968 claim that deconstruction should not
be identified with apophaticism:

> What I write is not "negative theology." First of all, *in the measure*
> to which this belongs to the predicative or judicative space of
> discourse, to its strictly propositional form, and privileges not
> only the indestructible unity of the word but also the authority
> of the name—such axioms as a "deconstruction" must start
> by reconsidering. . . . Next, in the measure to which "negative
> theology" seems to reserve, beyond all positive predication,
> beyond all negation, even beyond Being, some hyperessentiality,
> a being beyond Being. . . . No. I would hesitate to inscribe what
> I put forward under the familiar heading of negative theology,
> precisely because of that ontological wager of hyperessentiality
> that one finds at work in both Dionysus and in Meister Eckhart.
> (1987a, 7–8)

Here we can clearly see that Derrida understands the problem
with both positive and negative theology to be that neither avoids
onto-theological essentialism—whether such onto-theology takes
the form of a divine essence (kataphaticism) or a divine hyper-
essence (apaphaticism). Accordingly, the distinction between
apophaticism and kataphaticism, for Derrida, is not one of affirming or denying onto-theology, but simply two different ways of
being onto-theological (even if one is, nonetheless, more promising
as a resource for phenomenology than the other).

As we saw in the last chapter, exactly how to understand
onto-theology is a matter of some debate. Quite understandably,

Derrida's understanding of onto-theology as seeming linked to *any* conception of God understood *as a being* has been challenged by other new phenomenologists. According to Marion, for example,

> if an onto-theo-logy wants to attain conceptual rigor and not remain at the level of a polemical caricature, it requires first a concept of being, next a univocal application of this concept to God and creatures, and finally the submission of both to foundation by principle and/or by cause. If these conditions are not met, if in contrast being remains an inconceivable *esse*, without analogy, or even *penitus inconitum* [deeply unknown], then the mere fact that being comes up is not enough to establish an onto-theo-logy. (2002c, 145)

Even if one grants some ambiguity about onto-theology within new phenomenology, Derrida's radical phenomenological attempt is to think about that which *shows itself* only to the extent that it is not showable (as the very condition of appearance). In other words, what *is* yet does not exist and so must be crossed-out ("i̶s̶"). It is what is *presented* and *discussed* (i.e. Derrida is writing an essay about it *somehow*) and yet is "never offered to the present" (i.e. he is writing about the impossibility of saying what he needs to say). Derrida recognizes that such an attempt might require what he terms a "phenomenological conjuring trick" in *Specters of Marx* (1994, chapter 5) insofar as it tries to think and speak about "a space of invisible visibility" and "the dis-appearing of an apparition" (1994, 126).[21] It might be unavoidable that Derrida's account ends up sounding much like theological discourse about a God "transcendent to the point of absence" as Levinas will say (2000, 219–24), but it need not be understood as, therefore, necessarily landing Derrida (or the other new phenomenologists in their own considerations of that which excessively resists appearance/expression/comprehension) in directly theological waters. Or, even if it does, the proximity between new phenomenology and (apophatic) theology does not entail that the one is really just a particular way of engaging in the other. *One can swim in the ocean without being a fish.*

As in Marion, Chrétien, Levinas, and Henry, there is much in Derrida's authorship that plays at these complicated borders and swims in these deep waters. As an example, we will consider just one more passage that could also be cited as possible evidence of a slide from phenomenology to theology. This passage comes from *The Gift of Death* (Derrida 2008a). Here it would seem that Derrida offers a positive suggestion about how to understand God:

> We should stop thinking about God as someone, over there, way up there, transcendent, and, what is more—into the bargain, precisely—capable, more than any satellite orbiting in space, of seeing into the most secret of the most interior places. It is perhaps necessary, if we are to follow the traditional Judeo-Christian-Islamic injunction, but also at the risk of turning it against that tradition, to think of God and of the name of God without such a representation or such idolatrous stereotyping. Then we might say: God is the name of the possibility I have of keeping a secret that is visible from the interior but not from the exterior. As soon as such a structure of conscience exists, of being-with-oneself, of speaking, that is to say of producing invisible sense, as soon as I have within me, *thanks to the invisible word as such*, a witness that others cannot see, and who is therefore *at the same time other than me and more intimate with me than myself*, as soon as I can have a secret relationship with myself and not tell everything, as soon as there is secrecy and secret witnessing within me, and for me, then there is what I call God, (there is) what I call God in me, (it happens that [*il y a que*]) I call myself God—a phrase that is difficult to distinguish from "God calls me," for it is on such a condition that I can call myself or be called in secret. (2008a, 108, emphasis in original)

Surely, if anywhere, here we see Derrida sliding from a radicalized phenomenology to a determinate theology, even if a deconstructive one. Yet, as many scholars have suggested, Derrida's discussions of God and religion are not meant as theological attempts to articulate an account of positive religion, but phenomenological (and in this case deconstructive) attempts to make sense of what is going on in the accounts of religion that one might give. For example, Caputo explains that Derridian deconstruction should be understood as a "religion without religion" because, although Derrida often sounds religious, he does so in a way that "regularly, rhythmically repeats this religiousness, *sans* [without] the concrete, historical religious; it repeats nondogmatically the religious structure of experience, the category of the religious" (Caputo 1997, xxi). Caputo suggests that deconstruction definitely has theological import, but is not itself a determinate theological view. In this way, one could claim that Derrida is simply exploring the ways in which Husserl's own claim that phenomenology would be "mediately important" for theology (Husserl 1982, 117) in light of the admission of a depth of phenomenality that resists being phenomenalized—namely, the unapparent (Heidegger), *différance* (Derrida), the face of the Other (Levinas), the essence of manifestation (Henry), saturated phenomena (Marion), and the call and response (Chrétien). While we think that this is the right way to read what Derrida understands himself to be doing, there are reasons to doubt that "religion without religion" is the only possible framework for deconstructive philosophy of religion.[22] For now, though, what matters is that, regardless of their personal religious identities (or lack thereof), the new phenomenologists remain steady in their protestation against any confusion between phenomenology and theology. *Phenomenological heterodoxy is still not to be confused with theological orthodoxy.*

Phenomenology still . . .

The reason that the new phenomenologists give for differentiating between phenomenology and theology ultimately comes down to a robust phenomenological commitment to a particular notion of *evidence*. For the new phenomenologists, although there are reasons to radicalize or even sometimes to resist the specifics of Husserl's account of the "as such," they all maintain the importance of the Husserlian "principle of all principles" whereby that which gives itself should be engaged and considered on its own terms. Importantly, though, they endorse this principle while challenging the seemingly Husserlian articulation of the *limits* of such presentation as prescribable from the outset. The new phenomenologists thus agree with Husserl that phenomenological evidence is a matter of what presents itself in its very mode of presentation, but critically question any prima facie constraints on such presentation.

Jeffrey Kosky points out that such agreement counts in favor of the continued phenomenological status of new phenomenology:

> Husserl's "principle of all principles" claims that everything offered in intuition has the right to be taken as it gives itself (*Ideas*, §24); its Heideggerian revision claims that "phenomenon" is to be understood as what gives itself from itself (*Being and Time*, §7). To reject the religious phenomenon's claim to appear would therefore be something highly contrary to the principles of phenomenology, seeing as these principles mean to extend the right to appear to all that claims to appear. Stated positively, insofar as revealed theology, the Scriptures, claims to describe certain appearings and manifestations, theophanies, it belongs to phenomenology. (Kosky 2000b, 118)

With Kosky, we contend that when the new phenomenologists consider that which is "presented" as non-present (Derrida), or that which gives itself as absolutely other (Levinas), or that which shows up as the paradox of all paradoxes (Marion), or that which affects us without being an object (Henry), they are all attempting to think about appearance/givenness/presentation *as excessive* in particular ways. When discussing such excess, however, the new phenomenologists judiciously guard against allowing in evidence that comes from non-phenomenological sources—that is, from something other than what gives itself. This means that the new phenomenologists all agree with Levinas and Chrétien about the requirement of not admitting theological authorities to count as evidence for phenomenological inquiry. In other words, just because the Bible says that X, that doesn't necessarily count as evidence for X's truth—for the evidentiary structure that would admit the Bible as authoritative is beyond the phenomenological domain. The new phenomenologists also agree with Marion about the primary focus on possibility rather than actuality when it comes to religious phenomena. This is not something that should be seen as a challenge to phenomenological methodology, however. Rather, it might be seen as a more robust version of the Heideggerian insight that phenomenology is hypothetical when it comes to its consideration of religious life.

In *The Phenomenology of Religious Life*, after stating the "basic determinations" that will function as "phenomenological explications" to guide the inquiry to follow, Heidegger notes that "these fundamental determinations are for now hypothetical. We ask: If, with these, the basic meaning of Christian religiosity is hit upon, what follows from that methodologically?" (2004, 55). Notice the structure here: *if* such and such is assumed, *then* what follows for our inquiry into the phenomena under consideration? Heidegger reaffirms this hypothetical methodology just a couple pages later when he states that "the basic determinations are thus hypothetical: '*If* they are valid, *then* such and such results for the phenomenon'" (2004, 57, emphasis added). In light of this Heideggerian strategy, the new phenomenological focus on possibility should not be understood as a deviation from the original phenomenological path, but merely an attempt to walk further down that path. Now, as we have already indicated, this underlying agreement among the new phenomenologists on this front occurs in the context of robust debate and disagreement on the specifics of how things get cashed out. For example, consider again the debate between Marion and Derrida that we considered in Chapter Two regarding the horizonal conditions of givenness and appearance. What such a debate should indicate is that the new phenomenologists are all in different ways interrogating phenomenological orthodoxy, but doing so perhaps in the name of attempt to be orthodox. Again, the question about phenomenological limits is a question that phenomenology itself should ask.

That phenomenology and theology are distinct does not prevent the new phenomenologists from recognizing the possibility of significant mutual support for each other. Marion expresses this idea as follows:

Phenomenology cannot give its status to theology, because the conditions of manifestation contradict or at least are different from the free possibility of revelation. Yet the result is not necessarily a divorce, since a final hypothesis remains conceivable: could theology not suggest to phenomenology certain of method and process in virtue of its own requirements and only for formulating them? In other words, could one not inquiry into the (unconditional) conditions to which the phenomenological method would have to subscribe in order to attain a thought of revelation? Inversely, could not the requirements of theology permit phenomenology to transgress its proper limits, in order finally to attain the free possibility at which it has pretended to aim since its origin? (2008, 13)

Though asked in a way that reveals sympathy to an affirmative answer that might make some new phenomenologists less comfortable than others, Marion's questions reflect a fundamental aspect of a new phenomenological approach to the philosophy of religion. Simply put, *new phenomenologists recognize at least the possibility that phenomenological inquiry would push us to allow room in our inquiry for that which would require rethinking the very methodological procedures and discursive limitations with which one might have begun.* And, it is at least plausible, and perhaps unavoidable, that such a recognition will require speaking and writing in a way that borrows heavily from theological archives that have historically attempted to wrestle with versions of the problem of how to say the unsayable, which is a problem the new phenomenologists all face.

Accordingly, we can generalize the main meta-philosophical components of new phenomenological philosophy of religion as follows:

1 New phenomenology requires a notion of evidence that stays true to the givenness of what gives itself, though it goes beyond classical phenomenology in admitting of the possible givenness of that which does not appear (at least in straightforward ways).

2 New phenomenology does not allow theological authorities to count as evidence for phenomenological inquiry, though it does draw heavily upon theological archives as resources for phenomenological considerations of that which seems to exceed easy linguistic expression and conceptual articulation.

3 New phenomenology is limited to affirming only the possibility of religious phenomena rather than the actuality of such phenomena, though this does not mean that new

phenomenologists, as individual persons, must suspend
judgment about such actuality, which is something affirmed
internal to their own faith-lives.

In light of these basic commitments, Janicaud is right to say that
phenomenology and theology make two, but not for the reasons
that he offers. He assumes that phenomenological methodology is neutral while theological methodology is not. Moreover,
he assumes that phenomenology does not allow for considerations of vertical horizons (the absolutely invisible as in Levinas),
but only of horizontal horizons (the invisible of this world as in
Merleau-Ponty). Rather, and *this* is perhaps in part motivated by
their own individual religious perspectives and identities, the new
phenomenologists, in various ways, respect theology too much to
think it could be completely reducible to and fully accessible by
phenomenological philosophy—and in this way they agree with
Heidegger about there being both philosophical and theological
reasons to resist onto-theology.

Phenomenology can help theology to understand the requirements for Revelation to be given as revelation, and theology can
help phenomenology to understand that some revelation might
count as Revelation. Marion expresses such a view nicely when he
claims the following:

> Without any doubt, the phenomenological place of theology
> will necessitate . . . very particular protocols, conformed to the
> exceptional phenomena of which it is a question. For example,
> the event can take the figure of the miracle, the given becomes
> election and promise, the resistance of *l'adonné* is deepened
> into conversation of the witness, the transmutation from the
> *self*-giving into *self*-showing requires theological virtues, its
> progressiveness is prolonged in eschatological return of the
> eternal beginning, and so on. (2002c, 53)

As we have already said, going further and saying that such theological dimensions obtain and that these "figures" have been
"taken" or phenomenalized in history is to move from phenomenology to theology, and from the language of possibility to actuality. "Philosophy has neither the authority nor the competence to

say more," Marion admits, "but it leaves at least the right to appeal about it to the theologians" (2002c, 53). That one would have to make such "appeals" by leaving the domain of phenomenology is not necessarily a bad thing, however. It is simply to realize (as did Husserl and Heidegger) that phenomenology is not a totalizing discourse, but merely a way of getting clear on the stakes of discourse (even that about totality). In this way, the new phenomenologists remain concerned about a "fundamental" philosophical inquiry, even if not following the ontological formulations deployed by the early Heidegger. And, in this way, the new phenomenologists remain committed to a "rigorous" mode of inquiry, even if not following the specific "scientific" conception laid out by the early Husserl. Ultimately, then, new phenomenology is *still* phenomenology.

In the next chapter, we will continue our consideration of new phenomenological philosophy of religion by looking at the way in which the existence and nature of God is variously considered by the new phenomenologists.

CHAPTER FIVE

New phenomenology on the existence and nature of God

Our suggestion in the next few chapters will be that new phenomenology offers important resources to analytic philosophy of religion, and vice versa, such that philosophers working in both traditions (or, better, trajectories) would do well to engage in research that is willing to consider dialogue partners in traditionally unlikely places. Drawing on the notion of "mashup" music, which brings songs from different styles together to construct new music, we will propose that a strategy of "cross-traditional" or "mashup" philosophy of religion provides a promising future for philosophical inquiry in these areas.[1] In order to investigate the ways in which new phenomenology might stand as an important resource for mainstream debates in the philosophy of religion, in this chapter and the next, we will consider how new phenomenology approaches some traditional topics of relevance to these debates: the existence and nature of God, religious practices such as prayer, and the relationship between faith and reason as it concerns, in particular, the notion of "Christian philosophy."

New phenomenology and the questions of philosophy of religion

Though it is wrong to assume that religion must necessarily be theistic, the vast majority of debates in the philosophy of religion are engaged with a theistic conception of God—either attempting to defend such a notion (e.g. Alvin Plantinga, Richard Swinburne, and William Lane Craig) or to suggest that such a notion faces serious problems (e.g. Paul Draper, William Rowe, Kai Nielson). Traditionally, there have been three primary thematic foci in this literature.

1   The existence and nature of God (which would include classical arguments for God and philosophical considerations of theological doctrines).

2   The relationship of faith to reason (which includes debates in religious epistemology, religious language, and even the possibility of miracles).

3   Specific challenges to theism, such as the problem of evil.

While there have long been philosophical debates concerning other important issues such as the relationship of religion and ethics, in recent years discussions have begun to expand in two promising directions: comparative philosophy of religion (including debates regarding religious pluralism) and the impact of contemporary science on the philosophy of religion (including defenses of and objections to a variety of naturalisms). While the first helps to overcome what might be termed a theistic (and specifically Christian) privilege in philosophy of religion, the latter helps to keep philosophy of religion in dialogue with developments in theoretical physics, evolutionary biology, and cognitive science.[2] Nonetheless, as evidenced by some of the main textbooks in the field,[3] the three classic foci remain prominent. There are good reasons beyond simple historical precedent for the pervasiveness of these central themes. Asking into the existence and nature of God is essential if one is going to use the term *God* in one's philosophy, and even more so in one's faith life. At the very least, it is important to talk about what one talks about in order to avoid unnecessary ambiguity and opacity. Similarly, questioning how best to understand the relationship of faith to reason is as important to the life of faith as it is to the life of the mind. Finally, the fact that the world seems less good than it could be demands serious attention in light of continued atrocities and global crises.[4]

An important unifying meta-philosophical thread through all three of these areas is that they are deeply hermeneutically situated in relation to determinate religious traditions as well as philosophical perspectives. In other words, the terms and concepts in play have complicated histories. Further, and this is something premodern *and* postmodern thinkers understand, questions about God, faith, and evil do not easily admit of universal evidential standards and clear criteria for philosophical success. In light of these meta-philosophical realizations, new phenomenology's appropriation of philosophical hermeneutics and existentialism allows it to be a productive approach for the philosophy of religion. For example, philosophy of religion requires attending to a wide variety of "texts"—including practices, rituals, experiences, and vocabularies—all presenting hermeneutic difficulties that require careful philosophical scrutiny. Similarly, new phenomenology distinctively attends to the existential stakes of hermeneutic tasks themselves. We don't mean to suggest that new phenomenology is unique in these ways. Yet its starting point in lived experience and its concern with not only specific phenomena but phenomenality itself makes it especially well suited for philosophers of religion to engage. What Westphal says of his own investigations into the philosophy of religion could be said of new phenomenological philosophy of religion more broadly:

> Like any phenomenology, this one is about possibilities. It does not seek to establish the facts of the case but rather to explore possible modes of experience or being-in-the-world. But as such, these are existential and not merely phenomenological possibilities. They do not merely signify experiences I might have, but places I might dwell and ways that I might be. At issue is the meaning of my life. (2004, 12)

What Westphal realizes, and the new phenomenologists display throughout their work, is that at issue in the classic questions of philosophy of religion is not only how to make sense of God, but how to make sense of oneself in light of whatever sense one makes of God. New phenomenologists attend to this essential connection with care and rigor. Unfortunately, though, this care and rigor can sometimes be overlooked by scholars working in other traditions due to the frequent deployment of an overly technical and idiosyncratic vocabulary by many in continental philosophy, which can seem uninviting to those not already working in the area.

Having already considered the basic shape of new phenomenological God-talk in the last chapter, we will now look at the more
determinate claims about how God is understood therein. Two
specific ideas tend to unify the otherwise divergent new phenomenological discussions of God: (1) the relation between God and
being is problematized, and (2) the relation between God and justice is affirmed. We will consider each in turn.

God and being

The first thing to notice about new phenomenological accounts of
God is that they are certainly not homogeneous. This is understandable for a variety of reasons, including the diverse religious
identities of the new phenomenologists themselves. Nonetheless,
as we have seen previously, underlying the disagreement among
the new phenomenologists is often a generally coherent philosophical trajectory that allows their thought to be productively considered together. When it comes to God, such underlying coherence
emerges regarding the relationship of God to being, or more specifically, the attempt to think God *beyond* or *not contaminated by*
being (Levinas) or *without* being (Marion). Here one might ask:
what, exactly, is so wrong with thinking about God *as* a being?
Simply put: there are worries that derive both from theological traditions stressing the absolute transcendence of God and also the
philosophical tradition (after Heidegger) of viewing onto-theology
as something to avoid at all costs (for both philosophical and theological reasons). In both, the central problem amounts to the risk
of reduction. Theologically, the risk is that accounts of God as a
being would reduce God's mystery, majesty, and goodness to the
account of God offered by a determinate religious tradition—thus
forgetting the *historical and hermeneutic* situations in which such
traditions necessarily function. In other words, we would seem
to confuse God with "what we say about God." In such a case,
God would seem to be no more (and no less) than what we say
God is. Philosophically, the risk is that God could only be thought
according to *philosophical* conceptualities—thus forgetting the
existential and theological situations in which God-talk arises. In
both cases, onto-theology threatens insofar as it forgets these risks.
In light of these worries, it might seem sensible that Derrida, in

particular, appears to view any understanding of God as a being as straightaway onto-theological.

More than any other contemporary scholar, Westphal has carefully considered the precise meaning of onto-theology and ultimately concludes that there are many forms that onto-theology can take.[5] Nonetheless, Westphal proposes that

> all forms of onto-theology have a common purpose. Each puts its God, whether it be the Unmoved Mover, or Nature, or Spirit, or the Market to work as the keystone of a metaphysical theory designed to render the whole of reality intelligible to philosophical reflection. Thus, for example, those writers who identify freedom with free enterprise and make this the immanent *telos* of human history are onto-theologians in an era of the death of God. (2004, 18)

Rather than bringing its own conditions for reception, as in Kierkegaard's notion of encountering Christ and Levinas's notion of encountering the Other, onto-theology insists that "philosophy makes the rules that God must play by" (Westphal 2004, 34). Accordingly, it is worth repeating that onto-theology is both bad philosophy and bad theology. It is bad philosophy "because of its character as calculative-representational thinking," and, because of that very philosophical character, "it is bad theology" in that it "does not let God be God," but instead forces God to be a philosophical posit (Westphal 2004, 34). We can now better understand Heidegger's claim that in onto-theology, "the deity enter[s] into philosophy" (1969, 55) such that God becomes that before which "man can neither pray nor sacrifice . . . neither fall to his knees in awe nor . . . play music and dance" (1969, 72). Heidegger's encouragement of a "god-less" thinking that might be closer to God than all of the God-talk in the onto-theological tradition of western metaphysics can be understood as an encouragement toward both epistemic humility and theological receptivity in light of philosophical limitations (1969, 72).

It makes some sense, then, that in the attempt to let "God" be God, as it were, all philosophical concepts internal to which God has been thought would be problematized—especially the concept of being. Surely a non-onto-theological God would be a

God "not contaminated by Being," as Levinas says (1997, xlviii), would it not? And, if we should think God "without" being, as Marion suggests, then shouldn't we conclude that God does not exist? In this sense, even if theism and atheism are both options that assume the very metaphysical categories that we are trying to overcome, then perhaps the goal should be to "rightly pass as an atheist," as Derrida would say (1993, 155).[6] Here we ought to be very careful not to move too fast, because non-sequiturs abound in such reasoning. New phenomenological philosophy of religion would be misunderstood if interpreted as decisive encouragement toward atheism (even if of a postmodern variety). Instead, remembering that it is a discourse about possibility, *new phenomenology attempts to think what it would mean to talk about "God" without an onto-theological framework, not what it would mean to talk about life without God*. This should not be read as an affirmation of a tacit theism within new phenomenology, however. Instead, we understand new phenomenology to recognize the continued importance of "God" (and perhaps God) in the philosophical tradition in which the new phenomenologists find themselves.

That God is not reducible to being does not mean that God is not *at least* a being, but simply that being is probably not the best way to consider the divine, which is beyond philosophical categories. Moreover, saying that God is beyond such categories does not mean that we can *think beyond* such categories. Indeed, as Heidegger would likely point out, even the claim that "God is beyond being" requires the copula (*is*) in order for our claim to make linguistic sense. Hence, to say that the God beyond Being *is* not, such that God does not exist, would be to forget the paradoxical mode in which the claim operates. It is for these reasons that some postmodern philosophers of religion, such as Kearney, de Vries, and Caputo, have encouraged that we speak of something like "A/theism" in order to think God without being as not necessarily a straightforwardly atheistic thesis, but as a notion that realizes that onto-theology can show up in both theistic and atheistic forms. Overcoming onto-theology is a project to which all new phenomenologists are committed, and for all of them this overcoming involves rethinking God *and* being. How this gets worked out, though, varies across their authorships such that a spectrum begins to emerge regarding the models of God proposed by the various thinkers—not as theological accounts, which affirm the actuality of God according to a specific model, but as phenomeno-logical proposals regarding the possibilities of such models in light of the paradoxical status of religious phenomena.

At the theistic end of the A/theistic spectrum one finds Marion and Chrétien, and at the atheistic end of this spectrum one finds Derrida. Somewhere in between would be Henry (perhaps closer to Marion) and Levinas (perhaps closer to Derrida). This spectrum should not be seen as hard and fast, but instead as simply a loose way of making sense of how A/theism can tend toward theistic formulations (according to which God *is perhaps* a being, but in a radicalized way that differs from classical theism and the "omni" God found therein) and also toward atheistic formulations (accord-ing to which God *is not* a being, but nonetheless still an important idea in some sense and functionally operative in philosophy and lived existence). Given the apophatic tendencies of all new phe-nomenologists, another way to think about this spectrum is the degree to which apophatic discourse is deployed alongside what we might term "kataphatic correctives."

Jean-Luc Marion offers a model of God that quite prominently displays such kataphatic correctives.[7] In the English translation of his influential and controversial book, *God without Being*, Marion acknowledges that its title had created a confusion that he never intended:

> The whole book suffered from the inevitable and assumed equivocation of its title: was it insinuating that the God "without being" is not, or does not exist? Let me repeat now the answer I gave then: no, definitely not. God is, exists, and that is the least of things. At issue here is not the possibility of God's attaining Being, but, quite the opposite, the possibility of Being's attaining to God. With respect to God, is it self-evident that the first question comes down to asking, before anything else, whether he is? Does Being define the first and the highest of the divine names? . . . No doubt, God can and must in the end also be; but does his relation to Being determine him as radically as the relation to his Being defines all other beings? To be or not to be—that is indeed the first and indispensable question for everything and everyone, and for man in particular. But with respect to Being, does God have to behave like Hamlet? (1991, xx)

Here we can clearly see Marion's agreement with Westphal's understanding of onto-theology regarding the requirement that God be made intelligible according to philosophical standards and categories—that is, theology must be made to answer to philosophy. In the attempt to think otherwise than onto-theologically, Marion's final question in the above passage is rhetorically powerful because it demonstrates that understanding God according to the ways in which we understand everything else risks the ontological reductionism that good theology and good philosophy should both avoid. That is, if the question of being (to be or not to be?) is prior to God such that it is a question *for* God as well, then God is understood as having to answer to the dichotomy of this very question—even if this answer is articulated along the lines of God's "necessary being" as has traditionally been proposed. In other words, God is called to account by *our* questions, rather than our being called to account by God's love, grace, mercy, etc.

Westphal nicely conveys the problematic reversal of priorities that occurs in onto-theology in his philosophical consideration of the book of Job:

Job shouts, Where art Thou? And awaits the divine reply, *me voici* [here I am]. Here it is not science compelling nature to answer questions of its own determining, but a man seeking to compel God to answer his questions. We know how the story ends. God shows up by not to answer Job's questions. Rather, it is to insist on being the one who asks questions. . . . The narrative makes it clear that for all his steadfast piety, Job is on the verge of blasphemy when he insists that God enter his discourse on his terms, that God's job is to answer Job's questions. This is what happens to theology when it allows itself to be seduced by metaphysics. It assumes that the purpose of God talk is to render the whole of being intelligible to human understanding, in short, to answer our questions. (2002, 260–1)

For Marion, and for Westphal, whether God exists or not is surely important, but to begin with that question such that the highest name of God is a philosophical name—*causa sui*—is to start at the wrong spot. Onto-theology assumes that if there is a God, God must be first and foremost a principle of explanation, or as John

Sanders puts it, "the ultimate metaphysical principle" according to which everything else is then explained (Sanders 1994, 63–4; 1998, 26–34).[8] Yet, again, this way of framing things forces God to answer *our questions* on *our* (and Hamlet's) *terms*—"God do you exist or not?"—rather than allowing God to put our very questions/categories/terms into question. One might protest that only an existing being would be able to put things in question, since non-existent beings don't do anything at all. Marion does not consider such a claim as a genuine objection, however. For Marion, the fundamental question is not whether God exists, but whether *the category* of being and the dichotomy of existence/nonexistence is appropriately primary for God. Marion's answer is simply that God should be thought of as absolutely free and not constrained by the philosophical categories according to which we are bound. "Under the title *God Without Being*," writes Marion,

> I am attempting to bring out the absolute freedom of God with regard to all determinations, including, first of all, the basic condition that renders all other conditions possible and even necessary—for us, humans—the fact of Being. (1991, xx)

Marion's point here is fundamentally Kierkegaardian: what holds true for us might not hold true for God. A faithful relationship with God, for Marion, is an intimate, trusting, dynamic, and subjective personal relationship rather than a speculative, metaphysical, ontological, and objective relationship to a proposition or principle. Just "because *for us*, as for all the beings of the world, it is first necessary 'to be' in order, indissolubly, 'to live and to move' (Acts 17:28), and thus eventually also to love," we are tempted to think that this must be the case for God as well. However, "*for God*, if at least we resist the temptation to reduce him immediately to our own measure, does the same still apply? Or, on the contrary, are not all the determinations that are necessary for the finite reverse for Him, and for Him alone?" (Marion 1991, xx). These questions are crucial because they recognize the potential entailments of the apophatic gesture: if God is beyond our conceptualities of "God," then we should hesitate to assume that existence and being are categories that are adequate to the divine life. Yet, crucially, it does not follow that this potential inadequacy would yield the conclusion that "God does not exist." Marion's goal is to show the limitations of our conceptions of God while keeping open an idea of God *without* limitation, which might even mean keeping open the possibility of God's being a being.

Marion's kataphatic corrective goes on to suggest that the negative hesitation regarding being should be coupled with a positive affirmation about love (or at least the possibilities of love):

> If, to begin with, "God is love," then God loves before being, He only is as He embodies himself—in order to love more closely that which and those who, themselves, have first to be. This radical reversal of the relations between Being and loving, between the name revealed by the Old Testament (Exodus 3:14) and the name revealed, more profoundly though not inconsistently, by the New (First Letter of John 4:8), presupposes taking a stand that is at once theological and philosophical. (1991, xx)

This passage begins with a weighty "if." Marion understands that such a conditional statement is all phenomenology is able to say, but he also realizes that it is not all that one *can* say—not everyone has to be a phenomenologist and even phenomenologists can still be personally religious. Hence, he admits that philosophical and theological decisions are involved in the exploration of what would follow from thinking God as love rather than God as the highest being, or even the ground of being, etc. "I shoot for God according to his most theological name—charity," writes Marion (1991, xxi). The realization of the philosophical limitations occurring in light of the overcoming of onto-theological constitution of western metaphysics is something that Marion understands to be proper to postmodernism quite broadly. And, "in this precise sense," he claims, "I remain close to Derrida" (1991, xxi). But Marion does not see his project as "remain[ing] 'postmodern' all the way through," because he is willing to "refer to charity, the *agape* properly revealed in and as the Christ" (1991, xxi).

It is crucial to keep in mind the new phenomenological distinction between philosophy and theology that we considered in detail earlier—namely, the difference between possibility and actuality and also the difference between heuristically drawing on a theological archive, on the one hand, as opposed to allowing that archive to function as authoritative evidence in one's inquiry, on the other hand. What does Marion mean by "refer to charity"? If he simply means that the example of love presented in the Christ-narrative is one that should be available for phenomenological analysis, then it is not clear that he would be going any further than Derrida's own considerations of that narrative. Indeed, following Levinas, Derrida is quite comfortable with the notion of God as justice. Alternatively, if Marion means that this example is distinctive precisely because it is taken as authoritative, then he would be indeed leaning in the theological direction. In *God without Being*, in particular, we think that Marion is rightly understood occasionally to lean that way—notice his claim is that *agape* is "*properly* revealed" by Christ. However, this should not trouble us in trying to appropriate his thought for the philosophy of religion or return us to worries about a theological turn in French phenomenology. Since our concern here is with the models of God on offer in new phenomenology, it is understandable that such models will frequently operate at the border between phenomenology and theology, even while new phenomenology itself remains philosophical.

For Marion, rethinking God as love allows for good philosophy and good theology in that it overcomes the calculative and representational thinking that is characteristic of onto-theology. Marion's distinction between the "icon" and the "idol" is a helpful way of seeing how this overcoming might work. Simply put, an *idol* is something that serves to reflect one's focus back on oneself because it operates according to a conceptual object as the proper focus of one's intentional regard. In contrast, an *icon* is something that serves to draw one's focus beyond oneself by interrupting all objectivist reductionism. Onto-theological understandings of God are idolatrous in that they require God to be limited by human categories and, hence, say more about us than about God. According to Marion, the radicality of understanding God as love is that God shows up as a "gift" (1991, 3). Gratuity, love, and selfless giving all precede the necessity of being. Because God does not have to be,[9] God can give Godself freely and lovingly (1991, 3). This is important not only as a theological realization, but also as an epistemic one as well. Marion understands that God's self-giving would *not* occur according to the horizons in which everything else is "given" in the phenomenological sense. In this way, Marion suggests that the Word of God is "outside the text" (*hors-texte*) of the world in which we stand as the final arbiters of meaning.

Derrida's claim that there is no "outside the text," offered in *Of Grammatology*, should be read in productive contrast to Marion's account. As discussed in Chapter Two, Derrida and Marion appear to be at odds regarding the conditions of givenness. Yet there is reason to wonder whether they are really so far apart after all. That is, Derrida's appropriation of Levinas's distinction between the Same and the Other (which entails that the Other is never fully reducible to my conceptualities and horizons such that others could be universalized and completely objectified) admits that there are some phenomena that give themselves of themselves and not according to my preconceived horizons. Repeating the question of phenomenological heterodoxy, and maybe even flirting with heresy, Levinas recognized early in his authorship that we seem to "find ourselves at a level of investigation that can no longer be qualified as experience. And if phenomenology is only a method of radical experience, we will find ourselves beyond phenomenology" (1987, 54). Derrida's appropriation of this Levinasian gesture is displayed clearly in *The Gift of Death* when Derrida (2008a, chapter 4) articulates his paradoxical formula: *tout autre est tout autre* (every other is wholly other). References to the "wholly other," however, whether understood as the other person or God, can quickly become self-referentially incoherent. Westphal expresses this worry especially well as follows:

> It is sometimes argued that if any Other is Wholly Other then it is so completely outside the range of my experience that I can stand in no cognitive relation to it whatever. But obviously I cannot experience the *mysterium* as either *tremendum* or as *fascinans*, nor can I experience the ambivalence before the Sacred . . . if it falls entirely outside of my experience. (2004, 3)

Westphal's answer to this problem is to claim that "an other can rightly be said to be wholly other if it enters my experience on its own terms (*kath'auto*) and not on mine, if it *permanently exceeds* the forms and categories of my transcendental ego and *permanently surprises* my horizons of expectation" (2004, 3). Westphal, Derrida, and Levinas all eventually realize that the Other cannot be *absolutely* other to the point of eliminating the very possibility of encounter itself, for if that were the case then it wouldn't even make any sense to talk of the Other at all (much less as specifically being "wholly other").[10]

The possible distance and/or proximity between Derrida and Marion hinges on whether Marion's notion of "outside the text" is as radical as it might seem. Or perhaps we should say that it hinges on whether he is really as much of a phenomenological heretic as some have suggested. Marion does not give in to apophatic excess when he refers to the "outside of the text." His point is not simply that there is some hermeneutical "no-place" toward which we gesture but about which we cannot speak. Rather, Marion (heuristically drawing on his own Catholic tradition) claims that the outside of the text is not a non-existent abstraction, but can be productively understood as a concrete lived reality: the body formed by God's gift of love that is incarnate in creation and exemplified *par excellence* in Christ. Marion does not claim that the icon invites looking at the beyond such that nothing (no-*thing*) is seen (which, again, seems to quickly raise self-reference problems, but this time in the phenomenological rather than primarily the logical register). Instead, the icon calls us to look beyond ourselves in order to understand the very world in which we find ourselves as always already an expression of God's charity. This is epitomized, for Marion, in the bodily relation to Christ that occurs in the Eucharist. In this way, "if the Word is also made body, surely we, in our body, can speak the Word" (Marion 1991, 4). Marion's idea is nested in his general notion of "counter-intentionality," which is the concept that one takes oneself up as being-looked-at and being-put-in-question. Marion understands such thinking to yield both ethical and phenomenological results. At the ethical level, selfhood is radically challenged in all its egoistic pretensions. I see myself as seen-by, questioned-by. Accordingly, I am not my own origin and I am not able to rest secure in my own power. I *am* as constitutively interrupted by the Other. Phenomenologically, counter-intentionality challenges the privilege given to the first-personal account as a story that I tell. For Marion, the first-personal perspective might itself be a story that I receive to some extent from the Other. I find myself as always, already implicated in the Other's story.

Although we will return to this notion a bit later and ask whether counter-intentionality requires the theological framework that Marion appears to give it, one does not have to follow Marion's specific theological decision or be a part of his particular religious community in order to appreciate the phenomenological insight of his formulations. Indeed, while we recognize a significant difference in the specifics, we take Marion's distinction between the icon and the idol to be quite similar in its basic phenomenological orientation to Michel Henry's distinction between the Word of God and the Word of the World (cf. Marion 1991, chapter 5; Henry 2000a). Henry, Marion, and Derrida are similar in their appreciation of the excessiveness of givenness and the possibility of intuition that far outstrips (as Westphal says, *"permanently exceeds . . .* and *. . . permanently surprises"*) our intentional abilities and our conceptual frameworks. One of the upshots of new phenomenological philosophy of religion is the requirement of an infinite hermeneutic task (we take this to be as important to ethics and epistemology as it is to religion). Yet this hermeneutic task is not one that leads to a Wittgensteinian silence. Instead, "the extreme rigor of charity," Marion writes, "restores us to speech that is finally not silent" (1991, 4). Here we take Marion also "to remain close" to Derrida in that Derrida's account of how (not) to speak of God/the Other (*comment ne pas parler?*) is also a speech that is *finally* not silent.

Marion's model of God explicitly invites a consideration of God as giver and lover. Accordingly, we take Marion's God to be quite possibly personal, relational, and dynamically involved in the world (as found in creation, in general, and the Incarnation and Eucharist, in particular). Encouraging a *corps-à-corps* (body-to-body) relationship with God, Marion does not, thereby, preclude the idea of being in dialogue with God. Although Job was chastised by God for assuming that God ought to answer Job's questions, the biblical narrative still presents God as being in relation to Job such that conversation could occur—even to the extent that God might rupture Job's conceptions of "God." Such a rupture is brought about by the relationship itself. Without relationship, it is difficult to understand what a divine rupture would mean as opposed to being simply surprised by the unexpected, which could problematically leave the onto-theological framework in place.

God and justice

In contrast to Marion's account of God as possibly being a personal lover and giver, Levinas and Derrida both suggest that God is only impersonally found in the ethical relation to others. For Levinas and Derrida, thinking God beyond being means thinking God in terms of justice, but this is part and parcel of how they understand the "beyond being" itself. In order to focus our consideration a bit, let's consider the talk Levinas gave in 1976 titled "A God 'Transcendent to the Point of Absence'" (Levinas 2000, 219–24).

Levinas begins this lecture by pointing out that, when he uses the term "infinite," he does not do so as a negation of finitude, as in "non-finite," but instead a depth of subjectivity "behind, or prior to, intentionality" (2000, 219). How, then, would one think this infinite? "The not-able-to-comprehend-the-infinite-through-thought," Levinas claims, "would signify the condition (or the uncondition) of thought" such that the infinite "affects" subjectivity without there having to be a correspondence of *cogitation* to *cogitatum*, or *noesis* to *noema*, or *intentional act* to *intentional correlate*, etc. (2000, 219–20). Reminiscent of Henry's discussion of the pathetic affectivity of life, Levinas understands the infinite to "wake thought up" rather than to be a mere object for thought itself. Here, Levinas might indeed be read as close to Marion's own suggestion that "God can never serve as an object, especially not for theology, except in distinguished blasphemy" (Marion 1991, 139). In this sense, Levinas, Henry, and Marion are all trying to express that which would be the condition for expression, and yet simultaneously challenge the adequacy of all such attempts. This linguistic-epistemic problem might be decidedly theological for Marion, aesthetic for Chrétien, ethical for Levinas, political for Derrida, and existential for Henry, but it remains specifically phenomenological for all of them, even if insofar as it plays at the limits of traditional phenomenology.

So, what, exactly, does the affectation by the infinite yield? Levinas's answer is twofold. On the one hand, it contests all assumptions of self-sufficiency such that "the locks securing interiority's rear guard are burst open" (2000, 221). On the other hand, it gives rise to a very particular sort of desire. This is a *"Desire* that is a more within a less and that awakens with its most ardent and most ancient flame a thought given to thinking more than it thinks" (2000, 221).[11] What could Levinas possibly mean here? Levinas's basic point is that the desire that shows up as a result of the infinite encounter is a desire for the Good (as lying beyond myself and beyond Being) (2000, 221). If we understand the desirable par excellence to be what we term "God" (2000, 221), then God shows up (or as Levinas (1998a) will say elsewhere, "comes to mind" (*vient à l'idée*)) only in my directedness toward the needy other person. The desirable orders me to the undesirable. Similar to Marion, we might then say that "God is Love," but here we do not find an originary expression (i.e., gift) of God's love for us, but instead we find the awakening of our love of God only by taking up our love for others as a lived reality. For Levinas, this is a "love without eros" (2000, 223), and he uses the awkward term "*Illeity*" to get at this basic structure: God shows up as that which orders me to the Other, but only insofar as I take myself up as so ordered.[12] There is no relation to God as the one who orders me, except as the trace of the command that has preceded my own self-awareness.

Unlike in Marion, where God shows up as the one who gives good gifts, in Levinas God shows up as the depth announced by the ethical relation. Levinas does admit that it is possible, perhaps in retrospect, to think of the desirable (God) as "separate . . . from the relation to desire it called forth" (ethics) such that there would emerge a sense of "a He at the base of the Thou" (2000, 223). God is not to be confused with the Other, but is instead "other than the other" (2000, 224). Lest we think that Levinas is opening up the space for thinking of God as, in Marion's sense, at least a being, Levinas explicitly denies this possibility:

In this reversal and this referral of the desirable to the nondesirable, in this strange mission commanding the approach of the other person, God is torn out of the objectivity of presence and out of being. He is no longer an object or an interlocutor in a dialogue. His distancing or his transcendence turns into my responsibility. (2000, 224)

God is not merely another neighbor to whom one could speak or for whom one could be responsible, rather God is "prior to the ethical compulsion to the neighbor" (2000, 224). For Levinas, God is "transcendent to the point of absence, to the point of his possible confusion with the agitation of the *there is*" (2000, 224). To be sure, Levinas's notion of the "there is" is notoriously difficult, but for our purposes it can be defined as simply the anonymous space that would precede any specific instantiation of being. That there could be possible confusion between God and the "there is" means that we are not to think of God as *personal* in even the sense left open by Marion, but it does allow for God to be essentially *relational*. This relation is not straightforward, however. It is doubtful that, for Levinas, one could ever be in relation to God directly, but instead it seems clear that any God-relation would only be as a result of one's constitutive relation to the Other (see Westphal 2008). Accordingly, the God-relation seems best understood in Levinas as a relation to the depth-dimension of other people—that is, a relation to their ethical dignity. As Levinas claims in *Totality and Infinity*:

> The dimension of the divine opens forth from the human face. . . . A God invisible means not only a God unimaginable, but a God accessible in justice. Ethics is the spiritual optics. . . . There can be no "knowledge" of God separated from the relationship with men. The Other is the very locus of metaphysical truth, and is indispensable for my relation with God. (1969, 78)

It can be tricky, then, to pin down exactly how it is that Levinas's notion of the God-relation is "religious" or even "ethico-religious" as opposed to simply "ethical." Indeed, despite Janicaud's worries about the loaded dice of biblical theology, some have even suggested that "it is clear that Levinas's God is not the God of the Bible. For the God of creation and of covenant is not restricted. . . . The God of the Bible is clearly an interlocutor" (Westphal 2008, 47). Indeed, Westphal even wonders if "this is a theology without God? If God is only 'the he in the depth of the you', does this mean that God is not a distinct personal being but rather the depth dimension of the human person?" (2008, 71). Moreover, Westphal admits that although "there is plenty of God talk in Levinas' writings . . . it may well be that he is an atheist" (2004, 179). If one has reason to defend a truly personal conception of

God, then Westphal's questions seem to present serious problems for Levinasians.

Even if one has no *individual* motivation to defend such a personalist account, there are important *philosophical* reasons for at least leaving such a conception on the table as a legitimate phenomenological and theological possibility. These reasons have already been seen in our discussion of Marion: overcoming onto-theology means (at least in part) to allow theology to free itself of the metaphysical trappings of western philosophical categories. This does not mean that the account of God offered by classical theism is, therefore, false, but simply that such an account should not be assumed to be universal, objective, and rationally guaranteed. When God-talk is freed from such constraints it does not mean that one stops talking *about* God, or even *to* God. Instead, it just maintains the epistemic and theological humility that is crucial for "hearing a God not contaminated by Being." Even in Levinas, and perhaps more so in Chrétien, the importance of *hearing* God/the divine is maintained. While it might be that what one "hears" is simply the ethical call of the other person, it is also possible that one *might* also hear the powerful voice from the whirlwind, or the inquisitive voice in the Garden, or the invitational voice saying "come to me, all you who are weary" (Mt. 11:28), or even the assuring voice on the mountaintop (whether articulated by Abraham, Moses, or Martin Luther King, Jr).

Keeping the tension between God (the religious) and the Other (the ethical) is crucial for appreciating the essential connection between God and justice (the ethico-religious).[13] Whether one should then go on to affirm a notion of God who, in love, causes "justice to roll down like waters" (Amos 5:24), or a notion of God that is a functional name for the essentially human task of working for justice, phenomenology alone cannot finally decide. A God of justice, beyond being, might take on a more personal cast as in Marion and Chrétien, or an impersonal cast as in Levinas and Derrida, but the important phenomenological upshot amounts to an awareness of such possibilities as operative without the strictures of onto-theology. Such possibilities are crucial for philosophical inquiry regardless of where one ultimately comes down theologically.

A postmodern God?

Considering the philosophical limitations of God-talk and the important apophatic dimensions of new phenomenology, is it even possible to articulate some basic characteristics of a new phenomenological God who would come after metaphysics without sliding into a determinate theological position? We think that it is. In an essay titled, "Divine Excess: The God Who Comes After," Westphal offers three suggestions for how to think of God after onto-theology and in light of new phenomenology:

> We must think God as the mystery that exceeds the wisdom of the Greeks.
>
> We must think God as the voice that exceeds vision so as to establish a relation irreducible to comprehension.
>
> We must think God as the gift of love who exceeds not merely the images but also the concepts with which we aim at God. (2002, 265–6)

We like these three suggestions because they stress the epistemic dimensions of new phenomenological philosophy of religion. That is, these do not say that some models of God are off limits, but simply that some ways of *relating to* some models of God are. Namely, those approaches that would assume linguistic, epistemic, conceptual, and metaphysical adequacy are unsustainable. Thinking God as excessive mystery, as excessive voice, and as excessive love hits on the importance of rethinking the relation of God and being and stresses the importance of affirming the relation of God and justice, yet it does so without thereby closing down particular theologies. New phenomenology, as such, does not take a restrictive stand on who or what God is, or is not, but it does stress where we stand as embodied, finite, responsible, and relational persons speaking about or to God, which itself will impact the accounts we are likely to offer.[14]

For example, while we think that a Derridean notion of "religion without religion" is one way to understand new phenomenological God-talk (such that religious structures are maintained as phenomenological fodder without the determinate specifics of religious traditions being operative therein), we also recognize the value of a notion of "religion with religion" (Simmons and Minister 2012). Neither religion *with* religion nor religion *without* religion confuses phenomenology and theology. Both simply maintain the freedom of phenomenologists to be theological in a variety of ways—whether structurally (without) or determinately (with). Given the diversity of views within new phenomenology and the importance of the distinction between phenomenological possibility and theological actuality, it is important to realize that some influential readings of Derrida can seem to assume that atheism is the only real option left on the table. Yet Derrida himself is characteristically ambiguous about this point. Regardless of how one reads Derrida, though, other new phenomenologists, such as Marion, Chrétien, and perhaps Henry, are clear that theistic alternatives remain potentially viable. Accordingly, we take their account to be consistent with the phenomenological openness demanded by the principle of all principles, even if, as we have already noted, one has reservations about the Husserlian limits imposed upon presentation—that is, one can appropriate the principle (and the openness it entails) while possibly challenging the "as such."

In order to fill out such phenomenological possibilities as they concern religious phenomena, in particular, in the next chapter we will look at Jean-Louis Chrétien's sustained consideration of prayer. His account does not assume theological evidence, but does focus on prayer as articulated internal to one of the prominent guiding structures for new phenomenological discussions of religious phenomena—the call and response. Further, in anticipation of our direct engagement between analytic philosophy and new phenomenology in Chapter Seven, we will also consider whether the idea of "Christian philosophy" even makes sense in new phenomenology.

CHAPTER SIX

The call, prayer, and Christian philosophy

The call and response

Of central importance to new phenomenological philosophy of religion is the question of whether *religious* phenomena are even possible, *as such*. Responses to this question are diverse since so much hinges on the way in which one understands such phenomena (and how one understands the "as such"). For example, even if one admits that there are phenomena that have been culturally and linguistically labeled "religious," what is it about those phenomena that constitutes them as *immediately* religious (as opposed to something else)? In other words, are there truly distinctively *religious* phenomena? Or are there merely phenomena that we have decided *to term* "religious"? If the latter is the case, then new phenomenological investigations into religious phenomena seem to be more a matter of sociological analyses of cultural forms (see Ricoeur 2000).[1] Alternatively, if the former is the case, then it might seem that new phenomenology is, after all, not very far from the sui generis dimensions of classical phenomenology of religion, as proposed by Eliade and Otto, which we have already suggested would present its own problems.

In light of these general phenomenological difficulties, one of the loci of new phenomenological inquiry into religious phenomena is the "call and response" structure. For Levinas, Marion, Henry, Chrétien, Derrida, and even Paul Ricoeur (who is not usually considered among the new phenomenologists, but occasionally writes essays that significantly intersect with new phenomenological concerns), the possibility (or impossibility) of religious phenomena hinges, to some degree, on the difference between the call/response and the question/answer. The difference between these two alternatives can be summarized in two basic points: (1) call/response occurs in an essential relation of authority and obedience that supersedes all legality and cultural identities, (2) the call/response invites an existential transformation (and perhaps even constitution) and not simply an epistemic achievement (see Ricoeur 2000, 128–9). We can see this call/response structure in Levinas's account of the call of the Other to whom I simply respond "*me voici*" (here I am) and in Derrida's (2000) notion of absolute hospitality as the only proper response to the call of the Other. Similarly, we find this structure in Henry's discussion of how to understand the "Words of Christ" (Henry 2012a) and Christ's own proclamations of divine identity (Henry 2003). No new phenomenologist has offered as sustained and detailed an account of the call/response as Chrétien, in his book devoted to the topic: *The Call and the Response* (Chrétien 2004).

Chrétien emphasizes the way in which selfhood is a response to a prior call to being and beauty. Admitting that the "caller" might be identified as God, Chrétien claims that this structure would surely have theological dimensions, but need not lead to merely apophatic silence or to kataphatic arrogance. Indeed, the call itself is sufficient to challenge such arrogance and yet can be considered by phenomenology as a phenomenon of direct importance to all other experience:

> What must a call be if the one who is called springs forth only through this call? The inclusion of the call in the response—for in this case responding pledges our whole being but nevertheless falls short and fails to ever reach the level of corresponding—now takes on a whole new form. The form is no doubt theological, but this does not prevent it from dispensing a clear intelligibility. (Chrétien 2004, 3)

This constitutive call is not simply something directed to a "pure transcendental ego," but rather it is addressed to "the whole human being, body and soul" (Chrétien 2000, 3). Here we see

Chrétien perhaps going beyond Husserl in his emphasis on the *lived* dimension of lived experience. That move by Chrétien is similar to Henry's (1975) discussion of phenomenology and the body, which then gets cashed out in his notion of "material phenomenology" (Henry 2008a; see also 2004b, 70–1). It likewise fits with Levinas's idea (drawn from the Psalms) that one must believe "with your whole body" (2001, 258), and Derrida's (2008b) account of embodied animality, Chrétien does not understand phenomenology to be concerned with purely intellectual matters, but situates such matters in our fleshy materiality and the historical spaces we occupy. Despite Derrida's suggestion that deconstruction considers religious structures without the determinate religious content traditionally deployed in those structures, new phenomenology should generally be understood to follow Heidegger's resistance to abstraction such that they constantly move toward the concrete. *Back to the things themselves! . . . as lived, as felt, as affected, and as called.*

Yet phenomenological investigation does not find a "pristine and first call but encounter[s] instead what is already an answer" (Chrétien 2004, 5). It finds itself *in medias res*—in the midst of things. Just as in Levinas's account of the ethical encounter, in which I am always too late for the approach of the Other, Chrétien's notion of the call always positions the self as constituted by the call that precedes it. In a sense, hearing is already a response such that "that which is first resonates for the first time in our response" (2004, 6). Accordingly, the call simultaneously constitutes my very selfhood (calls me to being) and also challenges any pretensions to self-sufficiency by which I might be tempted. "This call does not actualize some prior potentiality," Chrétien writes. "It is not because I have the ability to hear or because of some virtual listening capacity on my part that I am called," he continues, "rather, I listen and have the ability to listen because I am called" (2004, 19). In this way, the complicated relation of God and being on the one hand, and God and justice on the other hand, both resound in the call. *The God who calls me to being is also the God who contests my egoistic preoccupation with my own being.* Here we can see, again, why God and the Other are so intimately related in new phenomenology—in relation to both, I am established *and* put into question. "The call that is sent to me makes me problematic to myself, uncertain of my own boundaries and of my power,"

Chrétien explains (2004, 48). The call does not merely contest egoism; it also demands justice:

> To sanctify the divine name is to struggle against letting it be profaned: more often than not, it is addressed to us under the opposite appearance, *sub contraria specie*. When a man is victimized and humiliated, the divine name of glory is humiliated, and to assist the man back up is to sanctify this same name. The injustice that we witness profanes the divine name of justice, and to fight against injustice is to hear the voice of the Word aggrieved in the event. To answer the voice of events is to speak, but also to act, by letting ourselves be transformed by it. (Chrétien 2004, 69)

We can begin to see a paradoxical logic here: the call only resounds *in my response* and yet I *am* only in light of the call. In other words, the call always precedes me and yet I devote myself to the task of properly hearing it. Chrétien summarizes the paradoxical situation as follows:

> To listen to the call is already to be, in response to the call. To listen to it is to be listening to it still. We never begin to listen to the call that makes us being. And if this instantaneous call is received by us only in time and with time, if we need a whole lifetime and more than our whole lifetime to fully hear it, we have nonetheless always/already heard it, in our answer, which is to be here—an answer that cannot be declined. (2004, 21)

This paradoxical logic is one that interrupts the ordinary way of making sense of the world and of understanding ourselves in it. This general approach to paradoxical logic, which Derrida will term "aporetic," is a frequent fixture in new phenomenology.[2] In his book-length consideration of the "Words of Christ," Henry explains that the phenomenological import of these words is a radical challenge to the fundamental dichotomies and oppositions that are so prominent in classical phenomenology itself. Henry claims that,

> The human condition hence can no longer be defined only in terms of the opposition of the invisible and the visible, understood

as an opposition of the self to the world and identified with it. Within the invisible itself, a chasm widens, a new relationship is established. The self is not linked only to the world and to others; it relates not only to itself in the secret of its thoughts and its acts. This secret is submitted to the gaze of a God. In this way, by this gaze which reveals humans to themselves and at the same time reveals them to God, they are linked to God in this interior relationship which now defines their reality. *In this way the human condition finds itself turned upside down at the very moment when it no longer receives its being from the light of the world in which men and women face each other, fighting for their prestige, but from the interior relationship to God and from the revelation in which this new and fundamental relationship consists.* (2012a, 31, emphasis in original)

We might say that when it comes to hearing the call, new phenomenology's stress on the invisible over the visible is itself an afterthought and, thus, not radical enough for the task at hand. The worry is that, if the new phenomenological account were to be fully adequate to the phenomena under discussion (whether visible, as in the particular historical responses to the call, or invisible, as in the call itself that only "shows up," as it were, *in* the response), then we would again face the risk of reductionism that we saw previously in onto-theology—that is, all excess would be evacuated in favor of philosophical mastery. This worry is not limited to Henry and Chrétien, but is expressed by all of the new phenomenologists: Derrida's discussion of the trace, Levinas's discussion of the Face, and Marion's account of the limits of language in relation to the icon are all gestures in this direction.

As we have seen, for the new phenomenologists divine discourse does not lead to apophatic silence, but to humble, yet confident, speech. This might be functional and evocative speech as in Derrida, or speech connected to determinate religious identities and traditions as in Chrétien, Marion, and Henry, or both evocative and occasionally determinate, as in the case of Levinas. Regardless of the specifics, however, all the new phenomenologists would agree with Chrétien that "the transmission of God's words makes itself dependent on the human word. God speaks by giving speech, by making men speak, not by imposing silence" (2004, 69).

For Levinas and Derrida, this speech shows up in a decidedly ethical register: when faced by the Other, quietism is not an option.[3] I must act and I must do so in a way that is itself available for further consideration and criticism. Levinas provides us with a basic epistemic insight of new phenomenology: that every *said* (ontological account) that attempts to say the *saying* (the ethical approach of the Other) must itself be *unsaid* (hermeneutically challenged as inadequate to the ethical demand itself) (Levinas 1997, 153–62). When we realize that absolute silence is not an appropriate response to the call we can begin to see why prayer becomes so important as a central example of *religious* phenomena.[4] As Chrétien notes: "Prayer is the religious phenomenon par excellence, for it is the sole human act that opens the religious dimension and never ceases to underwrite, to support, and to suffer this opening" (2000, 147).

A phenomenological approach to prayer

In a provocative and moving essay titled, "The Wounded Word: The Phenomenology of Prayer," Chrétien applies the broader notion of call and response to the specific phenomenon of prayer. He explains the centrality of prayer to any phenomenological approach to the philosophy of religion because it is there that we "address our speech to God or the gods" and without such an ability "no other act could intend the divine" (2000, 147). "With prayer," Chrétien concludes, "the religious appears and disappears" (2000, 147). Chrétien reminds us that the existence of God is not actually the most important thing about prayer. Indeed, even if there is no God, "actual and real prayer" would still occur whenever someone addresses the divine in whatever way. For the existence of the phenomena itself, only the address is required, not an existing addressee. This does not mean, however, that the addressee is irrelevant. Indeed, prayer only occurs when one speaks *to* God, not simply speaks *about* God. Since phenomenology is about possibility and not actuality,

> Even if, *as a phenomenologist*, the positing of existence is not achieved, it remains the case that the manner in which one addresses [the divine addressee], names him, speaks to him, the nature of what one asks and can ask of him, the fear or

the confidence with which praying turns toward him—all this depends on the being of this addressee as it appears to the faithful one. One cannot describe prayer without describing the power to whom it is addressed. (Chrétien 2000, 149, emphasis added)

Attempting to consider the various phenomenal impacts in light of different conceptions of the addressee, Chrétien claims that, at a minimum, "a first description of prayer can situate it in an act of presence to the invisible" (2000, 149). Similar to Kierkegaard's notion of "resting transparently" (1980, 14),[5] which he uses as the key metaphor for existing before God, Derrida's extended discussion of the God who asks for absolute secrecy (2008a), and Marion's notion of counter-intentionality, Chrétien understands prayer to allow one to be seen without necessarily seeing the one who sees you. Allowing for a wide variety of religious expressions (and forms of prayer), Chrétien admits that the "invisible before which man shows himself can range from the radical invisibility of the Spirit to the inward sacredness or power of a being visible by itself, like a mountain, a star, or a statue" (Chrétien 2000, 150). But, regardless of the specific addressee, its mere presence (as the one to whom the prayer is addressed) is enough to "put man thoroughly at stake, in all dimensions of his being" (2000, 150). The recognition of being put at stake in this way is something that occurs in the very physicality of prayer. As in the call and response more generally, prayer concerns more than one's intellect: it is a bodily act of engagement, receptivity, and often submission. As Chrétien explains, prayer

exposes [the person praying] in every sense of the word expose and with nothing held back. It concerns our body, our bearing, our posture, our gestures, and can include certain mandatory preliminary bodily purifications such as ablutions, vestimentary requirements such as covering or uncovering certain parts of our body, bodily gestures and movements such as raising the hands or kneeling, and even certain physical orientations. All these practices, whether they are obligatory or left to the preference of the one praying, can be gathered together in a summoned appearance that incarnates the act of presence. Even he who turns toward the incorporeal does so corporeally, with all his body. (2000, 15)

Essentially, then, in all its forms, prayer is a presenting, an exposing, and a revealing of oneself before the Other (perhaps whether or not that Other is identified as God). Given this phenomenological account of prayer as perhaps the religious phenomena par excellence, and in light of our earlier question about where to locate the "religious" dimension of Levinas's notion of the God-relation, perhaps we can now understand why Levinas would describe the "bond" of the ethical relation as "religion" (1969, 40).

The Other is essential for prayer—prayer cannot occur as a "pure soliloquy" without "doing violence to the phenomenon" itself (Chrétien 2000, 151). This interruption of my self-dialogue by the Other amounts to a "wound" to my speech and my subjectivity (2000, 153). As a particular way in which the call/response might be manifest, prayer fundamentally challenges the egoism that might tempt me to close my mouth and my ears in an isolationist expression of my own sufficiency. Because it does not "speak to me about myself alone," prayer forces me out of myself and toward the Other (2000, 153). Prayer, thus, wounds ontologically and epistemically. I am unable to ground myself—hence the challenge to egoism—and I am unable to understand prima facie how to pray and what such prayer will yield. Simply put, there is no algorithm for proper prayer to be found in philosophy of religion textbooks. Thus, Chrétien appropriates the Heideggerian hermeneutic circle and applyies it specifically to the philosophy of religion: "One can be turned to God only in praying, and one can pray only by being turned toward God. Only a leap makes us enter into this circle. There are no prolegomena or preliminaries to prayer" (2000, 157). Just as Kierkegaard opposes the notion that one could be brought into Christianity by social convention rather than by the risky decision of faith, Chrétien opposes the notion that prayer is something that could be learned through formulaic repetition or even social instruction.[6] Sure, we might learn what others do when they pray, but to actually pray, we must expose ourselves to God in our radical singularity and this is only possible *in prayer*—praying is the very condition for prayer!

At this point, our earlier discussion of God and being becomes especially relevant in the following question: should prayers be addressed to a divine "You"/"Thou," to an impersonal, anonymous "depth-dimension," or something else entirely? There are certainly reasons to think that we should prefer the depth-dimension option.

Excessive anthropomorphizing can quickly make the very God to whom we pray not much more than another being *like me,* but a stronger, better, and more perfect version of me. Such a concern could be expressed as follows: if God is approached as a "You" (even as a much bigger and better "You"), then this threatens the iconic status of God and makes our own personalized conception of God an idol of our own making. There have certainly been plenty of thinkers who have thought that this is the case both in the name of theistic opposition to idolatry and atheistic opposition to theism itself. Even though we saw that Marion is open to a personal notion of God, he also warns against problematically confusing one's idea of "God" with God. In this way, protecting the very transcendence of God would seem to require (or at least encourage) avoiding personal references to God. Basically, the worry is that such familiarity breeds contempt.

While Chrétien is certainly aware of these dangers of an excessive anthropomorphism, like Marion he rightly resists giving in to an excessive impersonalism in response. While there are dangers of seeming to bring God too close, there are also dangers of keeping God too distant. *While proximity would seem to invite disregard, distance would seem to invite irrelevance.* Chrétien sees the former danger to be a risk worth taking because it maintains the "ordeal" (again, think Kierkegaard) of prayer as a struggle with God and with oneself. "Only the second person singular," Chrétien explains, "can open the space of such an ordeal. It is only in saying *You* that the I can be completely exposed, beyond all that it can master" (2000, 161). As for Marion, Chrétien realizes that, even if God is beyond/without being, that does not mean that God does not exist. And, since it is only before other persons that we can be completely exposed, it is only before other persons that we can be truly wounded (either in good ways like when we open up to a loved one about something held very deeply, or in bad ways like when one is humiliated or embarrassed by the cold laughter of the crowd). Similarly, *if we refuse to allow God to be personal, we may refuse to be completely exposed.* Although such impersonal accounts might be offered for noble reasons (surely all religious persons would want to maintain God's glory, mystery, and transcendence), they risk making prayer not much more than a self-congratulatory practice. It is like singing in the shower when only one's cat can hear,[7] while never having the courage to stand on stage in front of other people who might either boo you off-stage or stand and cheer. Staying in the shower certainly eliminates the risk of embarrassment, but it also eliminates the possibility of real transformation and growth. Praying to "You" changes things because it eliminates my ability to hide within myself. No matter what I say, *You* hear me. No matter what I do, *You* see me. No matter if I know myself, *You* know me. Here *I* stand, exposed. There *You* stand calling me to further exposure. This is one of the important upshots of counter-intentionality. I see myself *as seen*—even when in the shower.

Chrétien's account of prayer is consistently phenomenological. While it does not move from possibility to actuality, that does not mean that it is not normative. Indeed, as we will discuss in detail in Chapter Eight, description is *always* normative in some sense—that is, it assumes a better way of understanding the phenomena being considered. Accordingly, while leaving open the question of whether there is a divine addressee, and whether or not one ought to pray, Chrétien does present reasons why one might want to engage in such activity and the stakes that would accompany it. Chrétien is himself a Christian and frequently draws upon Christian texts to work out his phenomenological accounts. Yet the accounts he offers—of the call/response and of prayer—are misunderstood if they are taken as of relevance only to those within the Christian community. Chrétien's willingness to take seriously the determinate practices of historical religious traditions without allowing his phenomenology to become simply a dogmatic proclamation of the truth of those traditions is a model to be emulated in all phenomenological approaches to the philosophy of religion.[8] Unlike some readings of Derrida (and perhaps even Levinas), Chrétien still opens plenty of space for phenomenological God-talk to lead well beyond phenomenology itself and perhaps even toward Christian (or Jewish or Islamic or Buddhist) philosophy, and even theology. Important questions remain, however, about what something like "Christian philosophy" might look like from a new phenomenological perspective. Even if new phenomenology is *not* "Christian phenomenology," it may offer important insight into the historical phenomenon of what has occasionally been called "Christian philosophy," as a practice in which one could legitimately engage as individual persons and professional philosophers.

Faith, reason, and Christian philosophy

Having looked at some of the basics of new phenomenological accounts of God and seen how specific religious practices can be legitimately considered phenomenologically, it is worth asking whether new phenomenology would reject the very idea of "Christian philosophy" as a confusion of spheres. As we will see, though Christian *phenomenology* might be problematic, given the specific tasks and methods of phenomenology, the idea of Christian *philosophy* need not be rejected by new phenomenologists. There are basically two ways that one might consider the idea of Christian philosophy from a new phenomenological perspective. On the one hand, one might phenomenologically investigate what it is that Christianity claims as its core phenomena. On the other hand, one might investigate the very idea of Christian philosophy as a practice in which engages *as* a phenomenologist. The first alternative—phenomenological considerations of *Christian* phenomena—is prominently displayed throughout new phenomenology: in Chrétien's account of prayer, Marion's discussion of charity as the core idea of Christianity, Henry's sustained discussions of life, and even Derrida's account of Christian hospitality, which he even takes to be crucial for thinking about justice and democracy (Derrida 2005, 41), etc. Such a strategy is less a new phenomenological *approach to Christian philosophy*, and more a new phenomenological *consideration of Christianity*.

Were such considerations an immediate indication of the presence of Christian philosophy, then assumptions that new phenomenology is merely Christian phenomenology would not be wide of the mark. However, we have seen that new phenomenological philosophy of religion does not deploy the authority and evidentiary criteria that would support the idea of Christian phenomenology. Now, this does not mean that there are not important intersections between new phenomenology and Christian theology at the level of core foci and even basic key ideas. For Henry, in particular, Christianity and "the phenomenology of life" share the same problems regarding revelation and expression. Indeed, the very question of whether "a phenomenological approach to Christianity" (*une approache phénoménologique du christianisme*) is possible is crucial to Henry's philosophical project in general, but especially as gets worked out in his trilogy on the philosophy of religion (2004b, 95–111).

While we have seen ample reason to think that such phenomenological considerations of Christianity are *legitimate* phenomenological investigations, it is not clear what the status of Christian philosophy is for a phenomenologist. Thus, the second approach—which considers whether a phenomenologist can engage in Christian philosophy—is very much an open issue. This is the case because, as Alvin Plantinga (and many other contemporary defenders of Christian philosophy) suggests, Christian *philosophy* is not necessarily the same thing as Christian *theology*, though such a distinction is not as quick and easy as some might think. In his essay, "Advice to Christian Philosophers," Plantinga lays out three suggestions for how Christians ought to understand themselves in relationship to philosophical inquiry:

> First, Christian philosophers and Christian intellectuals generally must display more autonomy—more independence of the rest of the philosophical world. Second, Christian philosophers must display more integrity—integrity in the sense of integral wholeness, or oneness, or unity, being all of one piece. Perhaps "integrality" would be the better world here. And necessary to these two is a third: Christian courage, or boldness, or strength, or perhaps Christian self-confidence. We Christian philosophers must display more faith, more trust in the Lord; we must put on the whole armor of God. (1998, 297)

For Plantinga, the Christian philosopher is neither a Christian who does philosophy, nor a philosopher who happens to be a Christian, but someone who actively lets her religious identity shape and influence the philosophy that she does. In such a case, we have a decidedly "Christian philosophy." Of course, one could equally imagine, say, a Jewish philosophy or an Islamic philosophy. Though it might seem that there is a mutuality here between philosophy and theology, Plantinga will go so far as to say that the allegiance of the Christian philosopher is first and foremost to Christianity and, only secondarily, to philosophy: "The Christian philosopher does indeed have a responsibility to the philosophical world at large; but his fundamental responsibility is to the Christian community, and finally to God" (1998, 305). Further, Plantinga even lays out a distinctive epistemic starting point for Christian philosophy: "The modern Christian *philosopher* has a perfect right, as a philosopher, to start from his belief in God. He has a right to assume it, take it for granted, in his philosophical work—whether or not he can convince his unbelieving colleagues . . . that this belief is true" (1998, 307). In stark contrast to something like A. J. Ayer's (1952) rejection of theological claims as meaningless and of no interest to philosophers,[9] Plantinga offers a view of philosophy as legitimately concerned with theological, and specifically Christian questions. Indeed, the radicality of Plantinga's claim lies in the fact that such questions can also be legitimately considered by starting with the truth claims of Christian theology. So, although Plantinga does not exactly collapse philosophy into theology, he certainly problematizes any easy distinction between the two areas of inquiry and practice.[10]

Hence, even if the distinction between Christian philosophy and Christian theology is perhaps quite porous, it is a distinction that remains in place (to some extent) for many who see themselves as Christian philosophers. For example, consider Nicholas Wolterstorff's discussion of how a naturalist and a Christian might engage each other:

> What does one say to the philosopher who has listened carefully to the arguments and counter-arguments and remains, or becomes, a convinced secular naturalist [or Christian]? What else can one say but to your deepest commitments and convictions be true as you engage in dialogue with your fellow philosophers on philosophical issues? Be a naturalist philosopher. Show the rest of us where naturalist [or Christian] thinking goes. Perhaps something will turn up that we can appropriate in our way. (2011, 265)

Here we see Wolterstorff stressing the fact that the dialogue occurring will be with "your fellow philosophers on philosophical issues." Even as a merely professional distinction, the distinction remains. As such, if Christian philosophy is not, necessarily, its own theological turn, what ought we to say about the possibility of new phenomenological Christian philosophy? Given his own frequent work at the border between philosophy and theology, it is not surprising that Marion is the primary new phenomenologist to take up this question, which he does in his book *The Visible and the Revealed* (Marion 2008). In an essay entitled "Christian Philosophy: Hermeneutic or Heuristic?" Marion starts his reflections by admitting that "the concept of 'Christian philosophy' can appear as problematic to believers (non-Thomistic as well as Thomistic) as to nonbelievers. The question remains entirely open, because the responses do not depend on the theological options. Should one give it up?" (Marion 2008, 67). In light of the prominence of Reformed Epistemology, it might seem that Marion's question is misplaced in the context of contemporary philosophy of religion: certainly "Christian philosophy" has been successfully defended as a legitimate philosophical possibility. Yet Marion asks a different question: he is not asking whether the concept of Christian philosophy is *logically* coherent, but instead whether one *should* continue to use such a concept today. Marion takes this to be an essentially philosophical question, as evidenced by his statement about the responses to Christian philosophy "not depend[ing] on the theological options." In other words, regardless of where one stands theologically, the very idea of Christian philosophy continues to press as an important challenge to the secular ideal of much of modern philosophy. This raises fundamental questions, though, about how to understand philosophy itself as a discipline distinctive from theology. Accordingly, Marion does not consider Christian philosophy as a primarily epistemic issue, as does Plantinga in the context of his critique of what he terms "the evidentialist objection to belief in God" (Plantinga 1998, chapter 5), but instead as a methodological (and perhaps even ethical) matter. Hence, we might restate Marion's question as: how ought philosophers to understand their practice and themselves given the historical proximity between western philosophy and Christian theology? We will return to the question of philosophical practice in detail in a later chapter, but for now, our guiding question is whether the notion of Christian philosophy has any traction within new phenomenology and, if so, how and to what extent?

Although Plantinga's work on this question is absent from Marion's consideration of Christian philosophy, he does say that "'Christian philosophy' is neither fragile nor marginal in our century" (2008, 69). Rather than looking to the Reformed tradition represented by Plantinga and Wolterstorff, Marion is primarily interested in alternative movements in twentieth-century Christian philosophy, which

> appea[r] to be the privileged method of a dominant part of Christian and Catholic thought. From de Lubac to Rahner, from Gilson to Blondel, up to Lonergan and Moltmann, Mascall and Tracy, even Ricoeur—our century has been that of "Christian philosophy" as hermeneutic par excellence. (Marion 2008, 69)

Importantly, here we see Marion add a crucial qualifier to the notion of Christian philosophy: *hermeneutic*. What does it mean to say that Christian philosophy is a hermeneutic? This particular understanding of Christian philosophy is one that "benefits" from "a theological interpretation of purely philosophical concepts, an interpretation that is possible but not necessary" (2008, 68). On this model, Christian revelation is not something that offers "themes to reason that otherwise would be unreachable," but instead "offers a radically original interpretation of them" (2008, 67). In other words, as hermeneutic, Christian philosophy offers philosophy an interpretive lens that is opened by Christian theology, which then allows for novel ways of making sense of prior philosophical content. This lens does not offer anything new as far as the content itself is concerned, however. To put this in more phenomenological language, hermeneutic Christian philosophy does not admit of distinctively *Christian* phenomena, but merely of Christian *understandings of* the phenomena already under consideration.

Marion says that there are three reasons to worry about Christian philosophy as a hermeneutic. First, as mere interpretive overlay, Christian philosophy would always "remain secondary, derivative, even elective in comparison with one instance, philosophy" (2008, 69). Christian philosophy would, thus, simply be a possible option in which philosophers could engage, but the category of philosophy would be essentially and normatively prior to any Christian interpretation of philosophical concepts. In other words, those concepts would be philosophical without the help of Christianity. Ultimately, then, reducing Christian philosophy "to a hermeneutic amounts to denying it the level of philosophy" (2008, 69). Second, hermeneutic Christian philosophy would face the same problems as all hermeneutic approaches (such as Marxism or psychoanalysis) in that they are all mere possible options among the many alternatives on offer. As such, "reducing 'Christian philosophy' to a hermeneutic leads to branding it as arbitrary" (2008, 70). Finally, the hermeneutic understanding of Christian philosophy fundamentally assumes dichotomies between "philosophy and theology," "nature and grace," and "the known and the revealed." Yet such dichotomies are inherently questionable. "To reduce 'Christian philosophy' to a hermeneutic," writes Marion, "thus exposes it to missing the specificity of creation and no less that of revelation—by locking faith in its *preambula*" (2008, 70–1).

In light of these three problems with a singularly hermeneutic understanding of Christian philosophy, Marion encourages an expansion/alteration of the concept itself. Instead of Christian philosophy *as hermeneutic*, Marion proposes Christian philosophy *as heuristic*. On this model, "Christian Revelation . . . [is] an indispensable auxiliary of reason. But from now on, the 'auxiliary' brought by Revelation not only assists in providing a new interpretation of phenomena that are already visible but also makes visible phenomena that would have remained invisible without it" (2008, 72). Christian philosophy, hence, "offers entirely new natural phenomena to reason, which reason discovers because Revelation invents them for it and shows them to it" (2008, 72). What are such "new natural phenomena"? Marion locates them all within the general rubric of "charity." Specifically, Marion claims that, under this hermeneutic of charity, the face of the other person is uniquely opened as relational by a "Trinitarian theology" (2008, 74). He also goes on to suggest that the idea of history as "a temporality free from any fate" is "born as a concept through St. Augustine" (2008, 75). And he additionally suggests that the "icon" that starts "with the revelation of Christ as 'icon of the invisible God' (Col. 1.10)" allows for a radical understanding of the "paradox of the gaze" that then makes possible a decided rupture of visibility. This last notion, Marion claims, enables him to "introduce a concept into phenomenology that was as unknown to Husserl as it was to Heidegger and whose absence precludes the phenomenology of intersubjectivity or of counter-intentionality almost entirely" (2008, 75). So, here we have three specific ways in which Marion thinks the heuristic of charity allows for new phenomena to be available for philosophical consideration.

There are serious questions that one might ask of Marion at this point. For example, though Marion positively references Levinas when he discusses the face of the Other that privileges relation over discrete substance (2008, 74), one might wonder whether Marion has a narrower notion of "relation" operating here that it might seem. Surely Levinas is not drawing on a specifically Christian Revelation in his account of the Face. Indeed, as we have already seen, there is reason to think that Levinasian ethics may not even need the determinate "religious" vocabulary in which it is frequently cast. Moreover, understanding history in that way may be more a matter of the contingent influence of St Augustine on the history of western metaphysics than an essential indication of novel phenomenal possibilities. In other words, maybe St Augustine does introduce a new concept into philosophy, but quite a bit of work is required to show that this concept would not, and indeed could not, be accessed without the Christian Revelation that St Augustine claimed as the source of his own thought. Finally, the notion of "counter-intentionality" is certainly distinctive to Marion's thought, but it is not clear that it has to be. Even if such an idea was absent from Husserl and Heidegger, it is quite plausible that it is present (in some basic form) in Levinas's and Derrida's notion of a fundamental exposure to the Other, and even in Jean-Paul Sartre's consideration of the experience of being-looked-at by others. These are all thinkers who read quite a bit of Christian theology, but again don't seem to draw upon that theology in the ways that Marion seems to require on the heuristic model of Christian philosophy.

Though Marion does not address these questions in particular, he importantly asks whether the phenomena opened by Revelation end up remaining specifically theological rather than decidedly philosophical. The way he answers this question is crucial to the viability of heuristic Christian philosophy and, we believe, leaves him with substantive potential responses to our above objections. Here we will quote him at some length:

> Concepts and phenomena obtained in the light of Revelation remain acquired by philosophy in the strict sense to the extent that once they have been discovered they are accessible to reason as such. The concepts of "face," "person," "history," "faith," etc.,

function philosophically even without the Christian convictions of their user. And this is why they may find themselves turned against their origin by non-Christian thoughts. The heuristic of charity itself is charitable: what it finds, it gives without reserve. And in this sense, the whole of philosophy could be called "Christian philosophy," so much is it saturated with concepts and phenomena that directly or indirectly were introduced in it by revelation. In this sense, Heidegger, Nietzsche, Marx, and Feuerbach practice "Christian philosophy" as much as Leibniz, Hegel, Schelling, and Husserl do. Recognizing the imprint of Christian revelation on philosophy, and thus the heuristic function of "Christian philosophy" in it, does not depend on a subjective believing or atheistic conviction: it is about facts that any competent historian of philosophy knows thoroughly. (Marion 2008, 76–7)

In this passage, it is clear that Marion does not mean to suggest that Levinas draws upon Christian Revelation as an expression of a Christian faith commitment (which would be odd, given Levinas's Judaism), but that the very concepts that Levinas uses are inherited from the deep and lasting influence of Christianity on philosophical thought. Further, Marion admits "concepts are mortal too" (2008, 66) such that they become part of one's tradition once they are introduced therein. So, even if St Augustine is responsible for a particular idea of history because of his own faith commitments, it is irrelevant whether those who read St Augustine are similarly religiously identified. That idea has now become a matter of philosophical debate. Marion's notion of heuristic Christian philosophy speaks only to the wellsprings for particular phenomena (all intimately related to charity) and not to the history of reception that accompanies those phenomena.

A new worry might emerge at this point to the effect that Marion overcomes the previous objections only by making Christian philosophy ubiquitous. If one appreciates the insights of postcolonial theory, there may be reason to worry about something like a meta-philosophical Christian imperialism occurring here in Marion's account. Similar to Karl Rahner's notion of an "anonymous Christian," it does seem that Marion understands all good philosophy to really be "Christian" at the end of the day (whether or not it consciously admits such an affiliation). While we do think that there are reasons to worry about any suggestion that an entire discourse can be neatly and homogeneously categorized, Marion does not finally give in to this temptation of what we might term *narratival totalization*. Marion explicitly says that "at least in regard to the disciplines" it is crucial to maintain a distinction between theology and philosophy. Here he deploys his arguments and definitions that we have already considered regarding theology being a discourse concerned with "truths that only faith can reach" while philosophy "discusses facts, phenomena, and statements accessible to reason and its workings" (2008, 77). When Marion claims that the whole of philosophy could be understood as Christian philosophy, it is important not to miss his qualifier "in this sense." The "sense" he has in mind is the historical influence of Christianity on western philosophy. Indeed, he repeats the phrase "in this sense" again to ensure that his reader not misunderstand his list of newly minted "Christian philosophers"—Heidegger, Nietzsche, Marx, etc. His point is that they are all participants in a tradition marked by Christianity and to ignore that context is to misunderstand their thought as well as the history in which they find themselves. That is why he presents his claim to the historian, not to the philosopher or theologian, for confirmation or refutation. Here we take Marion to be quite close to Gianni Vattimo (2002), who understands Christianity (and specifically the Christ-narrative) to be a defining event in western philosophy, regardless of where one stands on religious questions about the divinity of Christ. For Vattimo and Marion, we might say that all contemporary philosophy is a practice that occurs "after Christianity," whether positively or negatively.

In maintaining the philosophy/theology distinction, Marion admits that Christian philosophy will always be, to some extent, aporetic in that it uses the very "truths that only faith can reach" as the fundamental fodder for "reason and its workings." Nonetheless, this aporetic possibility is entirely appropriate given Marion's own refusal to allow new phenomenology to be a metaphysical sledgehammer meant to knock down particular theological perspectives. Marion's account of the specific tasks of new phenomenology as an inquiry into possibility that does not allow theology to function as an evidentiary source is consistent with a heuristic notion of Christian philosophy. Marion admits that there are phenomena available for phenomenological consideration that may have indeed be opened only by Christianity, but as we have already suggested, this is simply reflective of a heterodox appropriation of the Husserlian commitment to the principle of all principles. As a new phenomenologist, Marion appreciates the need to stop short of affirming the actuality of the "truths that only faith can reach," but he rightly allows for phenomenological consideration of such truths as historical phenomena worth taking seriously.

Nonetheless, Marion admits that "it is possible that the term *Christian philosophy* may turn out to be more of a handicap than an opportunity in the current state of the debate" (2008, 78). We applaud Marion's realization here and we are sympathetic to potential problems of dialogical insularity and professional cliquism that can tempt those who explicitly work within such a doctrinally distinctive frame.[11] One does not have to be a continental philosopher to appreciate the dangers of such approaches—even Plantinga worries about a potential "triumphalism" in "Christian and theistic philosophy" (2011, 268). Despite such worries, however, Marion concludes that "Christian philosophy" might be "inscribed in the most renovating developments of contemporary philosophy" and may also "contribute in a decisive fashion to the overcoming of the end of metaphysics and to the deployment of phenomenology as such" (2008, 78–9). Given the constitutive openness of phenomenological inquiry and the distinctive ways that new phenomenology, in particular, attempts to overcome onto-theology in the direction of love and justice, Marion's optimism about the future of Christian philosophy can be appreciated as consistent with a new phenomenological approach to the philosophy of religion broadly construed. And, given the specific way that Marion has worked things out, one can plausibly share his optimism regardless of whether one shares his specific Catholic heritage or his general postmodern brand of theism.

Having highlighted some possible points of resonance between new phenomenology and analytic philosophy of religion, in the next chapter we will pursue such intersections in more detail.

CHAPTER SEVEN

Proposals for new phenomenology and analytic philosophy of religion

Some analytic philosophers of religion are inclined to think of new phenomenology—to the extent they think of new phenomenology at all—as irrelevant to their work. Often this is due to a perceived "conflict" between continental and analytic philosophy. We think such a conflict simply does not exist. In the hopes of encouraging more work that takes both traditions into account, in this chapter we will consider John Caputo's seeming suggestion that there is a deep, and perhaps even insurmountable, divide between analytic philosophy of religion and continental philosophy of religion (specifically as found in new phenomenology, which is the philosophical trajectory in which Caputo's thought primarily operates—especially in line with a particular reading of Derrida). Then, we will offer brief suggestions for possible areas in which new phenomenology and analytic philosophy of religion stand as important resources for each other. Although there are many areas where such a dialogue is likely to be productive, we will focus on two representative examples: debates concerning apophaticism/kataphaticism and the possibility of postmodern apologetics. Given the specific goals of this book, these suggestions are simply meant as *constructive proposals*, but not as *conclusive accounts*. That is, we are not going to work out the details of such engagements, but simply sketch frameworks in which they might occur. Hopefully, though, our proposed "mashup" of new phenomenology and analytic philosophy of religion in these areas will encourage others to continue to pursue these important topics in more detail.

"Markedly different"?

Some prominent continental scholars, such as Caputo (2002b) and Philip Goodchild (2002b), have stressed the wide divergence between continental philosophy of religion and analytic philosophy of religion such that productive dialogue between these two discourses would seem to be a dim prospect indeed. For example, according to Goodchild,

> Philosophy of religion, in English-speaking countries, has a clear and distinct identity, and has been enjoying a resurgence: it focuses largely on the truth-claims, rationality, and coherence of religious propositions, and particularly those of "classical theism." Yet, for those who work in the tradition of philosophy derived from Germany and France, the problems, tasks, concepts, reasoning, and cultural location are *markedly different* from this identity. (2002b, 1–2, emphasis added)

Though such claims are certainly not found only in continental philosophy, our focus here is on ways in which continental philosophy of religion (CPR) has tended to situate itself in contrast to analytic philosophy of religion (APR), instead of welcoming it as an alternative and complementary mode of engaging questions of importance to both traditions.

We think that there are good reasons to push back against accounts that would emphasize the stark differences rather than the important intersections of CPR and APR. Although there are many examples of thinkers working productively at such intersections (e.g. Merold Westphal, Richard Kearney, Stephen Minister, Drew M. Dalton, Martin Schuster, Christina M. Gschwandtner, John Davenport, and James K. A. Smith, just to name a few), some recent attempts to bring analytic philosophy of religion and continental philosophy of religion together have made this important goal seem even more difficult. For example, Nick Trakakis (2008) suggests that we will quickly reach "the end of philosophy of religion" if the overly scientific approaches of analytic philosophy of religion are not challenged and supplemented by the more poetic approaches of continental philosophy of religion. While Trakakis (2013) has elsewhere offered an account that is much more charitable to the analytic mode, we want to be clear that we do not understand mashup philosophy of religion to be simply another way of saying that analytic philosophers should be continental philosophers—or vice versa. Instead, the direction of influence will likely be issue specific and will depend on what one is trying to do.

In contemporary mashup music, the two songs being "mashed-up" must remain recognizable in order that the desired effect can be achieved. Similarly, in "mashup philosophy of religion" (Simmons 2013), neither APR nor CPR can simply be reduced to the other. The benefit of such a mashup comes from allowing the insights and strengths of each tradition to continue to resound such that new possibilities might become available. In what follows, we will focus on Caputo's arguments since we take his basic reasons to be reflective of much of the literature in this area. Raising questions about Caputo's account should at least give us pause about concluding in favor of an absolute incompatibility between CPR and APR, quite generally, and also more specific engagements such as between new phenomenology and Reformed Epistemology, or even more narrowly between Derrida and Plantinga, say (see Simmons 2011, chapter 11; 2013; Trakakis 2013; and Westphal 2013).

Is dialogue even possible?

In his essay "Who Comes after the God of Metaphysics," Caputo offers what might be considered something of a mission statement for CPR by distinguishing it from "traditional philosophy of religion," in which he situates contemporary APR:

> The talk about God and religion in contemporary continental philosophy bears almost no resemblance to what passes for traditional "philosophy of religion." The latter has typically concerned itself with offering proofs for the immortality of

the soul and for the existence of God, and with identifying and analyzing the divine attributes. This tradition, which goes back to the scholastic debates of the high middle ages, is largely perpetuated today in the works of contemporary Anglo-American philosophers, who offer the old wine of metaphysical theology in the new bottles of analytic philosophy. Richard Swinburne alone can fill a blackboard with the symbolic logic of his proofs. All over Anglo-America, logicians and epistemologists, from the Dutch Reformed to the Roman Catholic confessions, hasten to stretch a net of argumentation under faith in the divine being, lest the leap of faith end up falling to the floor in a great crash. (Caputo 2002b, 2)

In response to the logic-chopping apologetic "proofs" of analytic philosophy, like Goodchild, Caputo positions continental philosophy as doing something else entirely:

We on the continental side of this divide have sworn off that sort of thing and taken our stand with the equally traditional objection to the ontotheological tradition, voiced in a prophetic counter-tradition that stretches from Paul to Pascal and Luther, and from Kierkegaard to the present, with honorary headquarters in Jerusalem that is constitutionally wary of visitors from Athens. The objectifying tendencies, the preoccupation with cognitive certainty, the confusion of the religious life with assenting to certain propositions, prove to be almost completely irrelevant to anyone with the least experience of religious matters, which beg to be treated differently and on their own terms. The God of the traditional philosophy of religion is a philosopher's God explicating a philosopher's faith, to be found, if anywhere, only on the pages of philosophy journals, not in the hearts of believers or the practice of faith. This philosopher's God is a creature of scholastic, modernist, and Enlightenment modes of thinking that deserve nothing so much as a decent burial. (Caputo 2002b, 2–3)

There are many things in Caputo's account of CPR that will sound familiar in light of our previous discussions of the problems associated with onto-theology, the existential attentiveness of new phenomenological God-talk, and the emphasis on lived praxis displayed in Chrétien's consideration of prayer and Marion's account of the Eucharist, etc. Accordingly, we want to make clear from the start that there is much in Caputo's account of CPR that is worth taking quite seriously and with which we certainly agree. Our critique is not primarily that Caputo understands CPR in such ways, but rather that his reading of APR as fundamentally at odds with the priorities and emphases of CPR ends up missing important ways in which CPR and APR can be resources for each other.

Caputo identifies two different "traditional" approaches upon which he finds APR and CPR alternatively to draw: we might term one *propositional* and the other *prophetic*. We share Caputo's belief that the prophetic tradition is an important one for contemporary philosophy of religion insofar as it helps us to realize that *philosophers often miss the existential forest for the speculative trees.* Caputo's appeal to the prophetic tradition is not an isolated phenomenon, however. Westphal (1973) has also famously defended such a notion. Indeed, Westphal's account calls for philosophers of religion to work from within the determinate religious traditions in which they find themselves and, although written over a decade earlier, strikes a similar tone as Plantinga's 1984 essay, "Advice to Christian Philosophers" (cited as Plantinga 1998, chapter 11) According to Westphal, prophetic philosophy of religion will be: personal, untimely, political, and eschatological.[1]

We grant that it is sometimes easier to see such "prophetic" traits in the work of continental philosophers of religion who have a distinctively literary, poetic, and occasionally almost memoir-esque quality to their writing (a quality that can express the personal and political dimensions of their thought in profound ways), than in the work of those analytic philosophers of religion who sometimes seem to be tied more to a logical *form* of writing than to *the existential impact and depth-dimension* of the thoughts being expressed. However, the particular way in which one expresses herself does not *necessarily* entail anything about what she is ultimately claiming.[2] Expressing one's thoughts in formal logic, say, does not necessarily lessen the existential depth of the thoughts themselves. Plantinga's own "advice" calls for an existential awareness (at both personal and political levels) to infuse philosophy of religion in ways that resonate with Westphal's account.

To be sure, Caputo's critique of problematic *tendencies* in traditional philosophy of religion is clearly warranted. However, the
question is whether CPR has exclusive rights to prophetic discourse, whereas APR is so mired in propositionally expressed,
onto-theological metaphysics that it has given up these rights.
We think the answer to this question is not as straightforward as
Caputo suggests. There is a further issue at stake. Caputo reads
the overly metaphysical tendencies of APR to lead it to what we
might term a *kataphatic excess*—affirming too much or affirming more about God, for example, than we can humanly know.
Such a problem has always been present in philosophy of religion
(and theology). And the opposite problem of *apophatic excess*—
claiming that too little (or nothing) can be said about God—has
also been present. Having acknowledged such tendencies, however,
scholars working on both sides can benefit from genuine appreciation of what the other side brings to the table. In this way, we agree
with Westphal suggestion that *all* philosophers of religion should
heed two important warnings: "the warning against philosophical
arrogance" (which reminds us of the limitations of philosophical
inquiry and that sometimes an incompatibility between philosophy and theology might cut *against* philosophy) and "the warning
against theological arrogance" (which reminds us of the historically situated context in which God-talk occurs) (Westphal 2001,
272). It is wrong to think that somehow CPR is less susceptible
to both sorts of arrogance than is APR, though it might be the
case that the shape of such arrogance would look different in each
case. For example, the theological arrogance of APR might have a
kataphatic tenor (namely, that we are arrogant about what we *can*
say about God), while CPR might have an apophatic tenor (namely,
that we are arrogant about what we *cannot* say about God). As we
will suggest later in this chapter, we think that one area in which
mashup philosophy of religion is likely to be quite productive is
in the relationship between kataphaticism and apophaticism. By
putting CPR and APR in dialogue, we might more readily introduce checks on sliding too far in either direction and, thereby, more
robustly and consciously heed Westphal's warnings.

Let's look a bit further at the specifics of Caputo's account
in order to better appreciate the stakes of it. It seems we can
extrapolate the following as his main characterizations of APR

as understood in light of traditional (*propositional* as opposed to *prophetic*) philosophy of religion:

1 APR is an exclusively professional discourse directed at a scholarly audience often detached from the existential realities faced by religious believers.

2 APR is committed to "cognitive certainty" and aimed at "propositional" assent.

3 APR operates according to a "scholastic, modernist, and enlightenment" framework.

4 APR is primarily engaged in a classically construed apologetic task (understood as an objectivist rational defense of the truth of the propositions affirmed by metaphysical theology).

5 APR affirms that without such classical apologetic stratagems, religious faith is in trouble.

According to Caputo's account, APR essentially depends upon a bankrupt metaphysics in order to provide objective defenses for a God that has been rightly declared dead (in various ways by Marx, Nietzsche, Freud, Heidegger, Thomas J. Altizer, Gabriel Vahanian, etc.). On Caputo's reading, APR's ultimate goal is to change the minds of other professional philosophers while leaving the existential issues of ordinary religious believers untouched.

However, it would seem that CPR is not simply about the business of reviving something that is better off given a "decent burial." According to Caputo, contemporary APR already amounts to the futile attempt to breathe life back into what he terms "metaphysical theology." For him, this very task is doomed to failure: "After Kierkegaard and Nietzsche, no major philosopher . . . has had the nerve to try metaphysics again, not in the classical manner, and not in such a way as to really catch on" (2002b, 1). How should we understand this claim? There are two primary options. On the one hand, the emphasis could be placed on the "*no major philosopher . . . has had the nerve to try metaphysics again,*" and, accordingly, Caputo could be saying that everyone who has attempted to defend metaphysical theology should be dismissed as, at most, "minor" philosophers. Yet this would require dismissing large portions of contemporary APR as not really being performed by major philosophers. The claim that Richard Swinburne, Eleonore Stump, Alvin Plantinga, Nicholas Wolterstorff, and William Hasker, among many others, all of whom do seem in one way or another to be engaged in what could be termed "metaphysical theology," are not really "major philosophers" is an assertion that we should be hesitant to affirm, regardless of whether one agrees with their philosophical views or methodology.

On the other hand, if we place the emphasis on the phrase "not in the classical manner," then Caputo could simply mean that the main figures in APR defend "metaphysical theology" but in a way that differentiates them significantly enough from what Nietzsche and Kierkegaard critique such that we can still recognize their work as important in contemporary philosophical debates. Such an interpretation is difficult to maintain, though, given Caputo's claim that "offering proofs for the immortality of the soul and for the existence of God, and with identifying and analyzing the divine attributes," is simply "the old wine of metaphysical theology in the new bottles of analytic philosophy." Even if some analytic philosophers of religion have resisted the classical mode of apologetic discourse, many continue to be engaged in projects that wrestle with the probability of God's existence in light of the problem of evil in the terms of advances in modal logic, quantum mechanics, and cognitive science.[3] Moreover, analyzing divine attributes continues to be a common task for many in APR—consider debates concerning Open Theism, for example. Hence, even if APR has moved beyond the specifics of traditional propositional philosophy of religion, Caputo does not appear to allow for it to be of any real value for CPR because he sees it as continuing to perpetuate the very thing CPR has absolutely rejected—"metaphysical theology," which seems to be simply another name for onto-theology.

While we think there are ultimately problems with each of the five characteristics of APR that Caputo puts forth, it is important to understand that his claims are also not without evidentiary support—that is, they do illuminate important stylistic and professional differences between CPR and APR. Anyone familiar with Richard Swinburne's rational defenses of Christian theism, William Alston's work in religious epistemology, Alvin Plantinga's modal version of the ontological argument, or Linda Zagzebski's critical Catholic response to Reformed Epistemology will certainly be sympathetic with Caputo's charge of professionalism in APR.

These ideas are developed in conversation with other scholars and deploy a technical vocabulary that is likely to turn off some readers. Additionally, the charge that APR is primarily after cognitive certainty and securing propositional assent does to some degree ring true of much of the work of William Lane Craig, J. P. Moreland, and Swinburne. Accordingly, it is certainly the case that there are some working in APR that may not have done all they can to avoid the charges Caputo offers from a generally continental perspective. Further, it is not only Westphal who warns against the possible arrogance that can accompany suppositions of objectivism and epistemic overstatement. As we noted in the previous chapter, even Alvin Plantinga (2011) expresses concern about the possible emergence of a triumphalist mode in contemporary theistic philosophy of religion. From Caputo's perspective, one of the contributing factors to such a triumphalism is what he sees as a particularly virulent strain of metaphysical realism in APR that is unresponsive to the critiques offered to scholasticism and modernity by Kierkegaard, Nietzsche, Heidegger, and Derrida among others.[4] Finally, in the work of some analytic philosophers of religion, Swinburne in particular, it is at least plausible to claim that, if the arguments for Christian theism fail, then faith would be in some trouble.[5]

Yet even if Caputo's claims are not without some merit, they need to be qualified in two important respects: on the one hand, Caputo generalizes across the whole of APR and, on the other hand, he assumes an onto-theological framework underlies APR's professional identity. First, although there is certainly no shortage of examples of APR presenting itself as a primarily academic and professional discourse, most analytic philosophers of religion also write essays for nonspecialists. When Nicholas Wolterstorff (1987) works through the personal trauma of losing his son, he is still doing philosophy of religion. Similarly, C. S. Lewis's probing consideration of the problem of evil is not found in his early *The Problem of Pain* (Lewis 1996), which is more clearly in what we might term an analytic style, but in his more mature and searching *A Grief Observed* (Lewis 1961), which might be read as an autobiographical testimony about the loss of one's beloved. Both of these are "existential" texts and they are clearly "relevant" for religious believers. But surely the wider problem is that much of APR *and* CPR is primarily geared toward an academic audience. If one were to focus on Christianity in particular and ask whether

APR or CPR were to be of more help to pastors as they consider how to help their congregations navigate the storms of existence, it is not clear that one tradition would emerge as any better suited than the other—it would all depend on who the pastor is (e.g. what sort of scholarly training she or he has, if any), what kind of church it is (e.g. Pentecostal or Episcopal) and what sort of question is being asked (e.g. problems of social justice or problems attending to the rationality of one's faith life).[6] Even Plantinga claims this of his own work when in his development of the free will defense he concedes that:

> Confronted with evil in [one's] own life or suddenly coming to realize more clearly than before the extent and magnitude of evil, a believer in God may undergo a crisis of faith. he may be tempted to follow the advice of Job's "friends"; he may be tempted to "curse God and die." Neither a Free Will Defense nor a Free Will Theodicy is designed to be of much help or comfort to one suffering from such a storm in the soul. . . . Neither is to be thought of first of all as a means of pastoral counseling. Probably neither will enable someone to find peace with himself and with God in the face of the evil the world contains. But then, of course, neither is intended for that purpose. (1998, 26)

In one sense, Plantinga helps make Caputo's case. But, given what Plantinga says, then that claim would also need to revised to read that *some* (or perhaps *much*) of APR operates this way. Such a revised claim, though, has considerably less force.

Ultimately, the charge of "professionalism" is one that can be made against either side. To critique APR's *particular cast* of professionalism doesn't work because it assumes that APR is a monolithic discourse, which is no more the case than to say that CPR is exclusively phenomenological. Both APR and CPR are loose descriptors that range across a wide variety of views and styles. While there might be more of a family resemblance between Alvin Plantinga, Peter Van Inwagon, and Paul Draper, on the one hand, and between Slavoj Žižek, Gianni Vattimo, and Jean-Luc Marion, on the other hand, this resemblance should not be seen as so pronounced that APR and CPR are set at essential odds with each other in terms of style and content. Indeed, when it comes to some philosophical commitments, we might find more resemblance between Plantinga and Marion (who are both Christians) than between Plantinga and Draper (who is an atheist), for example. Moreover, while the "God of the philosophers" sometimes found in the pages of Swinburne's version of apologetics, say, might indeed be at a far distance from the God found in the "hearts of believers" and "in the practice of faith," it would likewise be unlikely that Derrida's "messianism without a messiah" *is* found in such hearts and practices.

Let's take this idea a bit further. Though we find important resources in the deconstructive idea of "religion without religion," it would seem unlikely that such a notion would more closely resemble the beliefs and faith lives of historical Christian communities, in particular, than the classically theistic conception of God under consideration in APR. Ultimately, we think that both discourses are deeply philosophical and, as such, are already speculatively and linguistically abstract in ways that are likely to be at odds with much of determinate religious practice. This is only a problem if one thinks that one should primarily turn to philosophers when questions arise in such areas. While philosophers might have important things to say and might offer some aid to those struggling with existential problems concering the rationality of religious belief, for example, it is unlikely that philosophers of whatever tradition are the best place to look when one is attempting to calm the storms of the soul.

Second, regarding the requirement of "cognitive certainty," we will again quote from Plantinga, this time from *Warranted Christian Belief* where he offers a few examples of how postmodernism and Christian theism might be compatible:

> Postmoderns typically reject classical foundationalism, which has also been rejected by such doughty spokespersons for Christian belief as Abraham Kuyper, William Alston, and Nicholas Wolterstorff and, for that matter, in anticipatory fashion by Augustine, Aquinas, Calvin, and Edwards. . . . Many other themes of postmodernism can elicit only enthusiastic applause from a Christian perspective: one thinks of sympathy and compassion for the poor and oppressed, the strong sense of outrage at some of the injustices our world displays, celebration of diversity, and the 'unmasking' of prejudice, oppression, and

power-seeking masquerading as self-evident moral principle and the dictates of sweet reason. Another theme on which Christian and postmodern can heartily agree is the way in which, even in the best of us, *our vision of what is right and wrong, true or false, is often clouded and covered over by self-interest.* True, postmoderns tend to see these beams in the eyes of others, not in their own; but in this they don't differ from the rest of us, including Christians. (Plantinga 2000, 424, emphasis added)

Notice that Plantinga claims that resisting claims of cognitive certainty is not something to which deconstructive postmodernism has exclusive rights. If "our vision of what is right and wrong, true or false, is often clouded and covered over by self-interest," then suppositions of certainty would be out of place for *all* thinkers, or at least be quite rare. As many analytic philosophers point out, one does not have to be a deconstructive phenomenologist in order to be an epistemic fallibilist or an anti-realist. The recognition of the importance of existential contexts and perspectival locations for philosophical inquiry need not be viewed as sufficiency conditions for doing continental philosophy. While Caputo's model would seem to suggest that epistemic fallibilism and perspectival hermeneutic awareness are off limits to APR, the vast majority of APR's most prominent proponents display both of these commitments. A survey of APR might even lead us to say with Westphal (2013) that "we are all postmoderns now"—whether working in a continental or analytic professional style.

The second component of the second characteristic concerns the importance of propositional assent to APR. Here we think that Caputo hits on something quite important. APR *is* often concerned about defending true propositions and gaining assent from those who would deny such claims, but it is not clear what this means for the distinction between APR and CPR. Caputo is certainly correct to say that CPR resists the claim that religious belief and experience can be *entirely reduced* to propositional form, but we do not know of *any* analytic philosopher of religion who would disagree. Even Craig, who (at least in some essays) might be one of the most likely candidates within APR to affirm such a propositional reductionism, occasionally gives arguments for why personal testimony as a lived reality stands as crucial to the practice of philosophy of religion and the life of faith. As he writes in *Reasonable Faith*: "The ultimate apologetic is: your life" (1994, 302). So, while Caputo is right that APR is particularly concerned with propositional assent, the story is more complicated.

More problematic, though, is that Caputo's claim at least appears to situate CPR as not very concerned about asserting and affirming true propositions. If we consider what Caputo himself says in *The Weakness of God*, however, then it would appear that such a claim needs to be modified: "The modest proposal I make in this book is that the name of God is an event, or rather that it harbors an event, and that theology is the hermeneutics of that event, its task being to release what is happening in that name, to set it free, to give it its own head, and thereby to head off the forces that would prevent this event" (2006, 2). Here we find a series of propositions that, we assume, are meant to be proposed as worthy of our assent precisely because they are better descriptions of the phenomena than other alternatives on offer. So perhaps it would be better to say that Caputo does not think that CPR is *not* concerned about gaining propositional assent, but rather that the propositions CPR defends are meant to expose the limitations of propositional expression when it comes to religious experience and belief. As Wittgenstein and many others have demonstrated, one can give arguments for where arguments are likely going to run into some problems. The point is that such arguments are offered on *this* side of the limits being considered (hence the importance of context, perspective, fallibilism, etc.). If we are right in interpreting Caputo as making this point, then we think that he is far closer to APR than he might wish to admit. For APR is, at least often, invested in the same task—consider the prominence of analytic discussions of religious experience that stress the role of mystery and subjectivity in such encounters.[7]

Here we can naturally move to the third point we believe Caputo to be making: namely, that APR continues to operate within an enlightenment framework. For the previous discussion of cognitive certainty and propositional assent are best understood as particular expressions of this more general claim. As long as an enlightenment framework can be assumed to be operative in APR, then it is plausible to claim that epistemic certainty and totalizing propositional expression are achievable. Yet this assumption is open to serious question. Consider the previous passage from Plantinga in which he expresses his own resistance to classical foundationalism, which is often taken to be synonymous with the enlightenment project. Consider also the following account offered by Evans and Westphal:

> Twentieth-century epistemology, within both the "analytic" and the "Continental" traditions, can be described as the movement away from the Enlightenment view of reason as pure and self-contained to variations on this Humean theme of the indigence of reason. This in turn has created a new context for the philosophy of religion. . . . In the last thirty years there has been a marked resurgence of Christian philosophy, and this . . . has developed into a full-fledged assault on Enlightenment epistemologies and those philosophies of religion which rest on them. (Evans and Westphal 1993b, 2)

Here we find two rather explicit denials that contemporary philosophy of religion, whether understood as CPR or as APR, operates according to an enlightenment framework.[8] In light of the prominence of such evidence as presented by Evans and Westphal, it seems difficult to maintain such a claim as a general characteristic of APR, even though it may indeed be true for some analytic philosophers in particular.

Finally, we can consider points (4) and (5) together since they both concern the requirement of classical apologetics for APR. As noted, while it is certainly true that many within the analytic tradition do take apologetics seriously, it is not the case that everyone working in APR does so. Many within the Reformed tradition, in particular, claim that with a serious critique of particular forms of evidentialism comes a critique of the belief that apologetics of the sort defended by Craig or Swinburne are required for a robust (and philosophically defensible) religious existence.[9] The characteristic of "classical apologetics" (to follow David K. Clark's terminology) that would particularly invite Caputo's accusation is the tendency toward what Clark calls an "overconfidence in reason" (Clark 1993, 108). As Clark explains, defenders of classical apologetics "sometimes claim that a defense of Christianity must be airtight or useless" (1993, 109). As we saw in Plantinga's claim resisting absolute certainty above, and our discussion of Westphal's two warnings against arrogance, this problematic overconfidence is not thoroughgoing in all APR. It is also not entirely absent in CPR. We should assume that APR as a whole is fundamentally committed to this rather narrow sort of apologetic of a few. Moreover, as we will discuss below, CPR need not be necessarily opposed to something like a postmodern apologetics. Again, then, the distance between APR and CPR is not quite as great as Caputo would seem to suggest.

To make this point strongly, we can note that Plantinga, Wolterstorff, and Alston are all resistant to classical apologetics, at least as defined as objectivist arguments for the existence of God as necessary for religious belief. Nonetheless, Plantinga certainly engages in the practice of defending the rationality of religious belief and has also provided substantial arguments against possible philosophical defeaters offered to such belief. Yet we have seen that he does so while at the same time repudiating classical foundationalism and enlightenment certainty. Moreover, Alston (2005) suggests that a rigorous epistemological concern does not eliminate the importance of mystery when it comes to religious belief. Similarly, although Wolterstorff (1984) will defend the importance of holding specific things to be true of God internal to one's religious tradition, he also stresses the inescapable, and fallible, hermeneutic project that accompanies all such traditional affirmations. As Wolterstorff explains:

> The scholar never fully knows in advance where his line of thought will lead him. For the Christian to undertake scholarship is to undertake a course of action that may lead him into the painful process of revising his actual Christian commitment, sorting through his beliefs, and discarding some from a position where they can any longer function as control. It may, indeed, even lead him to a point where his authentic commitment has undergone change. We are all profoundly *historical* creatures. (1984, 96–7, emphasis in original)

Wolterstoff's claim that the historical realities of inquiry invite the constancy of hermeneutic tasks, although specifically addressing the practice of Christian philosophy in an analytic mode, could equally be proclaimed by Heidegger, Levinas, and Derrida. *One*

does not have to be a continental philosopher to realize the impor-
tance of hermeneutics for historically situated inquirers. Further,
Wolterstorff explicitly rejects what he terms "Kant-rationality"
as the primary goal of philosophical inquiry due to its presumptions of universality, and, instead, encourages a notion of "dia-
logic rationality," which is thoroughly contextual and existentially
aware (2011, 265–6).

While we have seen that the five main components of Caputo's
account of APR as distinct from CPR may have warrant to some
degree or another, we have also shown that they remain problematic. Accordingly, even while we admit of important stylistic
differences between the two modes, we think that it is more productive to show how one can draw upon both traditions in order to
address central questions in the philosophy of religion—questions
that press regardless of what stylistic cast one's philosophy might
take. Hence, we think a "mashup" approach to the philosophy of
religion is a promising way forward for scholars working in both
traditions. Such mashup work ought not to eliminate the distinctiveness of either perspective, but instead draw upon that very distinctiveness while attempting to explore new possibilities. In what
follows, then, we will simply consider two such areas in which
such mashup philosophy of religion might be especially productive
as one draws on both new phenomenology and particular strands
within analytic philosophy.

Apophaticism/Kataphaticism

In the last few chapters, we have seen how new phenomenologists make significant use of apophatic theological archives in
their attempt to articulate the excessiveness of religious phenomena. However, we also saw that some new phenomenologists offer
various sorts of what we termed "kataphatic correctives" to these
apophatic gestures. Nonetheless, such positive gestures are still in
the distinct minority within new phenomenological philosophy
of religion. For example, Caputo characterizes deconstruction as
"generalized apophatics" (1997, 28, 32, 41, 46, 55). And, drawing
upon Caputo's account, Westphal stresses the epistemic humility

of negative theology that resonates nicely with the contextual sensitivities of new phenomenology:

> Negative theology is a reflection on the transcendence of God rather than on the (quasi)transcendental conditions for language as such, it is a particularized apophatics. It tells us how not to speak of God, namely not to speak of God as if any images derived from our perceptual powers or any concepts derived from our intellectual powers, including the divinely authorized images and concepts of biblical revelation, were adequate to the divine reality. God is never at the disposal of our cognitive equipment. (2004, 115–16)

Westphal's basic suggestion is that negative theology deploys an antirealist epistemology that echoes the general worries about onto-theology that we have been discussing: onto-theology requires theology to answer to philosophy and God to answer to human ontological dichotomies (being or nonbeing, etc.). Westphal and Caputo, then, both stress the general apophatic tendencies of continental philosophy of religion. Their point is well taken and nearly ubiquitously affirmed by all of the new phenomenologists: human discourse about "God" is not likely adequate to God. Levinas (1997) will insist on the importance of un-saying what we say, Derrida (2008a) will stress the absolute secrecy and undecidability that attends all God-talk, Marion (2002b) will note the excessiveness of charity to any descriptions that one would give of the phenomenon of love, Henry (2000a) stresses that the Word of the World is never able to circumscribe the Word of Life, Chrétien's (2000) account of the "wounding" that results from an encounter with a divine call leaves us unable finally to respond once and for all, but instead calls forth a response that one perpetually lives out.

When faced with the general apophatic tendencies of new phenomenology, one might be tempted to conclude that new phenomenology is unable to help very much in the project of figuring out what *to say* or even what one *could say* about God. Despite the prominence of apophatic gestures, however, we have demonstrated that a careful analysis of new phenomenology does not turn up a thoroughgoing embrace of negative theological discourse. Indeed, Levinas is quite clear that an ethical discourse is going to be more adequate to God than a power discourse. Derrida stresses the endless translatability of the name "God," but stresses the particular importance of translating this name into such names as "justice," "secrecy," and "hospitality." Accordingly, for Levinas and Derrida, one is on better footing to refer to God as defined by "Other-seeking justice" rather than "self-serving egoism," say. Additionally, Marion is unambiguous that the claim "God is love" is better than a claim such as "God is exclusion and vitriol." Indeed, only by granting that there is a qualitative difference between such descriptors would Marion's fundamental distinction between the icon and the idol do the philosophical and theological work that he claims that it does. Finally, Henry understands that God is the one who names us as "sons," and Chrétien thinks that things change when one understands prayer to be addressed *to someone.* Understanding God as the one who names and the one to whom one prays means that God is not best understood as the *one who does not participate in naming* and the *one who is absolutely remote.*

Ultimately, new phenomenologists rightly demonstrate that, even if God is beyond all accounts of "God," not all accounts are *equally inadequate.* For new phenomenology, sometimes even despite itself (as when Derrida's occasionally slips from a claim about epistemic limitation to an affirmation of metaphysical negation), a singularly apophatic discourse is unsustainable because it risks being self-refuting. This is not something that only new phenomenologists understand. The history of apophatic theology is always located within kataphatic assumptions, which is to say that there cannot be *apophasis* without *kataphasis.* Specifically, Christian apophatic theologians are still working within the Christian tradition; Jewish apophatic theologians are still working within the Jewish tradition, and so forth. Apophaticism and kataphaticism are inherently connected and stressing epistemic, linguistic, and conceptual inadequacy does not amount to an "anything goes" relativism when it comes to God-talk.

The relationship between kataphatic affirmation and apophatic negation is not a matter of simply adding a tilde to one's "God is . . ." claims, however. Marion's extended consideration of negative theology in his essay, "In the Name: How to Avoid Speaking of It"

(2002c, chapter 6; see also 2008, chapter 6), explains that it is wrong to understand positive theology and negative theology as the only two options available. Stressing the importance of going beyond a dichotomy of simple affirmation and simple denial, Marion lays out a third alternative, which he claims to be a prominent strategy in Christian theology: *de-nomination*. De-nomination "bears the twofold function of saying (affirming negatively) and undoing this saying of the name. It concerns a form of speech that no longer says something about something (or a name of someone), but which denies all relevance to predication, rejects the nominative function of names, and suspends the rule of truth's two values" (2002c, 139). According to Marion, de-nomination ultimately "ends up as a *pragmatic theology of absence*—where the name is given as having no name, as not giving the essence, and having nothing but this absence to make manifest; a theology where hearing happens" (2002c, 155). Although we are not able to go into all of the details of Marion's account, and the theological history he offers in support of it, we want to highlight two important facets of it:

1 *Stressing divine ineffability is not an end in itself.* Rather, it is an invitation to what Marion will term, in a slightly different context, an "endless hermeneutic" (2002c, chapter 5). That is, saying that God is "never at the disposal of our cognitive equipment," as Westphal puts it, does not mean that we just throw our hands up in frustration and stop talking about God. Instead, Marion contends that the very unknowability itself would invite a novel relationship—of receptivity, of expectation, and of anticipation. Here we might say that the *eschatological* and *untimely* dimensions of the prophetic tradition are highlighted.

2 *Speech eventually gives way to hearing as philosophy gives way to praise.* Marion's point is that philosophy is not able to achieve totality: there is always a remainder. That remainder, or excess, might indeed be announced by philosophy, and new phenomenology, specifically (as, for instance, in the discussions of the (im)possibility of religious phenomena), but such an announcement would also signal the limits of philosophy and phenomenology. Here we might say that the personal and political

dimensions of prophetic philosophy of religion are on display. The personal dimension might be easy to see: after all, it is "I" who "hear." But the political implications are less obvious. As Chrétien and Levinas make clear, when one begins to listen and receive rather than to primarily speak and possess, one opens oneself up to the speech of the Other. Listening for the Word of God might (and probably will) entail listening to the words of others. As Levinas, Derrida, and Henry point out, the trace of God might show up most profoundly in the faces of one's neighbors.

These two points are offered from within an essentially phenomenological framework. In the first place, we are thrown back into the complicated discussions of religious phenomena. How could God show Godself? Although disagreement abounds among the new phenomenologists about the role of the horizon, they all contend in one way or another that religious phenomena would only be possible if intuition exceeds intentionality. For the new phenomenologists, religious phenomena are not meaningless, but *too meaningful*—"excessive," "saturated," and "overflowing." Ultimately, new phenomenology's appropriation of apophatic discourse is not primarily a way of expressing what is true of God according to the evidence provided by a determinate religious tradition, but instead a way of expressing the paradoxical status of the phenomenality of religious phenomena themselves. In other words, new phenomenology doesn't recognize apophatic theological evidence as any more evidentiary for phenomenological inquiry than kataphatic theological evidence. That the new phenomenologists draw upon determinate traditions primarily as something like phenomenological case studies, however, is an important illustration of the fact that the apophatic is historically located in relation to the kataphatic—and de-nomination occurs in relation to both. In the second place, the existential sensitivities of new phenomenology allow for more than merely an inquiry into the possibilities of *religious phenomena*, but also offer discussions of the possible *personal responses* of existing individuals when confronted with such phenomenal excessiveness. Here Marion's account of hearing is quite close to that found in Levinas (hearing a God not contaminated by being), Chrétien (hearing a Call that shows up only in the response), Henry (hearing the Word of Life as expressed in the Words of Christ), and Derrida (hearing the call of justice).

In light of all this complicated phenomenological discourse about the difficulties of expression accompanying God-talk, what might we conclude that is relevant to analytic philosophy of religion? We think that there are three main ideas worth noting:

1 Some analytic philosophers of religion offer reasons to think that the limits on human discourse about God might not be as prominent as new phenomenology seems to suggest.

2 New phenomenology offers reasons think that some of the prominent modes of discourse in analytic philosophy of religion would be productively enriched by an infusion of poetic sensibilities.

3 By reading analytic philosophy of religion and new phenomenology together, one is better able to appreciate the "endless hermeneutic" task of attending to the excessiveness of possible religious phenomena.

To put this another way, we might say that new phenomenology sometimes moves too quickly from the legitimate critique of onto-theology to the idea that *all* God-talk is inadequate—even if not all of it is *equally* inadequate. Thus, a potential problem is that, while new phenomenologists rightly believe that human conceptualities of God will likely miss *something*, it is all too easy to conclude that such conceptualities will likely miss *everything*. Yet such a conclusion does not follow.

Some thinkers working at the intersection of analytic philosophy of religion and cognitive science have begun to suggest that human brains are evolutionarily geared toward particular ways of conceiving the divine (see Alper 2008; Barrett 2004). If one then draws on the numerous analytic philosophers of religion who engage in thought-experiments about what would likely be the case about the universe if theism were true, it is not a stretch to conclude that, in such a case, God would have good reasons to create brains disposed to *religious* belief and that such brains might even be disposed to *true* religious belief. Consider, for example Plantinga's basic critique of naturalism on this front. To say that human cognitive functions are absolutely inadequate to God is to say more than we ought to say. Indeed, as Plantinga occasionally suggests, if there is a God who is all loving and relationally engaged with human history, it would be more unlikely that God would *not* show Godself than that God *would* show Godself. Accordingly, if our brains are designed to believe in God in particular ways, it is not implausible to think that they are designed in that way precisely so we could get some things about God quite right. While this might not *necessarily* be the case, many analytic philosophers of religion give us reason to pause before concluding in favor of absolute ineffability. New phenomenological philosophy of religion is helpfully supplemented, we think, by the willingness of so many within analytic philosophy of religion to weigh and consider the determinate truth-claims offered by members of religious communities. This need not mean that religion is *reducible* to propositional assertions, but it does mean that we should not take it as given that all religious propositional assertions are false. Some propositions might get very important things right about God: for example, that God is love, that God is justice, and that God is personal. *In this way, we think reading new phenomenology and analytic philosophy of religion together helps to avoid the apophatic excesses that seem to tempt the new phenomenologists.*

Nonetheless, the influence here should not only go in one direction. Although we have suggested that Westphal's warning against theological arrogance should be read as directed toward both continental and analytic philosophers, arrogance is plausibly more problematic in positive directions than in negative ones. While we have warned against what we might term an *apophatic orthodoxy* that might threaten to show up in new phenomenology (especially in Derrida's "religion without religion"), the deep hermeneutic awareness of the new phenomenologists helps to always put question marks at the end of sentences that might otherwise seem to be dogmatic affirmations (even if these are affirmations of what one *cannot* say). Alternatively, for those analytic philosophers of religion who understand themselves to be engaging in "Christian philosophy," the temptation is to claim that one is within one's "epistemic rights" to start philosophical inquiry by assuming quite determinate religious doctrines. One does not have to deny that such inquiry is philosophically legitimate to worry that it might inadvertently shut down dialogue with those who start from different assumptions. The poetic/prophetic apophaticism of many new phenomenologists can help to resist thinking that one's starting points are not themselves nested in a lifeworld, in which a whole host of background beliefs are already in play in a variety of ways. *In this way, we think reading new phenomenology and analytic philosophy of religion together helps us to avoid the kataphatic excesses that seem to tempt some analytic (Christian) philosophers of religion.*

If we understand that philosophy of religion, when prophetically situated, determinately located, and concretely aware, ought to walk the line between saying too much and saying too little, then we might see the importance of the important hermeneutic task announced by the new phenomenologists and analytic philosophers alike (consider our discussion of Chrétien and Wolterstorff in Chapter Four). Religious phenomena are difficult to make sense of regardless of what tradition, methodology, or history in which one finds oneself. Nonetheless, new phenomenology is distinctly suited to consider the stakes and complexities attending to such phenomena. However, since phenomenology is not all there is to philosophy, such analyses are likely productively enriched and expanded when then deployed in the context of analytic debates. Accordingly, stylistic questions will certainly remain for those engaged in mashup philosophy of religion. Just as kataphatic and the apophatic tendencies should be read as complementary, while critically related, there is room to draw mutually upon the logical style sometimes (but not exclusively) on display in analytic philosophy of religion and the poetic style sometimes (but not exclusively) on display in continental philosophy of religion. When engaging fundamental questions about the existence and nature of God, and the existence and nature of humanity in light of questions about God, continuing hermeneutic difficulties and epistemic limitations will invite varied stylistic expression. By reading widely in both new phenomenology and analytic philosophy of religion, we can help to protect against assuming that a particular philosophical style is natural and necessary.

Ultimately, engaging in mashup philosophy of religion in such ways opens the door for what we will term *Postmodern Kataphaticism. New phenomenology is right to say that what is said might indeed always need to be unsaid; yet, analytic philosophy of religion is right to say that some saids are surely better than others.*

Apologetics in postmodernity

As long as apologetics is exclusively understood as about the business of "offering proofs" for immortality, the existence of God, and "identifying and analyzing the divine attributes," in such a way as to garner universal rational assent, then we are quite sympathetic to Caputo's worry about apologetics. However, this is not the only way of understanding apologetics, nor even what most contemporary analytic philosophers of religion are up to. As we have already suggested, many associated with Reformed Epistemology have quite persuasively argued against the positive value of apologetics as a necessity for religious life. Nonetheless, while it may turn out to be that apologetics (of any variety) is not *primarily* what concerns continental philosophers of religion, is it *necessarily* the case that they cannot engage in such a practice, when appropriately reconstructed in a postmodern way? Simply put, is a postmodern apologetics anything more than a complicated oxymoron?

Caputo himself occasionally appears to defend something like a "postmodern apologetics," for he says that we can, and arguably should, give an "apology for the impossible" (Caputo and Scanlon 1999b).[10] As we see it, postmodern apologetics will be a multifaceted enterprise with quite local (as opposed to global) aspirations. For example, a postmodern apologist might attempt to critique a common religious conception as necessary for some particular religious identity (as does Kierkegaard in his reading of the Danish Hegelianism of his day).[11] Or a postmodern apologist might argue in favor of the legitimacy of determinate religious belief and identity in a philosophical tradition that seems to resist such determinacy (as does Westphal in his notion of prophetic philosophy of religion and those affiliated with the idea of "religion *with* religion" [Simmons and Minister 2012]). Given this plurality of postmodern apologetic approaches, it is no wonder that scholars such as Christina M. Gschwandtner (2012) and J. Aaron Simmons (2012) offer slightly different accounts of what such a practice might involve.

Though we are unable to work out the details here, we take the general new phenomenological interest in religious phenomena to stand as a particular sort of postmodern apologetic enterprise. The new phenomenologists (again on a spectrum from Marion to Derrida) give reasons to think that phenomenological inquiry and the postmodern framework in which such inquiry tends to be engaged need not abandon a concern for religious existence. Further, all of the new phenomenologists also at various points discuss their own identity in terms of religion (Catholic, Jewish, "rightly passing as an atheist," etc.). Accordingly, given its stress on the personal and political dimensions of religious existence, we find new phenomenology to be well suited to speak to an increasingly post-secular world. Given the specific methodological constraints of phenomenological inquiry, broadly construed, it is unlikely that new phenomenology will be the best resource for those wanting, say, to find arguments for the truth of Christianity or Judaism. Nonetheless, it offers important propaedeutic moves that might better situate such arguments as articulated by other philosophical trajectories. Specifically, new phenomenology's approach to givenness and receptivity allows the various beliefs or practices being analyzed to be considered on their own terms and constantly reminds us of the conceptual frameworks that can all too often be taken for granted within one's particular cultural context. Accordingly, positive apologetic projects would benefit from a better understanding of the situations in which the claims being defended have been and are being themselves articulated by religious persons.

Although we think new phenomenology can aid the apologetic discourse of some of analytic philosophy, it is also important for new phenomenologists to remember that one might legitimately engage in a rational defense of the truth-claims of a particular religious community. This realization helps to interrupt the possible assumptions by many in continental philosophy that rational defenses, as such, are impossible. Reading new phenomenology and analytic philosophy of religion together allows for an enriched vision of what is possible for philosophy because it reminds us that no one particular philosophical trajectory is sufficient to address all the questions asked by philosophers. While it is unlikely that a new phenomenological refutation of the modal approach to the ontological argument is going to be forthcoming any time soon, a phenomenological appreciation of how notions such as greatness, perfection, necessity, and contingency present themselves to consciousness might be worthwhile indeed.

Conclusion

While we have only looked at two areas in which new phenomenology and analytic philosophy of religion stand as important resources for each other, many other such areas might be pursued: the problem of evil as considered in light of skeptical theism and Levinas's notion of "radical evil" and "useless suffering"; commonsense views regarding historical evil and the rejection of the very idea of "theodicy" within Levinas and Derrida; discussions of God and time as situated in relation to phenomenological conceptions of "time-consciousness"; and even such specific questions as whether God can forgive in relation to Derrida's and Marion's consideration of gifts. Importantly, new phenomenology does not engage in philosophy of religion as a discrete subdiscipline for philosophical inquiry, but instead takes it to be merely an extremely important area in which a concern for appearance in its mode of appearance leads, as guided by a heterodox endorsement of the principle of all principles. Nonetheless, the new phenomenologists appreciate the deep interconnectedness between religion, ethics, and aesthetics, in particular. Accordingly, in the next chapter, we will explore normativity as it shows up in new phenomenology concerning moral existence, political philosophy, and social theory.

CHAPTER EIGHT

Normativity: Ethics, politics, and society

Normative resources in Husserl and Heidegger

Although Husserl becomes deeply committed to the centrality of intersubjectivity as his thought develops, his focus remains largely descriptive in nature. For example, Husserl's account of intersubjectivity is not meant to provide moral guidelines for how one ought to live with others or accounts of how best to structure social institutions. That said, although Husserl offers normative insights about understanding science, philosophical inquiry, and first-person experience of the world, it is not immediately apparent how one might appropriate his ideas for political philosophy and social theory. Nonetheless, it is important to appreciate Husserl's attempt to allow phenomenology to speak to the crises of his own time, and perhaps to speak to those issues and problems we face in *our* own time.[1] Even admitting of an increased existential awareness by the later Husserl, his task in *The Crisis of European Sciences and Transcendental Phenomenology* (Husserl 1970a) is still to defend the importance of phenomenology to life, and not to develop a normative phenomenological ethics or political theory.[2]

Given our previous discussions of Heidegger's existential and hermeneutical revisions to Husserlian phenomenology, it is certainly plausible that his work would be a sensible place to look for ethico-political insights that might be drawn from phenomenology. However, in *Being and Time*, Heidegger makes it clear that his task is, like Husserl, solidly phenomenologically descriptive and not morally normative. For example, despite the fact that a notion like "authenticity" (*Eigentlichkeit*) seems to introduce a normative judgment about the best way to life—surely one *ought* to be authentic—Heidegger is careful not to allow such assumptions to abound for long. When he first introduces the authentic/inauthentic distinction in *Being and Time*, he makes clear that inauthenticity does not name a moral or existential failure:

> The two kinds of being of *authenticity* and *inauthenticity*—these expressions are terminologically chosen in the strictest sense of the word—are based on the fact that Dasein is in general determined by always being-mine. But the inauthenticity of Dasein does not signify a "lesser" being or a "lower" degree of being. Rather, inauthenticity can determine Dasein even in its fullest concretion, when it is busy, excited, interested, and capable of pleasure. (2010, 42)

Rather than signaling how Dasein *ought* to be, authenticity/inauthenticity is a pairing that names the phenomenal distinctiveness of Dasein's ontological status. That is, Dasein *is* in a way other than those beings that are merely "objectively present" (*Vorhandenheit*). Accordingly, Heidegger's account of authentic Dasein is not one of achievement, but of possibility—a possibility that ontologically defines a way for Dasein to be as *being-in-the-world*.

Just as authenticity does not stand as an ethical category, Heidegger's conception of sociality as worked out in his notion of "the They" (*das Man*) is a matter of distinctive ontic possibilities available to Dasein in light of the descriptive realties that attend to its mode of being, rather than a positive conception of social existence.[3] Although Heidegger locates the reality of "being-with" (*Mit-Sein*) as constitutive for Dasein, such an account does not entail how one *ought* to live with those others. The They amounts to the anonymity of no one in particular, and it names the public dimensions of the historical lifeworld in which Dasein finds itself. Heidegger's goal is to describe, with phenomenological rigor, the fundamental possibilities for Dasein and not necessarily to recommend which particular possibility is better than another:

> Everyone is the other, and no one is himself. The *they*, which supplies the answer to the *who* of everyday Dasein, is the *nobody* to whom every Dasein has always surrendered itself, in its being-among-one-another. . . . The self of everyday Dasein is the *they-self*, which we distinguish from the *authentic self*, that is, the self which has explicitly grasped itself. As the they-self, Dasein is *dispersed* in the they and must first find itself. (2010, 124–5)

Heidegger goes on to forestall the claim that an authentic life that rises above the They is a normative achievement such that one could escape the "idle talk, curiosity, and ambiguity" that characterize one's "falling-prey" (*Verfallen*) to everyday existence and the public opinion that defines it. As Heidegger explains:

> This term [falling-prey], which does not express any negative value judgment means that Dasein is initially and for the most part *together with* the "world" that it takes care of. This absorption in . . . mostly has the character of being lost in the publicness of the they. As an authentic potentiality for being a self, Dasein has initially always already fallen away from itself and fallen prey to the "world". . . . Inauthenticity does not mean anything like no-longer-being-in-the-world, but rather it constitutes precisely a distinctive kind of being-in-the-world which is completely taken in by the world and the Dasein-with of the others in the they. Not-being-itself functions as a *positive* possibility of beings which are absorbed in a world, essentially taking care of that world. . . . Thus the falling prey of Dasein must not be interpreted as a "fall" from a purer and higher "primordial condition." Not only do we not have any experience of this ontically, but we also do not have possibilities and guidelines for such an ontological interpretation. (2010, 169)

Clearly, in *Being and Time*, Heidegger understood phenomenology to remain a mode of inquiry with thoroughly descriptive conclusions.[4]

That said, there is at least one place in *Being and Time* where Heidegger's descriptive account does seem to open the door to normative moral judgment in determinate ways. During his discussion of "taking care" (*Besorgen*), Heidegger distinguishes between two positive modes of "concern" (*Fürsorge*): "leaping-in" (*Einspringen*) and "leaping-ahead" (*Vorausspringen*) (2010, 118–19). Leaping-in for the other takes away the other's freedom and decision by taking care of the issue and handing it over as finished and completed. For example, consider a mother who, when asked for assistance by her daughter on a science project, just completes the project and hands it back to her so she doesn't have to do any work on it. Alternatively, leaping-ahead does not take the care of the other away from her, but instead frees the other to true investment regarding that about which she cares. Returning to our previous example, were the mother to leap-ahead of her daughter, she might assist her just enough to allow her to see her own possibilities and grasp her own abilities. In the distinction between leaping-in and leaping-ahead, Heidegger does appear to go beyond mere description and presents leaping-ahead as a *better* alternative because it presents authentic relationships with others as defined by freedom (which is hard not to see as a positive thing in this context). "This *authentic* alliance," Heidegger notes, "first makes possible *the proper kind* of objectivity which frees the other for himself in his freedom" (2010, 119, emphasis added).

In his later work, especially in the "Letter on Humanism" (1993, chapter 5), "The Question Concerning Technology" (1993, chapter 7), and *Poetry, Language, Thought* (Heidegger 1971), Heidegger will more directly address questions of how best to inhabit the world in which we find ourselves as it concerns such topics as human dignity, personal freedom, and historical destiny. Nonetheless, as with Husserlian phenomenology, Heideggerian phenomenology faces difficulties in easily moving from a descriptive account of what *is* the case to a normative hope for what *might be*. Although there have been many thinkers who have attempted to work out a Heideggerian political theory, such projects are difficult and are made even more challenging given Heidegger's own concrete and complicated political history.[5] That said, our task in this chapter is not to get into the debates about Heidegger's own ethico-political thought, but to sketch some components of the new phenomenological trajectory as it concerns ethics, politics, and society. We have begun this chapter by looking at Husserl and Heidegger, though, because nearly all of the new phenomenologists take up ethical and political topics in critical conversation with Husserl and Heidegger about the function and limits of phenomenology. As we have seen on nearly all the topics we have considered, the new phenomenologists receive significant inspiration from these classical sources while being propelled to original conclusions by wrestling with what they took to be the shortcomings of their phenomenological predecessors.

In our extended discussion of new phenomenological philosophy of religion in the previous chapters, we saw that the new phenomenologists offer a coherent trajectory while significantly disagreeing about the specifics of where that trajectory leads. Similarly, when it comes to ethics and politics, the new phenomenologists are agreed on some basic ideas concerning the importance of alterity and responsible existence, but they disagree sharply when it comes to how they cash out such responsibility in both theory and practice. In what follows, then, we will be careful not to overstate the points of resonance, but instead lay out a general framework and then look to two specific areas that illustrate particular ways forward for new phenomenology as it concerns ethics, politics, and society: Jacques Derrida's account of the "democracy to-come" and Michel Henry's controversial take on society and culture in his book, *Barbarism*. These examples reflect the specific views of the new phenomenologists under consideration and ought not to be too broadly generalized across new phenomenology as a whole. For example, Derrida's specific view of democracy is not reflective of anything like *the* new phenomenological view of democracy. Indeed, when it comes to ethics, politics, and society, there is no such thing as "the" new phenomenological view. Instead, there are a range of alternatives that share characteristics such that they might be understood as new phenomenological *views*. Despite this diversity, however, these examples are productive for understanding the important possibilities for new phenomenology as a contributor to debates in such areas.

Is new phenomenology a propaedeutic?

If phenomenology is primarily about description rather than normativity, as proposed by Husserl and Heidegger, or about possibility rather than actuality, as explained by Marion, then it is worth asking whether issues of practical moral, political, and social concern are available for phenomenological analysis at all. That is, although not all normativity is *moral* normativity, is phenomenology able to go beyond something like methodological or hermeneutic normativity and contribute to debates about how to understand goodness, justice, and cultural progress? We should not be too quick to decide in favor of new phenomenology as a sensible place to turn for help in thinking through such topics. And yet, moral life, political organization, and social theory are not unconnected from the sorts of descriptive accounts that phenomenology is well suited to address. How one articulates what it *is* to be in relationship with others affects what sorts of prescriptive visions one might subsequently propose for such relationships. Similarly, getting clear on what it means to be responsible, or to be in community, or to participate in a particular culture is a crucial first step for thinking about how responsibly to act, or how to set up institutions, or how to judge cultural expression. Accordingly, it is quite plausible that the real contribution that phenomenology makes to these debates is at the level of propaedeutic stage setting. In this sense, phenomenology might be a prolegomena to applied philosophy, but not a direct contributor to such philosophy. In this sense, Husserl's notion of intersubjectivity as found in his later thought, or Heidegger's account of being-with in *Being and Time*, say, are plausibly viewed as important contributions to ethical and political philosophy not because they tell us how to live, but because they articulate the stakes of what it means to be the sort of beings we are as we experience others and live with them in a space of shared meaning.

There is much to say in favor of this way of understanding phenomenology. Indeed, in the "Letter on Humanism," Heidegger directly challenges traditional philosophical conceptions of value, ethics, logic, and the holy. He does this not in the defense of moral nihilism or theological atheism, however, but in the attempt to open spaces for thinking well about such topics. We might say that he is concerned to get clear on what it is that we are talking about when we talk about such things. As he explains regarding "values":

> To think against "values" is not to maintain that everything interpreted as "a value"—"culture," "art," "science," "human

dignity," "world," and "God"—is valueless. Rather, it is important finally to realize that precisely through the characterization of something as "a value" what is so valued is robbed of its worth. . . . Every valuing, even where it values positively, is a subjectivizing. It does not let beings: be. (1993, 251)

Notice that Heidegger is not articulating a prescriptive account of what ought to be valued, but instead saying that "value" has been misunderstood in the history of philosophy because we have not attended carefully enough to the ontological questions that underlie such inquiry. In this way, Heidegger offers something of a defense of the importance of his ontological project as a necessary corrective to our own philosophical history. This is surely not surprising given Heidegger's recommendation in the introduction to *Being and Time* that in order to open the space for restoring the meaning of the question of being, we first need to "destruct the history of ontology" (2010, §6). In effect, Heidegger's point is that we need to catch up to where we already are in order to attend carefully to where it is that we want to go. Similarly, Husserl's *Crisis* is surely normative insofar as it lays out an argument for the importance of phenomenology for all other science, but it is not obviously viewed as a *direct* social intervention that lays out proposals for new social institutions and educational policy. Hence, in both Heidegger and Husserl we find that the descriptive projects in which they are engaged certainly entail normative implications, but it is not clear that those normative implications are straightaway moral and/or political. The question of whether phenomenological ethics or phenomenological political philosophy is even possible remains an open question in light of their work.

If understood as a prolegomena to moral and political philosophy, then phenomenology is *inappropriately* criticized for not being more prescriptive or proscriptive regarding moral and political life. Moral normativity may not be the business *of phenomenology*, but it may indeed be the business of those *who start by reading phenomenology*. Moreover, even among the new phenomenologists who do offer sustained considerations of such topics as ethics, politics, society, culture, community, intersubjectivity, and economics, it is not clear that their task is immediately normative. It is quite likely that they are still engaged in a fundamentally

Heideggerian sort of project such that they are trying to get clear on the descriptive stakes that attend to such topics. For example, Levinas claims: "My task does not consist in constructing ethics; I only try to find its meaning" (1985, 90). Similarly, when Derrida discusses his authorship, he does so in terms of describing the phenomenon of an "originary response," not prescribing what responses are to be judged right or just: "If I had to summarize, using an elliptical paradox, the thinking that has unceasingly permeated everything that I say and write, I would speak of an *originary response*: The 'yes', wherever this indispensable acquiescence is implied . . . this 'yes' is first of all a response. To say *yes* is to respond" (2002, 355). Further, Marion's consideration of evil in *Prolegomena to Charity* is offered as an analysis of the "logic of iniquity" rather than its repudiation—though such repudiation is perhaps more plausible when one understands the underlying logic (2002b, chapter 1). Moreover, when Chrétien discusses loss and hope (2002) he does so by trying to be descriptively adequate to the phenomena under consideration rather than trying to offer therapeutic solace or instructive guidance. Finally, Henry's account of "material phenomenology" is not one that necessarily speaks to the material needs and struggles of historical individuals, but instead attempts to "seek out the mode according to which [pure phenomenality] becomes a phenomenon—the substance, the stuff, the phenomenological matter of which it is made, its phenomenologically pure materiality. . . . [M]aterial phenomenology is devoted to the discovery of the reign of a phenomenality that is constructed in such a surprising way that the thought that always thinks about the world never thinks about it" (2008a, 2). In all of these examples, we find evidence that new phenomenology is still appropriately guided by the (classical) aim of phenomenological description, even if admitting that *new* phenomena (or even novel dimensions of phenomenality as such) are available for such description: the face of the Other (Levinas), the originary response (Derrida), the logic of iniquity (Marion), loss and hope (Chrétien), and pure materiality and affectivity (Henry).

Although we think that patiently interrogating the expectation that philosophy must be normatively prescriptive is a crucial step in postmodern ethics, ultimately we do not think that new phenomenology is best understood as *merely* a prolegomena to ethical and political philosophy—even if classical phenomenology is perhaps

more appropriately understood in that way. There are two important reasons to think that new phenomenology does more than
merely anticipate or invite further work on ethics and politics, but
actually offers important (and perhaps *direct*) contributions to the
current work on such topics.

First, as we have briefly suggested, the new phenomenologists all
understand that description is always a normative venture and that
this connection is likely morally and politically invested. Second,
some new phenomenologists—Levinas, Derrida, and Henry,
in varying ways—are *explicitly* morally, politically, or socially
normative.

The normative stakes of description

Whether classical or new, phenomenology *is primarily* a descriptive endeavor. Yet phenomenological descriptions are not ethically
innocuous. It can make a moral difference *how* one describes a
situation, an experience, a person, and even a practice. To illustrate this point, let's consider a distinction made by Mircea Eliade
regarding the academic study of religion. In the last paragraph of
The Sacred and the Profane, Eliade claims that two "divergent
but complementary methodological orientations" are present in
religious studies, "one group concentrate primarily on the characteristic structures of religious phenomena, the other choose to
investigate their historical context. The former seek to understand
the essence of religion, the latter to discover and communicate its
history" (1959, 232).

Although this basic distinction is not implausible, the key thing
to realize is that there is not normativity without some*one* for whom
the norm is supposedly binding and without some*thing* or some
state of affairs affected by the constraints of the normative claim. In
particular, then, religious phenomena occur in historical contexts
and those historical contexts are shaped by the phenomena identified as significant. As such, those who claim to be doing exclusively
descriptive work, whether social scientific, cognitive scientific, historical, or whatever, are deceiving themselves if they don't admit
the normative ways in which descriptive claims work in public discourse and professional practice. Richard Rorty (see 1989; 1999)
explains this when he advocates the importance of "narratival

redescription" as the key to social justification. Alternatively, those who might assume that normative work could occur in isolation would do well to realize that they could only get a normative project off the ground if they assume a particular state of affairs, whether historical or ontological, from which *the ought* can be considered, even if not *derived*. As Thomas Nagel (1989) notes, in agreement with the hermeneutic sensibilities of new phenomenology as well as Kierkegaardian insights on the epistemic confines of existence, the "view from nowhere" is a standpoint that no existing person can occupy. As Kierkegaard rightly suggests, existence might be "a system—for God, but it cannot be a system for any existing [*exister-ende*] spirit" (1992, 118, see also 190). Existence continues to get in the way of purely normative claims just as it interrupts the idea that description is normatively neutral. Norms happen, appear, impinge, and function only within specific contexts and understanding those contexts is crucial to thinking well about how one "ought" to live within them and what one "ought" to affirm as true given the relevant options for one's assent.

The problem with Eliade's distinction is that it assumes the difference between description and normativity really does some sort of critical work. Instead, the very claim that there *is* a difference between description and normativity turns out to be questionable. For such a claim assumes that there are two different domains of academic inquiry such that the philosophers and theologians, for example, can hang out on the normative side and the social scientists and historians, say, can occupy the other side, or that the descriptive phenomenologists stand in opposition to the normative ethicists. Importantly, though, such claims are themselves both descriptive and normative.

They are descriptive because there is certainly a marked difference between the stuff that goes on in departments primarily engaged in the scientific study of religion, say, and departments primarily engaged in the philosophy of religion and or theology. Yet this descriptive difference doesn't tell us anything, immediately and obviously, other than that people study things in a variety of ways, which is surely an underwhelming realization.

They are normative because those who care to take such distinctions seriously almost always do so implicitly and occasionally explicitly insofar as they consider a particular approach as the "right" way to study the specific content being investigated. For example, those who think that "religion" is best understood as nothing more than culture may find descriptive analysis to be the best, and perhaps only, way of moving forward, since there is nothing being studied that is not a matter of sociology. Those who think that "religion" involves truth-claims, distinctive religious phenomena, ways of life that are not necessarily objectively available to analysis, and existential risk that gets expressed as subjective commitment may find that normative assessment seems to make a lot of sense as the primary approach. On the one hand, the question is a matter of *what* is going on. On the other hand, the question is a matter of whether what is going on is what *ought* to be going on.

Framed this way, one might simply say that the distinction between the different approaches is due to a distinction between the objects of study. Whereas the normative folks might study the truth-content of the claims made by "religious persons," descriptive folks might study those who are identified as "religious persons" as historico-cultural artifacts. Regardless, there is no innocuous reading of the data that is not already normatively laden and politically, epistemically, ontologically, implicated. Similarly, there is no decision on this regard that is not invited and informed by what we take to be given as a matter of descriptive "matter of fact." As the whole of the phenomenological tradition understands: *history and science are already philosophically committed; philosophy is only done in history and with a concern for what will count as science.*

Given the deeply hermeneutic dimensions of new phenomenology, many of the new phenomenologists realize that their descriptions will be normatively weighty in moral and political ways. In fact, when it comes to Levinas in particular, the concrete weightiness of reality is affirmed as the key message of phenomenology (as opposed to the problematic message of idealism regarding the centrality of representation). Speaking of Merleau-Ponty's idea of the "flesh of the world," Levinas says:

> That is an excellent formula. Reality has weight when one discovers its contexts. This is the phenomenological message. The deduction pertains not only to the analysis of concepts; things are not content to appear; they are, rather, within the circumstances that give them the weight of their horizons. And this weight is their richness. (2001, 60)

This weightiness can be seen in Marion's account of the status of being constitutively called by the Other/God such that one's very identity is understood as *"interloqué"*—that is, put into question. Similarly, Derrida's description of the way in which texts function is not simply a theory of language and writing, but of ethical and political practice such that deconstruction can be said to be "justice." For Henry, getting clear on the Truth of Life expressed in the words of Christ (as opposed to the Truth of the World expressed in public opinion) announces a different way of relating to one's own existence such that one can be named as a "son of God." Additionally, Chrétien's key distinction between the call and the response and the question and answer is more than an account of different speech acts, but amounts to a performance of two different orientations for subjectivity. In all these cases, attending to the depth of phenomenality—even at the cost of remaining faithful to some aspects of classical phenomenology—leads to accounts of the self, the Other, the world, God, and experience that invite serious questions about how to take oneself up in the world while standing before God and others. Even if the new phenomenologists stop short of laying out prescriptive guidelines for action and resist the very possibility of adequate algorithms for moral life, that does not mean that they are concerned with phenomenal description at the cost of disregard for moral and political normativity.[6]

Perhaps what is needed is a notion of phenomenological normativity whereby what one claims ought to be the case is presented as a call for reflection, commitment, and decision rather than mere obedience to an imperative deductively presented. In something of a radical revision of Ludwig Wittgenstein's claim that "the limits of my language mean the limits of my world" (1974, §5.6), the new phenomenologists understand that how one speaks about the world can literally change the world in which one lives. Attending directly to the "unapparent," the "invisible," the "excessive," the "saturated," and the "absolutely other," the new phenomenologists *do describe* reality, experience, and consciousness differently than Husserl and the early Heidegger, but in so doing, they crucially announce the relation to others as central to selfhood, rather than as merely an important aspect of how intentionality operates with regard to objectivity and evidence (viz., Husserl's notion of intersubjectivity), or how one understands the ontic possibilities of social existence as ontologically situated (viz., Heidegger's notion of being-with).

So where does all of this get us as it concerns a new phenomenological approach to ethics, politics, and society? As a way of
setting up the specific discussions of Derrida, and Henry to follow,
we want to offer three basic characteristics of new phenomenology
that we take to bear upon such questions:

1 *New phenomenology affirms the centrality of a constitutive
relation to alterity such that sociality is prior to individuality.*
The idea here is that we are always already beyond ourselves
as a result of the call of the Other. Exactly how this call
gets cashed out is a matter of debate among the new
phenomenologists, but all of them challenge the stasis and
self-sufficiency of modernist subjectivity. When it comes to
ethics and politics, we contend that the constitutive relation to
alterity also serves to challenge something like liberal selfhood
as proposed by thinkers from John Locke to John Rawls.

2 *New phenomenology does not see moral and political
normativity as an algoithmic recommendation for proper
action, but as the weightiness of reality such that decisions
about what actions will count as proper are inscribed into
subjectivity itself.* As we will suggest, however, this does
not prevent the new phenomenologists from occasionally
offering what rightly can be considered prescriptive claims.
The point is that even such prescription is presented as a
further invitation for critical engagement with others.

3 *New phenomenology understands that attention to the
excessiveness of phenomenality leads to important questions
being asked about social structures and political institutions.*
In light of the new phenomenological attention to excess
and the invisible, we are invited to what we might term an
epistemic and ethical humility regarding our own view of
reality. There is always more than what we can say, more
than what we can imagine. New phenomenology should
propel us to critical engagement, but it should admit that such
engagement is never finished. Just as Husserl saw himself as a
perpetual beginner, the new phenomenologists offer models
of what it might mean to apply such an idea to social life. As
we will see, for Levinas and Derrida, it is this basic idea of
phenomenal excessiveness when coupled with the call of the
Other that leads to a sustained defense of democratic politics.

In the previous chapters, we have seen all of these three aspects show up in implicit ways. Levinas's notion of the "face," Chrétien's notion of the call and response structure, Derrida's formulation of *"tout autre est tout autre,"* and Marion's idea of the *interloqué* have all been considered in the context of new phenomenological philosophy of religion, but they are all models of how to understand identity as constitutively interrupted/established by alterity. In Chapter Two, we suggested that there are links between such ideas and Husserlian notions of intersubjectivity and phenomenological openness. Selfhood is never stable, but always already responding to the call of the Other/Life/God/Being. This pre-originary response is not simply a matter of logical mutual constitution—as might be the case for the relational ontologies of Hegel or Spinoza—but instead signals what has been termed elsewhere an "ontology of constitutive responsibility" (Simmons 2011).

One might object here that Henry's philosophy is devoted to immanence and, as such, he seems to be critical of the role that transcendence plays in the work of the other new phenomenologists. Indeed, we have seen that Henry seems to be going in a direction counter to Levinas, for example: auto-affectivity seems a far cry from being held hostage by the Other. But if we consider Henry's appropriation of themes in apophatic theology, it is not so clear that Henry and Levinas are as opposed as it might seem. Henry's repeated tropes of the "night," as occur in his discussions of Novalis and Meister Eckhart, can be read as indicating the overflow of that which affects us to our understanding of being-affected. In brief, *I* am not life, even if life always shows up in *my* living it. That excessiveness may not indicate a Levinasian transcendence, but it does indicate that, even for Henry, selfhood is never self-sufficient. I am always beyond myself in a pathos-filled relation to my own existence. I am never adequate to myself, but instead inhabit my own subjectivity ever more fully by turning to what calls me to being: life. Further, for Henry, it is by attending to the Truth of Life that we are best able to see the failure of our ordinary way of living with each other. Henry's *Barbarism* is a book-length chastisement of the failure of human society to live up to the demands of life. Auto-affectivity may not be the same thing as absolute alterity, but both ideas invite serious reflection about who it is that we are and how we ought to live in light of the constitutive relation that defines us.

In the remainder of this chapter, we will look at a couple examples of how these three general characteristics have been worked out by new phenomenologists. This is not meant to be a comprehensive look at the wide range of views of ethics, politics, and society offered by new phenomenology, for such a project would require a book all its own.[7] Instead our goal is to provide examples of what moral and political normativity might look like according to a new phenomenological framework.

Political theory after Levinas and Derrida

As we indicated in Chapter Two, Derrida's particular contribution to new phenomenology has been decidedly hermeneutic. His considerations of language, conceptuality, writing, discourse, and identity have been as controversial as they have been influential. Over the past couple decades, however, there has been much discussion about the "ethico-political" (or "ethico-religious") turn in Derrida's thought. To this suggestion, Derrida responds: "There never was in the 1980s or 1990s, as has sometimes been claimed, a *political turn* or *ethical turn* in 'deconstruction', at least not as I experience it. The thinking of the political has always been a thinking of *différance* and the thinking of *différance* always a thinking *of* the political, of the contour and limits of the political, especially around the enigma or the autoimmune *double bind* of the democratic" (2005, 39). In light of Derrida's account, we propose that Derrida's early critiques of logo-centrism and presence are already political. *Différance* affects much more than simply how we read texts; it is a matter of how we live with others.

Readers familiar with Derrida's famous claim that "there is nothing outside of the text" might assume that Derrida deconstruction to be limitless (1997a, 158). That is, if there is no way to get outside of a text, if everything is textual, then interpretation would not be bounded and hermeneutics would be the very condition for lived experience. Although this passage has received an enormous amount of attention in the literature, both positively and negatively, we find that the best way to understand it is in tension with another famous Derridean passage from his essay "Force of Law" (Derrida 1992b). Therein Derrida strikingly claims:

> The structure I am describing here is a structure in which law (*droit*) is essentially deconstructible. . . . The fact that law is deconstructible is not bad news. We may even see in this a stroke of luck for politics, for all historical progress. But the paradox that I'd like to submit for discussion is the following: it is this deconstructible structure of law (*droit*), or if you prefer of justice as *droit*, that also insures the possibility of deconstruction. Justice in itself, if such a thing exists, outside or beyond law, is not deconstructible. No more than deconstruction itself, if such a thing exists. Deconstruction is justice. (1992b, 14–15)

What is remarkable about this passage is that Derrida appears to offer limits to the deconstructive enterprise. He seems to suggest that there are boundaries beyond which hermeneutics does not extend. If we read textuality as the space in which deconstruction is possible, then Derrida can be read as insinuating that justice resides *hors-texte*. Notice, however, that deconstruction does not have its *foundation in* justice, but deconstrudtion *is* justice. The *practice* of deconstruction is the *task* of justice. Would this mean that justice is nothing other than a way of reading texts? To assume this to be the case would be misunderstand deconstruction and to ignore the phenomenological context in which Derridean deconstruction occurs. In "Force of Law," Derrida decidedly presents the project of deconstruction as a *way* of holding positions rather than its being a particular position itself. Deconstruction is the task of hearing the call of alterity in whatever we investigate, be that the legal structure, the university system, or textual narratives. In this way, we can see Derrida's deep phenomenological focus: he rigorously continues to inquire into phenomena, but attends in particular to the way that some phenomena challenge easy inquiry. We have already seen how this plays out in the connection that Derrida draws between "God" and "justice," but now we will consider how Derrida understands his entire phenomenological project to be a matter of enacting justice, or at least trying to lay out the stakes of what such an enactment would involve.

The distinction between law and justice is key for understanding Derrida's argument. *Law* (droit) is the term Derrida gives to the necessity of calculation internal to one's social context and interpersonal relationships. This would include both law as normative codes according to which society is structured and also such operations as reading, speaking, and writing. Repeatedly in his authorship, Derrida recognizes that his speaking in French, writing about certain figures rather than others, and choosing to read some books rather than others are all decisions that make him guilty of exclusion and marginalization. To do philosophy can be seen as a failure to feed the poor, say. For Derrida, however, even feeding the poor can be failing to care for the widows and the orphans. What matters is not which activity one chooses to engage in, but the ways in which all action faces structural problems in light of the infinite call of each and every other person (and even nonhuman animals). The deconstructive logic that Derrida understands is that to act in one way is to fail to act in another way. This is neither just a bit of rhetorical flourish nor a trivial statement about action, but a deep phenomenological realization about finitude of action itself. Decision is always required and yet always frustratingly inadequate to the tasks at hand. For Derrida, following Levinas, "justice" is the name for the obligation that underlies *all* activity. It is what continues to press even when we feel like we have done enough. Indeed, justice perpetually challenges the idea that "enough" could ever be done. It is, thus, *incalculable* because it is the constant reminder that calculation itself tends toward violence:

> Justice is an experience of the impossible. A will, a desire, a demand for justice whose structure wouldn't be an experience of aporia would have no chance to be what it is, namely, a call for justice. . . . Law (*droit*) is not justice. Law is the element of calculation, and it is just that there be law, but justice is incalculable, it requires us to calculate with the incalculable; and aporetic experiences are the experiences, as improbable as they are necessary, of justice, that is to say of moments in which the decision between just and unjust is never insured by a rule. (1992b, 16)[8]

Justice, then, operates according to an *aporetic logic*. To move according to the strictures of law is to be guided by a particular sort of norm, which is itself often rooted in appeals to a foundation or rationale beyond the discursive community—to human rights, say. Alternatively, justice repeatedly puts such firm foundations in question. "The questioning of foundations," Derrida reminds us, "is neither foundationalist nor anti-foundationalist" (1992b, 8). What would lie between these two options? It would not be some deeper logos that would simply serve to expand the initial horizon of onto-theological speculation. Rather, it would be the *experience of aporia* understood as the very possibility of the impossible as occurring in every experience. Here we can see the apophatic tendencies and the ethical sensibilities of Derrida come together since God/Justice/the Other is always given *as* excessive.

In light of the aporetic experience of the tension between law and justice, how are we to understand the conditions of possibility for a just society? Derrida does not claim that such conditions do not exist, but instead that the conditions are not available as a guarantor of experience—justice claimed might be justice denied. As Derrida says in *The Other Heading*, "These conditions can only take a negative form (without X there would not be Y). One can be certain only of this negative form. As soon as it is converted into positive certainty . . . one can be sure that one is beginning to be deceived, indeed beginning to deceive the other" (1992c, 80–1). Similar to Levinas, Derrida understands justice, or the "undeconstructible," always to be prior to the legal manifestations that a particular historical conception of justice might takes in the political arena. If there were not such a thing as justice, then there could be no deconstruction—for there would be nothing in the name of which we would necessarily continue to interrogate our experience, our language, and ourselves. But, as just indicated, the idea that one could have knowledge of justice is deeply problematic because it would ignore the excessiveness of the phenomena itself. Justice, then, is that in which Derrida claims we must put our trust or faith. Derrida will often speak this way about the Other more broadly. Due to the very alterity of the Other, the Other is not something that one "knows," which would assume that somehow the distance between sameness and alterity has been effectively crossed, but instead the Other is someone in whom one trusts. Intersubjectivity is more than merely a matter of achieving objectivity in subjectivity regarding one's intuitions; it is a matter of who one is in the first place. Far from yielding epistemic confirmation regarding judgment, intersubjectivity is risky because it is always a matter of justice—of doing justice to the Other with whom one speaks, to whom one listens, and from whom one receives oneself.

Accordingly, Derrida's primary focus is not on what we are justified in believing, but what we must trust in order for deconstruction to be possible. In this way, Derrida (with Levinas) helps to illustrate the ethical stakes of epistemology itself. Hence, there is no absolute legitimacy that could be obtained for the assertion that "there is such a thing as justice." Instead, it is only justified by acting *in the name of justice*. The only way in which law is actually about social justice (and not simply a power play) is for justice to exist. Yet such existence is what constantly overflows our knowledge, while remaining that in relation to which we constantly risk ourselves. This basic structure is fundamentally phenomenological: Derrida constantly asks how it is that that which gives itself does so. His discussions of justice are not disconnected from his work on language. It is all of a piece internal to an authorship concerned about being open to the excessiveness of phenomenality and the challenges that accompany attempts to express such excess.

Hence, as a phenomenologist, political life is more than politics for Derrrida. To live as a member of society is to be constituted by the tension between the demand for singular recognition and the necessity of generalization—another aporetic experience:

> How are we to reconcile the act of justice that must always concern singularity, individuals, irreplaceable groups and lives, the other or myself *as* other, in a unique situation, with rule, norm, value or the imperative of justice which necessarily have a general form, even if this generality prescribes a singular application in each case? (1992b, 17)

This question is the central question for not only deconstructive political theory, but contemporary debates concerning contemporary political liberalism as well. For Levinas and Derrida, the liberal self is problematically isolated from the outset. On this model, there is no way for liberalism to conceive of the move from oneself to the other as anything other than an act of original freedom. In light of the call of the Other, however, the new phenomenologists all indicate that the self is not prior to its relationships, but its relationships constitute the self. Indeed, this can be viewed as the hermeneutic upshot of taking the lifeworld seriously. Perhaps, then, this is simply a complicated version of something like civic-republicanism or communitarianism? Certainly such thinkers as Michael Sandel, Alasdair MacIntyre, and Charles Taylor claim that the unencumbered liberal self is a problematic fiction. Though we would resist any simple identity or confusion between new phenomenology and communitarian political theory, we think that there is important work to be done bringing these two discourses together in productive ways.[9] Although we are always enmeshed in social relationships, the notion that these relationships actually lay some sort of ethical claim upon us is not necessarily required by the relationships themselves. The debate between liberalism and communitarianism, for example, is itself perhaps too late for the ethical/ontological articulations of new phenomenology.[10]

Justice, then, must be conceived otherwise than merely legally, even though justice will always require legal structures. Rules, norms, values, and imperatives are all attempts to give presence to the excessiveness of alterity. We cannot do without law, as Derrida clearly insists, but this does not mean that we must be content with it. That the law is "essentially deconstructible" is cause for a reserved optimism. *Optimism* because there is always hope for making tomorrow better than today; *reserved* because such hope is essentially contingent upon my action here and now—action that is not guaranteed by the law, but a challenge to it. It is crucial that we realize that this decision is not merely a choice between two otherwise legitimate actions. Rather, "a decision that didn't go through the ordeal of the undecidable would not be a free decision, it would only be the programmable application or unfolding of a calculable process. It might be legal; it would not be just" (1992b, 24). Derrida's point here is that, as long as our decision is made under the horizon of universality and objective certainty, there is no real decision. Drawing on Marion, we might say that Derrida finds an "endless hermeneutic" in all political decision (see also Simmons 2011, 118). Here, then, we can see the radicalization that Husserlian intersubjectivity receives in the hands of Derrida. The Other calls me to justify my beliefs, my action, and my very selfhood, but this task is not one that can be finalized; instead, it stands as the task of one's entire existence (similar to Kierkegaard's notion of faith). The conversation with others continues as long as decisions are required.

The *Other* for Levinas, *Life* for Henry, the *Call* for Chrétien, *Justice* for Derrida, and *Charity* for Marion are names given to that which outstrips the domain of nomenclature. These are names that operate as placeholders for that which is not localizable in one place. In relation to the Other, I stand (am) without a place because of the transcendence that constitutes me—even, as for Henry, if that transcendence is best understood as the depth of lived immanence. As Marion, Henry, and Chrétien understand regarding their respective ideas of being oneself as the *"interloqué,"* "the son of God," and "the called," when one's very being is put in question, it affects how one then relates to oneself, others, and the world. When the world doesn't revolve around us, we inhabit the world differently. As "undecidable," decision is, for Derrida, always an attempt to inhabit the world as best as possible—yet risk remains. This is a phenomenological realization and an ethical reality. Derrida writes that, "the undecidable remains caught, lodged, at least as a ghost—but an essential ghost—in every decision, in every event of decision" (1992b, 24).

Because justice is always at stake in every decision, as its condition and its contestation, justice is never something that can operate as merely a past occurrence, but always signifies a continuing task. The "event" of decision is always a moment that anticipates the future by attempting to enact it here and now. Thus, deconstruction is always about critiquing the present in the name of the "to-come" (*à venir*). It is in light of this basic idea that one can understand Derrida's robust defense of what he terms the "democracy to-come." Here we must hear the "to-come" as echoing with what Derrida understands to be the first words of deconstruction: "Come, yes, yes" (*Viens, oui, oui*). The idea is that the inaugural call of the Other ought to cause us to inhabit the world guided by what Derrida (2000) will term "absolute hospitality." This hospitality gets worked out in political theory as an argument for the constancy of critique. Such critique, Derrida thinks, is maximally encouraged within a democratic structure. "The expression 'democracy to come,'" he writes, "does indeed translate or call for a militant and interminable political critique" (2005, 86). For both Levinas and Derrida, democracy is "the only system, the only constitutional paradigm, in which, in principle, one has or assumes the right to criticize everything publicly, including the idea of democracy, its concept, its history, and its name" (Derrida 2005, 87–8).

Here we find Derrida affirming democracy because of its constitutive openness to critique—a constitutive openness that, we suggest, is rooted deeply in Derrida's own appropriation and appreciation of Husserlian phenomenological openness as a methodological necessity.

We should understand, however, that this openness is not simply an abstract task for speculative philosophy. In *Rogues*, Derrida works out what seem to be prescriptive guidelines in the task of self-critically striving toward justice. A community/state/institution that is concerned about justice must:

1 Criticize dogmatism that is unaware of itself and "cultivat[e] the virtue of such critique, of the critical idea, the critical tradition, but also submi[t] it, beyond critique and questioning, to a deconstructive genealogy that thinks and exceeds it without yet compromising it" (Derrida 2005, 77).

2 View democracy not merely as a historical given, but as something that "remains to be thought and *to come*" (Derrida 2005, 78).

In these prescriptions, Derrida offers a positive vision of how to strive for an ethical politics. If the undeconstructibility of justice forms the framework of a deconstructive political theory, these prescriptions might begin to articulate its content.

As a final point, perhaps we might suggest that Derrida understands democracy to serve as something of a "regulative ideal" for political life. Would such a characterization be sustainable? Almost everywhere Derrida mentions the democracy to-come, he is quick to distance it from a supposed Kantian notion of regulation. While this resistance to "regulative ideals" remains undeveloped in the majority of his work, in *Rogues* he offers a lengthy rationale for it by offering three "reservations" about conceiving of the democracy to-come in such ways. The first is that regulative ideas all operate within the sphere of the possible, whereas the democracy to-come should only be conceived of as "im-possible" (we hyphenate this term in order to convey that, for Derrida, possibility and impossibility are always intimately related such that the conditions of one might also be the conditions for the other). Interestingly enough, however, Derrida goes on to explicitly reject the idea that such an impossibility would be unreal. The im-possible "is what is most undeniably *real*. And sensible. Like the other. Like the irreducible and nonappropriable *différance* of the other" (Derrida 2005, 84). What Derrida is going to great lengths to make clear (albeit in a deconstructive fashion) is that the im-possible is not a concept. It is an experience. It is sensible *like* the Other. However, as Levinas repeatedly insists, the Other is never just another sensible object. It is concrete by being that which overflows its sensible representation. And, *as such*, it is available to phenomenology—albeit a potentially heterodox phenomenology that has challenged the "as such."

The second reservation Derrida has to regulative ideas is that, whereas such ideas function as rules to be followed, the democracy to-come is not an instruction manual to be followed. If it were such a manual, then justice would be eliminated because there would be no risk. As we have seen, new phenomenological prescriptivity will often show up as an invitation to continued critical engagement about how to be prescriptive. Derrida fleshes this claim out further as follows:

> The responsibility of what remains to be decided or done (in actuality) cannot consist in following, applying, or carrying out a norm or rule. Wherever I have at my disposal a determinable rule, I know what must be done, and as soon as such knowledge dictates the law, action follows knowledge as a calculable consequence: one *knows* what path to take, one no longer hesitates. The decision then no longer decides anything but is made in advance and is thus in advance annulled. It is simply deployed, without delay, presently, with the automatism attributed to machines. There is no longer any place for justice or responsibility (whether juridical, political, or ethical). (2005, 84–5)

Two points are worth highlighting here. First, Derrida again resists too closely aligning justice with knowledge. This opens the second point—namely, Derrida's concern for not eliminating the humanity of human beings. A human is never merely a machine that operates according to ethical algorithms—this will become important when we turn to Henry's notion of barbarism. Even desiring such a codified normativity is to desire no longer to be oneself. Derrida's contention is that regulative ideas function as rules according to which we can act and as such evaporates the justice the resides in action.

Derrida's final resistance is due to the Kantian metaphysics seemingly underlying the notion of regulative ideas. Regulative ideas, Derrida says, seem to require us to "subscribe to the entire Kantian architectonic and critique" (2005, 85). The ideas of practical reason are linked to the "Transcendental Unity of Apperception," which signifies within the vast systematic project of critical deductions. Derrida indicates a worry about the status that this gives to reason, the conception of the self that it requires, and the ontological horizon that epistemological reflections presuppose.

Although we are sympathetic to all of Derrida's three reservations, we suggest that none of his claims indicate traits that are intrinsic to regulative ideals generally, but only to the traditional Kantian articulation of them. Derrida's understanding of the im-possibility of the democracy to-come is only intelligible *as* im-possible when expressed within the terms of possibility. We should guard diligently against *reducing* the democracy to-come to the story we tell about it—just as we should never confuse the face of the Other with the specific ontological narrative that articulate the ethical encounter. What Derrida seems to indicate is that because something outstrips the linguistic form in which it is presented it cannot be presented in that form. However, according to Derrida's own admission, there would not be words available for accurately representing the im-possible. To express it is already to betray it, at least to some extent.

Crucially, we must be diligent to continue to learn from Levinas's insistence that we much unsay everything that is said and to Husserl's encouragement of phenomenological openness. If we deploy the term "regulative idea" and then go on to suggest that it is an idea that cannot be adequately thought and a regulation that does not actually guide action in the way a legal statute would, we will have more success in opening the space towards which Levinas and Derrida are directing us. Regarding the im-possibility of the democracy to-come, what needs demonstrated is the way in which im-possibility is not impractical—that is, the democracy to-come must not just be an excuse for quietism. Conceiving of the democracy to-come as a regulative ideal actually offers resources for such a project. The im-possible ideal is what signifies a critique of all our particular interpretations and so it must be undertaken as part of a lived hermeneutic. Moreover, this unending hermeneutic project is always particularly situated and socio-historically embedded. Hence, the regulative ideal is not content-less, but merely forces the specific content to run up against the conditions of its im-possibility.

Similarly, regulative ideals need not be read as simply rules to be followed. The nonrule that this ideal would offer is one of constant criticism as a type of ethical positivity instead of either pure negativity or a rationalistic imperative. The value of conceiving the democracy to-come as a regulative ideal is that it demands action here and now and yet contests any supposition that this action would discharge or fulfill my obligation. The regulative idea is not a rule, but it may be a calling-forth to serious conversations about how to draw up rules that will remain sensitive to the call of each and every other.

Finally, to suggest that we cannot affirm regulative ideals without simultaneously "subscribing to the entire Kantian architectonic and critique" is an unhelpful exaggeration. Derrida is right to remind us of the origins of this notion and warn of the potential dangers that lurk around every corner, but this does not mean that we will of necessity give in to the philosophical roots and be overtaken by the dangers that haunt us. We should reanimate the notion of a regulative ideal in the way that Derrida does for so many other terms that Heidegger might claim have been "used-up" (Heidegger 1999, 3).[11] By doing so, as we have attempted to do here, we are better able to understand the way in which the democracy to-come is not a mere possible political future, a generally accessible rule, or a remnant of an outmoded metaphysic. Instead, it is the demand that we get down to the messy business of working to build political institutions that function as constant reminders of the limits of the political itself.

Before turning to Henry, we want to offer two suggestions for how this Derridean account might find fecund conversation partners in contemporary political philosophy. In addition to the idea that there is much work to be done thinking through the possible resonance between communitarianism and new phenomenological sociality, recent attempts by some political philosophers to stress the importance of continued critical conversation to democratic societies strikes a similar chord as does the Derridean notion of democracy. For example, Robert B. Talisse (2009) offers an epistemic argument for democracy such that, even in light of significant (and perhaps intractable) moral conflict, democracy stands as the political structure best able to foster real debate and dialogue. Talisse's account has much to offer to Derrideans who support democracy because of its hospitality to critical discourse, but who might too quickly abandon the importance of epistemology to democratic life and society. Similarly, Derrida has much to offer in return, because, as stated previously, he helps to articulate the ethical stakes of all epistemology. Moreover, the Derridean idea that democracy is fundamentally agonistic—that is, defined by disagreement and debate—stands as an important contribution to contemporary debates about agonistic democracy, broadly construed (see Minister 2012). Alternatively, political thinkers working within a new phenomenological legacy should more frequently attend to theorists of agonistic democracy (see, e.g. Mouffe 2000; Connolly 2008; Schaap 2009; and Wingenbach 2011) regarding the ways in which one might move from deconstructive critique to a plausible public policy.

On the destruction of culture: Henry on barbarism

Since its publication in French in 1987, Henry's short book, *Barbarism* (cited as Henry 2012b), has caused significant controversy. Alternatively received by some as a thoroughgoing luddite critique of science and technology and by others as a prophetic challenge to the leveling tendencies that result from the devaluation of the humanities in contemporary culture, this book is an unflinching look at the phenomenon of a culture in crisis as a result of the "omnipresent objectivism of modernity" (2012b, xvii). Indeed, Henry is unambiguous about his assessment when he notes that his book is not really about "just a question of a crisis of culture but of its destruction" (2012b, 2). In the attempt to get a sense of how new phenomenology might speak to normative concerns regarding social existence, we will offer a brief consideration of Henry's text as a complementary account to the Derridean political theory discussed above.[12]

While Derrida advocates a democracy to-come and celebrates the importance of continued critical conversation about the im-possibility of justice, Henry considers the practical cultural context in which democratic institutions could be instantiated. For Henry, the rise of barbarism, which signals the possible destruction of culture, is closely connected to the question of democracy. With the loss of culture comes the loss of true selfhood and intersubjective relationship, which "prohibits all free thought and all 'democracy'" (2012b, xvii). We might say that, if the democracy to-come is to have any chance of "coming," then culture must be protected against the assault of objectivism and reductionism of which Henry warns. Something of a latter-day version of Husserl's *Crisis*, *Barbarism* clearly goes beyond merely a neutral description of the contemporary situation and, instead, offers a dire warning of where we are headed if things don't change. Unlike Heidegger's denial of the normative status of "authenticity," Henry's conception of "barbarism" is explicitly meant to be normative such that it encourages transformed life and action.

Let's take a closer look at Henry's diagnosis of the contemporary cultural disease that he sees to have been inaugurated by modern science, and in particular, by Galileo. Although modern science has certainly allowed for a host of creature comforts and has transformed medicine, communication, and travel, among many other areas of human life, Henry claims that science has brought with it an epistemological reductionism such that "the universe" is understood "as reduced henceforth to an objective set of material phenomena" (2012b, xiii–xiv). The basic idea, here, is that modern science does not respect scope restrictions for its inquiry; everything becomes a matter of scientific investigation, or what Henry terms "geometric-mathematical knowledge" (2012b, xiii). Though this epistemological reductionism primarily concerns knowledge such that everything that is knowable is only knowable in one (scientific) way, it has implications for how we envision reality itself. When science gives way to scientism, it is no longer primarily engaged in the task of understanding reality, but is engaged in the business of delimiting what reality can even be. "Since the modern era," Henry explains,

we are witnessing an unprecedented development of the knowledge that forms "science" and is worthy of claiming this title. This means a rigorous, objective, undeniable, and true knowledge. It is distinguished from all the approximate and dubitable forms of knowledge, belief, or superstition that preceded it by the power of its evidence, proofs, and experiments as well as by the extraordinary results to which it has led and which have revolutionized the face of the earth. (2012b, 1–2)

Rather than opening up new possibilities for human existence, the scientism of modernity has eliminated the very possibility of being human because it has brought about a "revolution of the human being" (2012b, 2). Similar to Marx's claim that the alienation form the product of one's labor leads to an alienation from one's own being, Henry's point is that, when the only knowledge that counts is scientific knowledge and the only truth is scientific truth, then the only thing that is valued is science.[13] What happens to art, ethics, and religion in such a context? Henry believes that science has not simply superseded the humanities; it has destroyed them. Given the erasure of art, ethics, and religion, science is the only way of knowing what it is to be human. Hence, humanity is reduced to an objective phenomenon essentially available for scientific inquiry. A deadening materialism emerges that leaves no room for what Henry terms life. Since culture is the "auto-revelation of life in its self-growth" (2012b, xv), culture is not merely transformed—as one cultural expression gives way to another as in the transition from the Romanesque to the Gothic, say—but instead it is eviscerated as we move from culture to barbarism. Life, culture, and humanity stand together. As Henry explains,

Every culture is a culture of life, in the dual sense whereby life is both the subject and the object of this culture. *It is an action that life exerts on itself and through which it transforms itself insofar as life is both transforming and transformed.* "Culture" means nothing other than that. "Culture" refers to the self-transformation of life, the movement by which it continually changes itself in order to arrive at higher forms of realization and completeness, in order to grow. (2012b, 5)

"We are faced with something that has never really been seen before," claims Henry: "the explosion of science and the destruction of the human being. This is the new barbarism, and this time it is not certain that it can be overcome" (2012b, 3).

It is worth spending just a little time figuring out what Henry means by "life" since it bears so heavily on his discussion of culture, and is really the key term in his entire phenomenological project throughout his authorship. He makes clear that by life he is not speaking about "the life that forms the theme of biology and the object of science" (2012b, 6). Instead, life is not a matter of objectivity but of subjectivity. Accordingly, there is no epistemic oligarchy that has some sort of special access to life. "The life that we are speaking about," Henry claims, "cannot be confused with the object of scientific knowledge, an object for which knowledge would be reserved to those who are in possession of it and who have had to acquire it" (2012b, 6). Instead, drawing on his early phenomenological discoveries in *The Essence of Manifestation*, Henry thinks that life is something that "everyone knows, as part of who we are" (2012b, 6). Consistently rejecting what he has termed "ontological monism," Henry contends that life is not something over and against us such that it is an object to/for our subjectivity. Life fundamentally challenges the objectivism of a scientific approach to material phenomena: "Life feels and experiences itself in such a way that there is nothing in it that would be experienced or felt. This is because the fact of feeling oneself is really what makes one alive" (2012b, 6). Attempting to avoid all confusion between phenomenological life and biological life, Henry claims that "this is life not in the biological sense but in the true sense—*the absolute phenomenological life whose essence consists in the very fact of sensing or experiencing oneself and nothing else*—of what we will call subjectivity" (2012b, 6).

Whereas Henry believes that Husserl understands the priority of subjectivity to objectivity—even if inadequately (see 2012b, 40–1, see also 60, 67)—"Galileo's illusion, like all those who came after him and considered science to be absolute knowledge, was to have taken the mathematical and geometrical world, which provided univocal knowledge of the real world, for this real world itself, is the world that we can intuit and experience only in the concrete modes of our subjective life" (2012b, 8). Simply put, Galileo, and those who work in his wake, have left no room for a lifeworld underlying the world investigated by science. Given the priority of subjectivity and the fundamentality of life, Henry argues that science is only possible on such bases. Scientism is problematic because "*science . . . has no idea of what life is; it is in no way concerned with it; it has no relation to it and never will.* There can only be access to life in and through life, if it is the case that only life is related to itself in the Affectivity of its auto-affection" (2012b, 17, emphasis in original). In effect, science provides a third-person account of a first-person world and ends up remaking the world in its own image at the cost of no longer have a first-person image with which to make the world, which leads to what we might term an existential version of self-referential incoherence. Henry explains the situation as follows:

> The view from above over all of external-being internalizes what it has learned about things and then tries to adjust to it as best it can. This is what one calls wisdom—the wisdom of historians, sociologists, ethnologists, and biologists, and all those who trust in what they see. But one does not yet know anything about life when one "philosophizes" in this way. Life is discovered as an unauthorized (*sauvage*) principle within oneself that has to do with a knowledge that one does not have. (2012b, 21)

Just as Husserl (1970a) argued that the "crisis of European sciences" required phenomenological insight if it was to be remedied, Henry also claims that "we phenomenologists" (2012b, 57) might potentially have the cure to the disease of barbarism, or what he terms "the sickness of life" (2012b, chapter 4). According to Henry, the "*inner contradiction*" that defines science "*is a phenomenological contradiction. It is on the place of its phenomenality, as an original phenomenality of life, that we can discern its true sense, but what we must seek out first is its own possibility*" (2012b, 66, emphasis in original). A new phenomenology that attends to the auto-affection of life is, for Henry, the only hope for arresting our current momentum toward the cultural brink.

In a nearly Levinasian vein, Henry indicates that contemporary phenomenology ought to turn away from science as the exclusive source of knowledge and instead begin to realize that the "primitive and primordial knowledge" that we require if we are to save culture is found in "the domain of ethics" (2012b, 95). We might say that, as in Levinas, Henry affirms that ethics is something like *first philosophy*. However, the priority here is not the same as the Levinasian notion of a pre-originary encounter with absolute alterity. Rather, Henry's move is to locate all theory as rooted in praxis. Life is only theoretically available when we attend to the living of life itself. Despite the specifics of how they cash out the idea of ethics, Henry and Levinas walk together when it comes to the idea that phenomenological ethics cannot be reduced to traditional normative ethics as found in the history of western moral philosophy. In a passage that resonates with some of Heidegger's "Letter on Humanism," Henry explains: "If one defines ethics as a relation of action to ends, norms or values, one has already abandoned the site in which it stands, that is, life itself. In life, there are neither goals nor ends, because the relation to them as an intentional relation does not exist in what does not have in itself any ek-stasis" (2012b, 96).

This "ethical" emphasis on lived praxis as the source for reflection about the world is something with which Levinas would immediately concur. Consider the following claim Levinas makes in response to a question about his being a phenomenologist who also lives in a determinate Jewish context: "Every phenomenological experience rests upon a pre-philosophical one. In Jewish thought, I encountered the fact that ethics is not a simple region of being. The encounter with the other offers us the first meaning, and in the extension of this encounter, we discover all the others. Ethics is a decisive experience" (Levinas 2001, 160). Levinas announces a strikingly similar account of the priority of praxis as does Henry. For Henry and Levinas, the attention that is required to address our moral failures and our cultural degradation "is essentially phenomenological" (2012b, 98). Just as we previously noted that Levinasian phenomenology yields an awareness of the "weightiness of reality," Henry's phenomenology conveys a similar weightiness: "Something is a burden *through its subjectivity which is burdened with itself up to the unbearability of this weight*" (2012b, 99, emphasis in original). Ultimately, Henry concludes that only if "we phenomenologists" begin to speak ever more loudly about the destructiveness of modern science as currently operative in society can we perhaps open up the possibilities for a truly *human/humane* future.

As we saw in Derrida, law is the required institutional structures that give justice a voice in the world, yet law is also where justice is perpetually differed because of its attempt to calculate the incalculable—that is, it reduces the infinite alterity of each and every other to a conception of social exchange. Henry also seems to recognize a similar distinction, though not in Derridean terms. After discussing the ideologies and practices of barbarism, Henry turns to the notion of the "university" and claims that it is the site where much of the real culture wars must be fought. If the university becomes exclusively the domain of the sciences, then we are lost. Accordingly, Henry calls for a reinvigorated university structure internal to democratic societies. In this way, Henry recognizes the importance of practical action in light of phenomenological attention. As we have already said, the new phenomenologists understand that description is already normative. *Barbarism* is Henry's attempt to convey the fact that when we properly understand our diseased situation, we are better able to envision the needed correctives for it.

Conclusion

This chapter is merely an outline of ways in which new phenomenology might approach normative ethics, political philosophy, and social theory. Ultimately, new phenomenology attends to life as lived in a variety of ways. Accordingly, our hope is that those working in new phenomenology and also those working in mainstream moral and political philosophy will begin to see in each other important opportunities for dialogue and mutual support, even as they mark out sites of dissonance and distance. In the next chapter, we will conclude our discussion of new phenomenology by summarizing where we have come to and where new phenomenology might continue to go.

Conclusion:
Possible futures for new phenomenology

We have gone a long way down the "path" that Heidegger claims phenomenology has opened up for all those who would choose to follow it. But where are we, then? Briefly, we will summarize the main points of our discussion and suggest two other productive areas for further research: aesthetics and epistemology. Our hope is that, by briefly sketching these other areas of possible research, we can illustrate that new phenomenology has a promising future as a dialogue partner for mainstream debates in contemporary philosophy in a wide range of areas: philosophy of religion, philosophy of mind, philosophy of language, epistemology, aesthetics, ethics, political philosophy, and social theory, among others. Although we have focused primarily on philosophy of religion, we are confident that future work on new phenomenology can open it up to a host of contemporary philosophical conversations.

Catching up to where we already are

Let's begin by returning to our original three theses as announced in the introduction:

Thesis 1: *New phenomenology can be legitimately considered an heir to historical phenomenology when understood as a general path of inquiry into phenomenality, rather than a rigid perspective that holds a set of stable doctrines regarding phenomenality and the modes in which particular phenomena appear.*

Thesis 2:   *New phenomenology should be weighed and considered in light of a variety of contemporary philosophical problems.*

Thesis 3:   *New phenomenology can be productively put into conversation with other contemporary philosophical perspectives regardless of whether those perspectives are traditionally associated with "continental" philosophy.*

In regard to thesis 1, we have argued that new phenomenology is rightly considered phenomenology. Our argument has been guided by the notion that part of phenomenological "orthodoxy" is the patient analysis of what ought to count as phenomenological orthodoxy. Accordingly, in light of new phenomenologists having been dismissed as heretics by such critics as Dominque Janicaud, we have suggested that we should look closer and ask whether the problem is with the new phenomenologists or with the expectation that phenomenology is static enough as to provide a clear orthodoxy from which clear heresy could be distinguished. New phenomenology *does* challenge such fundamental phenomenological ideas as the "as such," horizons, intentionality, and even the reduction. However, such challenges have not come in the name of dismissive rejection, but critical attention. By attending to phenomena in their very mode of presentation, the new phenomenologists have opened up phenomenology to the "unapparent," "excess," "saturation," "overflow," and "invisibility." Such moves need not be read as a turn to theology, but as a deepening of phenomenology itself in response to givenness, phenomenality, and intuition that seem to outstrip the frames according to which classical phenomenology operates.

Responding to thesis 2, we have demonstrated that new phenomenology is productively approached and considered in terms of philosophical debate rather than merely figure-based analysis. In particular, we have offered an extended discussion of new phenomenology as it concerns philosophy of religion, but also as it concerns ethics, political philosophy, methodology, hermeneutics, and even questions of normativity more broadly. One of our guiding thoughts has been that new phenomenology displays a coherent philosophical trajectory. As evidence of this, we have drawn extensively on the texts of the new phenomenologists to show that their contributions to debates in these thematic areas operate with basic underlying commitments that give rise to specific disagreements among the new phenomenologists themselves. An understanding of this unity in diversity is one of the things we hope to have provided. Nowhere have we indicated that new phenomenology is monolithic, homogeneous, or static. Rather, we have argued that the new phenomenologists can be rightly read as being part of a philosophical family, even if there are familial disagreements.

Regarding thesis 3, we have demonstrated possible points of resonance between such diverse thinkers as Jean-Louis Chrétien and Nicholas Wolterstorff concerning matters of hermeneutics. In our chapters on philosophy of religion, we showed important ways in which new phenomenology could learn from analytic philosophers, while simultaneously offering important insights that might benefit analytic thinkers. Although we looked at debates concerning kataphaticism/apophaticism and postmodern apologetics, in particular, we noted many other areas in which new phenomenology and analytic philosophy of religion might be productively considered together as part of a project we term *mashup philosophy of religion*. Further, in our presentation of new phenomenological approaches to ethics, politics, and society, we suggested links between new phenomenology and agonistic approaches to democratic theory. Additionally, a variety of other possible dialogue partners have been mentioned throughout the book: scholars working in "theories of religion," philosophers of language, Christian philosophers, communitarian critics of liberalism, and comparative philosophers of religion. While we have pointed out that new phenomenology is sometimes unnecessarily opaque and unclear, we have called for more hospitality to be shown toward new phenomenology by those not operating within its domain and deploying its vocabulary. In the same way that new phenomenologists try to approach phenomena on its own terms and be open to whatever is given, we hope that dialogue between analytic philosophy and continental philosophy might similarly display such openness.

Prospects for further research

In any introductory book, there are always tradeoffs between breadth and depth. While arguments could be offered for preferring one or the other, we have tried to offer a broad survey of new phenomenology as a coherent philosophical trajectory by focusing primarily on philosophy of religion and, to a lesser degree, on ethics and politics. Since there is much more that could be said about all of the topics we have considered, we want to offer a few reflections on two other areas that we especially see as promising for further research.

Aesthetics

When Chrétien considers the call and response structure, he offers a series of important questions that one might ask regarding this fundamental phenomenological investigation. "In order to investigate these lofty questions," Chrétien writes, "we will follow a diagonal path and interrogate the origin not of speech, but of a single word, the Greek word *kalon*, the beautiful" (2004, 6). In a careful linguistic and conceptual analysis that is as historically attentive as it is philosophically rigorous, Chrétien demonstrates that "the origin of the word 'beautiful', *kalon*, does not constitute an etymology among others, but is the very origin of language. The word *kalon* is the name of naming: it names that which, in speech, calls" (2004, 7). Given the centrality of the idea of the call to new phenomenology, it is not unimportant that Chrétien links the idea of calling to the notion of beauty. As usual with Chrétien, he demonstrates both the philosophical and theological dimensions of such a fundamental connection.

Chrétien is not alone in his focus on the centrality of beauty and aesthetic judgment for new phenomenological inquiry. Henry offers careful analyses of art and aesthetics, paying special attention to the abstraction of Wassily Kandinsky's paintings (see 2004a, part 2; 2009). Moreover, Marion writes essays in which he uses aesthetics to illustrate such fundamental conceptions in his thought as the idol, saturation, and givenness. Namely, Marion's *In Excess* contains an essay titled "The Idol or the Radiance of the Painting" (2002c, chapter 3). Similarly, in *The Visible and the Revealed*, Marion considers Mark Rothko's painting "Number 212" during a discussion of what he terms the "banality of saturation" (2008, 128). Further, Derrida devotes an entire book—*The Truth in Painting* (Derrida 1987b)—to aesthetics. Indeed, Levinas is really the only new phenomenologist who does not spend a significant amount of time dealing with art and aesthetics, even though he does bring an aesthetic sensibility to his discussions of Talmudic texts.

In light of the prominence of such examples in new phenomenology, we think that there is important work that remains to be done to bring new phenomenology into dialogue with contemporary philosophies of art and aesthetic theory.[1]

Epistemology

Several times in this book we have mentioned the importance of openness and hermeneutic sensitivity to phenomenological inquiry. As one example of how this shows up in Husserl's thought, consider his notion of "the self-realization of reason" (1970a, appendix IV). There Husserl speaks of the

> struggle of the generations of philosophers, who are the bearers of this spiritual development, living and surviving in spiritual community, in the constant struggle of "awakened" reason to come to itself, to an understanding of itself, to a reason which concretely understands itself in understanding the existing world, existing in its whole universal truth. [To say that] philosophy, science in all its forms, is rational—that is a tautology. But in all its forms it is on its way to a higher rationality; it is rationality which, discovering again and again its unsatisfying relativity, is driven on in its toils, in its will to attain the true and full rationality. But finally it discovers that this rationality is an idea residing in the infinite and is *de facto* necessarily [only] on the way. (1970a, 339)

We think that in Husserl's account, one can find an implicit defense of epistemic infinitism—the theory that justification is always an ongoing process. Notice that Husserl stresses the importance of philosophical rationality seeking that which it cannot finally achieve, but can ever move toward while constantly being "on the way." Similar to Peirce's notion of a "community of inquiry," Husserl locates the philosophical task of reason to be something undertaken by philosophers while "living and surviving in spiritual community." Later in the same essay, Husserl refers to "mankind understanding itself as rational" as something that "signifies an infinity of living and striving toward reason" (1970a, 341). Again, Husserl describes the task of philosophy as infinite insofar as we continue to live and strive. Here, we think that Husserl has much to offer such contemporary epistemic infinitists as Scott F. Aikin (2009), Jeremy Fantl (2003), and Peter Klein (1999; 2000; 2003).

Although Husserl will spend a great amount of time thinking about the relationship between phenomenology and epistemology (see especially Husserl 1975), the new phenomenologists spend significantly less time addressing epistemological issues. Perhaps connected to the generally postmodern suspicion of epistemology, new phenomenology has not frequently been viewed as a productive resource for contemporary epistemology. Though this might be largely due to new phenomenology's seeming disregard for epistemology, we think that it is a missed opportunity. There may be ways of reading new phenomenology as operating with an implicit "modest foundationalism" similar to that of Robert Audi (1993; 2001) or William Alston (1989; 2005b).[2] Similarly, Levinas can be read as following Husserl by offering an unstated (and perhaps even unrecognized) epistemic infinitism.[3]

As with aesthetics, it is not clear where discussions of new phenomenology and epistemology will lead, but we think that there is ample reason to think that such discussions are worth having. They are valuable because any philosophical trajectory should be able to give good reasons for preferring it over competing alternatives and new phenomenology is no different. Moreover, being in relationship with other ideas and thinkers requires approaching the claims, actions, and practices of those others with care. Such care, however, demands that we take seriously the epistemic requirements of justification both when we critique others and when we are convinced by them. As such, new phenomenology can continue to help us see the ethical stakes of epistemological debates.

Conclusion

In the introduction, we noted that part of the challenge of writing this book is that new phenomenology is still part of the contemporary philosophical landscape. As such, we claimed that writing a book that articulates the key aspects and characteristics of new phenomenology actively contributes to what new phenomenology will someday be. What is truly exciting about the future of new phenomenology is that it is genuinely open—it is not clear what will happen to new phenomenology as a philosophical trajectory. On the one hand, new phenomenologists remain alive and philosophically active. As such, the future of new phenomenology is still unfolding insofar as some of the texts that will make up the complete new phenomenological archive remain to be written. On the other hand, the future of new phenomenology is open insofar as the relationship between new phenomenology and continental philosophy, as well as the relationship between continental philosophy and other philosophical traditions, continues to be a matter of current debate. Will our hopes for mashup philosophy of religion find fulfillment? Will the hospitality that is called for in new phenomenological ethics find expression in our professional relationships with philosophers working in alternative traditions and drawing on alternative archives (both philosophical and theological)? We are not sure, though we remain hopeful. As we have attempted to demonstrate on a variety of topics, new phenomenology and analytic philosophy ought to be read as important resources for each other.

The future—l'avenir—of new phenomenology is uncertain, for it is an open future. New phenomenology remains a gift that is given to its readers and which lays claim to them. Thus, the philosophical trajectory of new phenomenology calls out to all of us: for a charitable hearing, serious consideration, and critical engagement. As with all aspects of new phenomenological discussions of lived existence—which focus on the priority of praxis to theory— meaning is found and made in the living of life itself. Similarly, what will become of new phenomenology has everything to do with how its readers encounter it and live it out. In the spirit of St Augustine, we bid the reader: "take and read." We believe that such reading will be time well spent.

NOTES

Introduction

1 We want to distinguish this group of French phenomenologists from the "New Phenomenology" (*Neue Phänomenologie*) of Hermann Schmitz, who uses this term to describe his own version of phenomenological inquiry, which is both inspired by and critical of Husserl and others such as Merleau-Ponty. For more on this alternative philosophical perspective, see Schmitz (2002; 2003); for a brief introduction to Schmitz's thought, see Blume (2010).

2 As we have already noted, Hermann Schmitz also used the term "new phenomenology" to describe his work, but in a way that does not overlap directly with our use here. Additionally, Enzo Paci (1970) wrote an essay titled "Towards a New Phenomenology," which attempts to think in light of the possibilities opened by Husserl's *Crisis*, but, as with Schmitz, Paci's use of the term is not a specific reference to the French phenomenologists with whom we are concerned. It is for these reasons that we locate the origin of the term, in the way we mean it, in Janicaud's essay.

3 For scholarly consideration of the so-called theological turn, see especially the work of Hent de Vries (in particular 1999, but also 2002 and 2005).

4 Paul Audi (2006) refers to the "philosophical trajectory" (*trajectoire philosophique*) of Michel Henry to indicate the general direction in which his thought leans, and even leads.

5 We also want to note that, given the impressive nature of Gallagher and Zahavi's (2012) own introduction to the way in which phenomenology and analytic philosophy of mind can be brought into productive conversation, we have chosen not to retread that ground and instead merely recommend that readers interested in that particular intersection consult their excellent book. See also Smith and Thomasson (2005).

Chapter 1

1 For just a few examples, see Bernet et al. (1993), Zahavi (2003a), Hermberg (2006), Russell (2006), Smith (2007), Mohanty (2008), and Lewis and Staehler (2010). For a couple of older introductions that might offer instructive indications of how approaches to phenomenology have changed over the past few decades, see Elveton (1970) and Lauer (1978).

2 As Evan Thompson notes, "mental events do not occur in a vacuum; they are lived by someone. Phenomenology is anchored to the careful description, analysis, and interpretation of lived experience" (2007, 21). Or, as Shaun Gallagher and Dan Zahavi explain, for phenomenologists, "only insofar as the object appears in one way or the other can it have any meaning for us" (2012, 24).

3 As Zahavi explains, "Husserl wants to describe our experiences as they are given from a first-person perspective, and it is no part of my experience of, say, a withering oak tree, that something is occurring in my brain" (2003a, 13).

4 Importantly, however, we should remember that Husserl does not claim to be antimetaphysical as such, but simply not naively metaphysical: "Finally, lest any misunderstanding arise, I would point out that, as already stated, phenomenology indeed *excludes every naïve metaphysics* that operates with absurd things in themselves, but *does not exclude metaphysics as such*" (1999a, 156, emphasis in original).

5 David Woodruff Smith nicely describes the basic four steps involved in the transition from the natural attitude to the phenomenological attitude as follows: "The general thesis of the natural attitude is the implicit thesis that there exists a world around me, in which I and my activities occur. In order to shift my attention away from things of the world around me, I bracket, and so make no use of, the general thesis of the natural attitude. I then attend to my consciousness of things in the world. In this modified attitude toward the world, I give phenomenological descriptions of various types of experience just as I experience them" (2007, 242).

6 For a good defense of Husserl on this point, see Zahavi (2003a, 45).

7 For a consideration of skepticism and new phenomenology, especially as proposed by Levinas, see Aikin and Simmons (2009).

8 There are significant questions as to exactly how Heidegger's account of Dasein differs from Husserl's notion of the transcendental consciousness, but these questions will not concern us here.

9 Lee Braver argues that "although a number of important continuities persist across the two phases [of Heidegger's thought], the differences are significant enough to make the *Kehre* a genuine break" (2009, 3) from Heidegger's earlier thought.

10 This phrase is translated by Andrew Mitchell and François Raffoul as a "phenomenology of the inapparent" (Heidegger 2003, 80). We will use the terms "unapparent" and "inapparent" interchangeably because we do not think that anything significant hinges on choosing one over the other.

11 Since this is a quotation, we maintain the capitalization of "Being," but, in general, we will follow the style of Joan Stambaugh's translation of *Being and Time* and not differentiate between a capital-B Being (*Sein*) and lowercase-b being (*Seindes*). This is especially important, we believe, in the context of new phenomenology because of the temptation to read capital-B Being as a double for something like God. Moreover, when it comes to the thought of Derrida, in particular, the ambiguity between the capital and the lowercase is itself philosophically significant.

12 For a couple general introductions to Heidegger's philosophy, see Polt (1999), T. Clark (2002), and Greaves (2010). For extended considerations of *Being and Time* in particular, see Kisiel (1993) and Large (2008). For a couple more wide-ranging engagements, see Dreyfus and Wrathall (2005) and Guignon (2006).

Chapter 2

1 See Derrida (1988, 146).

2 Whether Husserl is correct in his reading of Kant here is open to debate. In any case, it is beyond our concern here.

3 Of course, as we hinted at in the previous chapter, one can argue that such a shift *is* what takes place even in Husserl as he develops his idea of intersubjectivity. Whether that is true, however, is at the very least open to question and not a decisive factor in the way in which many of the new phenomenologists read Husserl.

4 Indeed, Levinas will even say that "it is Husserl above all who brought up the idea of a program of philosophy" (1985, 90).

5 As we will suggest in the conclusion to this book, Husserl's move here may even give rise to something like an epistemic infinitism.

6 For more on Levinas and desire, see Dalton (2009).

7 See Henry (2012b), and also (2000b, 143).

8 In *Being Given*, Marion (2002a) makes clear his indebtedness to Michel Henry's *Phénoménologie matérielle* (Henry 1990). See also the preface to Marion (1998, xi).

9 Chrétien clearly has this idea of the "Here I am" in mind since, elsewhere, he speaks of "the gift to which one is opened without recourse, about being the only one who can say *Me voici*, here I am" (2002, 120).

Chapter 3

1 Of course, one of the present authors has argued that Nietzsche may not quite be an atheist after all. See Benson (2008).

2 For a consideration of the relationship between philosophy and theology in the twentieth century (and especially concerning the continental tradition), see Grønkjær (1998). For an historical consideration of the ways in which philosophers have held a variety of positions regarding religion and God, see Edwards (2009).

3 For more on Husserl and religion, see J. Hart (1994) and Bello (2009).

4 For an excellent analysis of Heidegger's philosophy of religion, see Vedder (2007).

5 Iain D. Thomson admits that "on hearing the expression 'onto-theology', many philosophers start looking for the door" (2005, 7).

6 Matheson Russell gets at both the metaphysical and epistemic dimensions as follows: "Heidegger eventually came to define the dominant tradition of Western metaphysics in terms of its coordination of the question of being and the question of God: (i) God is defined . . . as the highest being and the ground of being; God is thus understood by reference to being. (ii) But equally, being is accounted for by appeal to the highest being and the ground of being. The reason, ground or account (*logos*) for being (*on*) is found in the highest being (*theos*); hence the description of metaphysics as 'onto-theologically constituted'" (2011, 644).

7 As to how a notion of "the highest" might stand in relation to Heidegger's conception of transcendence, see Crowell and Malpas (2007).

8 Though it might require going beyond theism and atheism as the only available options. See Gall (1987), who argues that thinking in light of Heidegger would invite such an attempt to reconceive religious belief and existence. See also Gianni Vattimo (2002) on how postmodern thought invites a movement beyond the dichotomies of theism and atheism.

9 For more on Heidegger's own relation to Christian theology, see Caputo (1982; 1986; 1993a). See also De Paulo (2006).

10 Heidegger repeats this point at various places in his lectures. See especially his claim that "equally mistaken is the thought of a theological system in Paul. Rather, the fundamental religious experience must be explicated, and, remaining in this fundamental experience, one must seek to understand the connection to it of all original religious phenomena" (2004, 51). See also Russell (2011), who clearly distinguishes between "theism in the metaphysical mode" and "faith in the primitive Christian mode."

11 See Dahl (2010) for an argument that there might be a more robust connection between Husserl, Heidegger, and the phenomenologists of religion such as Otto, van der Leeuw, and Eliade.

12 This reading of onto-theology has many detractors who understand onto-theology to exclude particular notions of God and not simply particular ways of appropriating such notions. See, for example, Caputo (1997; 2006; 2012). For a consideration of the distinctions between these two different readings of metaphysical and epistemic postmodernism, see Simmons (2012). For more on the relation between onto-theology and deconstruction, see Ruf (1989).

13 Greisch is not, himself, thinking of new phenomenologists here, but instead of such thinkers as Pierre Rousselot, Joseph Maréchal, Ambroise Gardeil, Jacques Maritain, Edith Stein, and Bernard Lonergan.

Chapter 4

1 For representative essays from his later period that consider such topics, see Heidegger (1971; 1996). For an in-depth analysis of Heidegger's relationship to poetry as displayed primarily in his late thought, see Fóti (1992).

2 Of course, such decisions about fundamental commitments are not distinctive to phenomenology. If Heidegger and, even more so, Gadamer and Ricoeur, are right about the inescapability of hermeneutic obstacles for all inquiry, then historical decisions about how to move forward in light of such obstacles and about what to take as fundamental as opposed to accidental to a given discourse would also be inescapable. Simply put, what one grants at the beginning affects what is open to one as an end. Nicholas Wolterstorff's (1984) discussion of "control beliefs" and the reflexive relationship between such beliefs and what will count as evidence and data internal to a particular community of inquiry is extremely helpful here.

3 Of course, even his early thought worried about this to some degree as it relates to the question of being. See Chapter One where we discuss Heidegger's revision of Husserl's project.

4 As Jeffrey Bloechl claims, "The expression 'Christian phenomenology' has become common currency in a debate between those who consider it a barbarism and those for whom it signifies the simultaneous fulfillment of both Christian thought and phenomenology" (2002, xi, n7). We resist not only the phrase, but also the notion that thinkers such as Marion and Chrétien see things in such a teleological way as such a categorization could indicate. Although Marion will say such things as "recognizing the saturated phenomena comes down to thinking seriously *'aliquid quo majus cogitari nequit'*—seriously, which means as a final possibility of phenomenology" (Marion 2000, 216), this does not mean that he takes Christianity to be the fulfillment of phenomenology, which such a description seems to suggest, but merely that the final goal of phenomenology will concern the saturated phenomenon, good examples of which are found in theological sources. Hence, while Marion and Chrétien certainly stress the important possibilities for both phenomenology and Christian theology when these two discourses enact a mutually enriching dialogue, they don't go as far as to see a necessity of such an intersection in such a strong way as to claim that phenomenology represents the "fulfillment" of Christian theology on the one hand, and Christian theology represents the "fulfillment" of phenomenology on the other hand. Though they don't deny that such a co-fulfillment is possible, their thought displays more disciplinary humility and historical contingency than such a description would appear to indicate.

5 Many have challenged the specifics of Derrida's account. See Olthuis (2002) and Simmons and Minister (2012).

6 See, for example, Kosky (2001), Katz (2003), Purcell (2006), and Cohen (2010).

7 Though we will suggest that there might be room for a postmodern apologetic enterprise in new phenomenology (see Chapter Seven), such a project would still endorse the distinctions between actuality/possibility and various authority/evidentiary structures operative in phenomenology as distinguishable from theology. That said, even if Chrétien is not engaged in the sort of thing about which Janicaud worries, this does not mean that he might not be a resource for a different sort of *postmodern* apologetics.

8 As Husserl states in *Ideas I*: "Our immediate aim is not theology but phenomenology, however mediately important the latter may be for the former" (1982, 117).

9 See, for example, Horner (2001; 2005) and Gschwandtner (2007).

10 As Jeffrey Kosky claims, "What phenomenology can attest to is a possible religion, never a historically actual religion" (2000b, 118).

11 Marion stresses that there are "third way[s]"—the "path of eminence" (2008, 103–4), and "de-nomination" (2002c, 134–42)—but we will not pursue such alternatives here simply because our task is merely to consider the way in which apophatic discourse shows up in new phenomenology and discuss whether that amounts to a theological turn. To go further and engage in the debate, an important one to be sure, regarding the different theological approaches to divine discourse is more than we are able to do here. We will return to the discussion of apophaticism and kataphaticism in Chapter Seven and discuss Marion's notion of "de-nomination" in more detail.

12 Marion prefers the descriptor "mystical theology" over "negative theology" for historical as well as theological reasons (2008, 104). Marion's sophisticated argument regarding the various ways of understanding negative theology lies beyond the scope of our aims here (see also 2002c, chapter 6).

13 Marion's note: Martin Heidegger, "Protocole á un séminaire sur la conference *Zeit und Sein*," *Questions IV*, ed. Jean Buffret (Paris: Gallimard, 1976), 83.

14 Marion's note: Wittgenstein, *Tractatus Logico-philosophicus* 6.522 (see also 6.432 and 6.44).

15 Marion's note: Jacques Derrida, "Comment ne pas parler: Dénégations," in *Psyché: Inventions de'lautre* (Paris: Galilée, 1987), 535–95.

16 See Kosky (2000a).

17 See Rubenstein (2003) and Carlson (1999).

18 For responses to Trakakis's objection to new phenomenology on this front, see Simmons (2013) and Westphal (2013).

19 For sustained considerations of these aspects and themes in Kierkegaard's thought, see Podmore (2011) and Mahn (2011).

20 For a consideration of this Derridean essay, see Wolosky (1998). For more on Derrida and negative theology, see Caputo (1997, 31–4) and Coward and Foshay (1992).

21 Derrida will, following Marx, admit that such a conjuring trick will have to deal with the specter of "the Man-God" such that we eventually might have to entertain the idea that "Jesus is at once the greatest and most 'incomprehensible of ghosts'" (1994, 144).

22 See Simmons and Minister (2012); see also Olthuis (2002).

Chapter 5

1 J. Aaron Simmons proposed the idea of a "mashup philosophy of religion" in Simmons 2013. Importantly, there are many other ways to engage in cross-traditional work than simply to draw upon new phenomenology, on the one hand, and analytic philosophy of religion, on the other hand. Our account here is merely meant as a narrow suggestion internal to a larger general framework of possible dialogical engagements in such areas.

2 We want to be clear that we are not saying that Christian voices are problematic, nor are we trying to defend a vague pluralism here. Rather, we are simply saying that debates in philosophy of religion are productively expanded when they attend to the varieties of religious expressions and identities that exist in global society. Insularity and exclusivism can emerge in any discourse that assumes homogeneity when, in fact, there is robust diversity. Accordingly, we are not rejecting "Christian philosophy," but simply suggesting that the philosophy of religion is benefited when we attend to world religions in a more dynamic and hospitable way (at least as concerns the phenomena under consideration, even if not the truth-claims being affirmed). For just a few examples of thinkers who have, to varying degrees of success, we believe, begun to explore a more comparative approach to the philosophy of religion, see Schilbrack (2004) and Wildman (2010).

3 The thematic similarity in such textbooks is striking. Cahn (2009) is divided up into the following parts: The concept of God, The existence of God, Religious Language, Miracles and Mysticism, Belief in God, Resurrection and Immortality, Religious Pluralism. Oppy and Scott (2010) features the following main sections: Religious Language; Arguments about the Existence of God; Evidence, Argument, and Belief in God; Divine Attributes; Religious Diversity. The influential text by Pojman and Rea (2012) has more parts, but they also largely repeat those previously mentioned: The Concept of God; Traditional Arguments for the Existence of God; Religious Experience; The Problem of Evil; Miracles; Death and Immortality; Faith and Reason; Science, Religion, and Evolution; Religious Pluralism. For other examples of such thematic similarity, see Peterson et al. (1996) and Zagzebski and Miller (2009). For a slightly broader, and more comparative, approach see Quinn and Taliaferro (1999).

4 Of course, the prominence of such topics does not mean that one must accept traditional conceptual frameworks for approaching them. This is part of what strikes us as productive about a more comparative approach to the philosophy of religion in general.

5 As Westphal writes: "Onto-theology is thus a bit like Baskin-Robbins or Heinz. It comes in thirty-one flavors or fifty-seven varieties or who knows how many different versions" (2004, 18).

6 For a consideration of Derrida's claim on this front, see Caputo (1997, 288).

7 In light of our claims in the last chapter that new phenomenological God-talk should not be understood as evidence for a theological turn, it is important to admit that Marion frequently articulates his model of God in his works that occur "at the border between philosophy and theology" (1991, xix). Even if Marion's account of God is one that seems to sometimes slide into philosophical theology, however, that entails neither that Marion's entire phenomenological project is really just disguised theology, nor that his account is irrelevant to the philosophy of religion.

8 Sanders distinguishes "the ultimate metaphysical principle," which he takes to be operative in much of Greek philosophy (specifically Anaximander, Plato, and Aristotle) and "the ultimate metaphysical category," which was proposed by the Cappadocians (Basil, Gregory of Nyssa, Gregory of Nazianzus) and was decidedly personal and relational rather than detached and explanatory (see 1994, 78; 2007, 142–8).

9 For an alternative formulation of this idea that God neither is, nor is not, but "may be," see Kearney (2001).

10 Indeed, as we mentioned in the previous chapter, Derrida (1978, chapter 4) himself raises this worry about Levinas's notion of "absolute alterity" in *Totality and Infinity*.

11 For more on Levinas's notion of "metaphysical desire," see Dalton (2009).

12 *Illeity* is a complicated and difficult notion. For some good attempts to think it through, see Peperzak (1997, 106–8), Kosky (2001, 191–3), and Purcell (2006, 131–4).

13 For sustained arguments on this point, see Westphal (2008) and Simmons (2011).

14 We are siding with Westphal's epistemological understanding of postmodernism here over against that of Caputo, who does seem to require postmodernism to say more about what models of God are still viable (see Caputo 2005; Westphal 2005). For a more extended consideration of their divergent views, as well as an argument in favor of Westphal's formulation, see Simmons (2012).

Chapter 6

1 Here, again, we think that productive engagement is called for between philosophers of religion and those scholars working in "theories of religion," such as Jonathan Z. Smith, Timothy Fitzgerald, and Russell McCutcheon.

2 This emphasis on *"aporia"* (an ancient Greek term that literally means "without a way") goes back to Socrates, who even describes himself as in the *Theaetetus* (149a) by saying "I am utterly disturbing (*atopos*) and I create only perplexity (*aporia*)." Socrates is constantly raising difficult questions, which eventually leads to his death. So we should read this concern for *aporia* in new phenomenology not as something *new* but a retrieval of something *ancient*.

3 Yet, as Diane Perpich (2008) rightly notes, the weight of this ethical demand is found in my taking it up as binding. In other words, even if understood as the word of God, as it were, ethical obligation is fragile and dependent on my response and action.

4 See Benson and Wirzba (2005).

5 For an extended discussion of Kierkegaardian transparency and its relation to Levinasian exposure, see Simmons (2011, chapter 4).

6 Chrétien even draws directly upon Kierkegaard's notion of struggle (Chrétien 2000, 158).

7 Of course, Derrida (2008b) will make quite a bit of being seen by one's cat.

8 As with our claim earlier about the possible problematic privilege of Christian assumptions in philosophy of religion, our point here is that such defenses lie beyond the scope of phenomenological inquiry, though not necessarily beyond the scope of individual phenomenologists (when operating according to other methodologies).

9 An alternative example here might be Bertrand Russell, who advocated philosophical atheism and not simply logical positivism. Yet since we are more interested in the meta-philosophical understanding of how philosophy and theology might be related than we are about particular views on the existence or nonexistence of God, we have chosen to use Ayer because his thought provides a nice meta-philosophical contrast with that of Alvin Plantinga. For more on philosophical atheism, see Thrower (1999), Joshi (2000), and Aikin and Talisse (2011).

10 Recently, however, the very distinctions between philosophy and theology that Plantinga himself attempted to maintain (even if tenuously) have become even more porous within the movement known as "analytic theology" (see Crisp and Rea 2009). Though we are unable to argue the case here, we think that there might be good reasons to push back against such trends in the name of disciplinary specificity and dialogical invitation.

11 One might indeed be within one's "epistemic rights" to engage in Christian philosophy, as articulated by Plantinga, but there still might be good dialogical and strategic reasons to be hesitant to engage in such a practice. See Simmons (2013).

Chapter 7

1 For a good discussion of Westphal's essay, see Trakakis (2008, 54–8).

2 This is not to say, however, that some styles are not better at some things than others. There are good reasons why Levinas and Derrida, say, choose a particular style as they attempt to express

the limits of expression. There are also good reasons why Dean Zimmerman and William Hasker, say, choose a different style as they engage in careful analysis regarding the relationship between temporality and omniscience.

3 For example, see the following special journal issues: *Faith and Philosophy* 22(5) (Special Issue 2005); *Modern Theology* 27(2) (April 2011).

4 See Caputo's (2000) defense of what he terms Derrida's "hyper-realism."

5 In an essay that is meant to be something of a spiritual autobiography, Swinburne articulates his philosophical "program" as follows: "to use the criteria of modern natural science, analyzed with the careful rigor of modern philosophy, to show the meaningfulness and justification of Christian theology" (1993, 186).

6 For a few examples of what might be considered a more existentially engaged version of philosophy of religion, see K. J. Clark (1993) and Morris (1994). For examples geared specifically toward apologetic thinking, see Murray (1999).

7 For example, see Holley (2010), and also the special journal issue on the epistemology of religious experience: *Faith and Philosophy* 22(4) (October 2005).

8 For more on the question of how modernism and postmodern stand in relation to each other, see Marsh et al. (1992). Additionally, for considerations of exactly what the critique of the Enlightenment means in postmodernism see, Boeve et al. (2006).

9 As just one example see, Plantinga and Wolterstorff (1983). See also Westphal (2003).

10 Consider also Caputo's claim that "deconstruction is a passion and a prayer for the impossible, a defense of the impossible against its critics, a plea for/to the experience of the impossible, which is the only real experience, stirring with religious passion" (1997, xx).

11 See Backhouse (2011), Barnett (2011), Mahn (2011), and Podmore (2011).

Chapter 8

1 For example, Henry's *Barbarism* (2012b), which will be considered in what follows, occurs quite directly in light of space opened by Husserl's *Crisis* (1970a).

2 See Husserl (1970a; 1999a, 89–150). For an excellent account of the importance that intersubjectivity plays in Husserl's thought, see Zahavi (2003a). For a good consideration of the lifeworld, see Held (2003).

3 To be sure, there are certainly subsequent attempts to use "the They" as a springboard for thinking such sociality—see Nancy (2000).

4 For a sustained consideration of Heidegger and ethics, see Hodge (1995). See also, Raffoul and Pettigrew (2002).

5 See, for just a few examples, R. Wolin (1990), Bourdieu (1991), Dallmayr (1993), Ward (1995), Beistegui (1998), and Young (1998).

6 For more on normativity in continental ethics (particularly concerning Levinas), see Perpich (2008).

7 For some considerations of continental ethics and politics that involve (to some extent) new phenomenologists, see the following: Caputo (1993b), Haverkamp (1995), Mouffe (1996), Bernasconi (1997; 1999), Dudiak (2001), Dooley (2001), Burggraeve (2002), Butler (2005), Horowitz and Horowitz (2006), Batnitzky (2006), Patton (2007), and McQuillan (2007).

8 Derrida echoes this sentiment in *Rogues*: "Justice can never be reduced to law, to calculative reason, to lawful distribution, to the norms and rules that condition law, as evidenced by its history and its ongoing transformations, but its recourse to coercive force, its recourse to a power or might that, as Kant showed with the greatest rigor, is inscribed and justified in the purest concept of law or right" (2005, 149–50).

9 As another productive possibility, see Minister (2012). Minister suggests that Levinas should be read in close proximity with the "agonistic" political theory of Chantal Mouffe. For alternative proposals, see also, Perpich (2008) and Simmons (2011).

10 Consider the following passage from *Rogues*: "In political philosophy the dominant discourse about democracy presupposes . . . freedom as power, faculty, or the ability to act, the force or strength, in short, to do as one pleases, the energy of an intentional and deciding will. It is thus difficult to see, and this is what remains to be thought, how another experience of freedom might found in an immediate, continuous, and effective way what would still be called a demo*cratic* politics or a demo*cratic* political philosophy" (Derrida 2005, 44).

11 For an example of how to reanimate "used-up" words, see Simmons (2006).

12 For a discussion of Henry's social theory, see Gély (2012). See also Henry (2004a; 2004b).

13 For Henry's reading of Marx, see Henry (2008b).

Conclusion

1 For an example of such existing work, see Benson (2013).

2 For an argument on this front, see Simmons (2011, chapter 11).

3 Simmons and Aikin (2012) have argued this point at length.

BIBLIOGRAPHY

Aikin, Scott F. 2009. "Prospects for Peircean Epistemic Infinitism." *Contemporary Pragmatism* 6(2): 71–87.

Aikin, Scott F. and J. Aaron Simmons. 2009. "Levinasian Otherism, Skepticism, and the Problem of Self-Refutation." *The Philosophical Forum* 40(1) (Spring): 29–54.

Aikin, Scott F. and Robert B. Talisse. 2011. *Reasonable Atheism: A Moral Case for Respectful Disbelief.* Amherst, NY: Prometheus Books.

Alper, Matthew. 2008. *The "God" Part of the Brain.* Naperville, IL: Sourcebooks, Inc.

Alston, William. 1989. *Epistemic Justification. Essays in the Theory of Knowledge.* Ithaca, NY: Cornell University Press.

—. 2005a. "Two Cheers for Mystery." In *God and the Ethics of Belief: New Essays in Philosophy of Religion.* Ed. Andre Dole and Andrew Chignell. Cambridge: Cambridge University Press, 99–114.

—. 2005b. *Beyond "Justification": Dimensions of Epistemic Evaluation.* Ithaca, NY: Cornell University Press.

Audi, Paul. 2006. *Michael Henry: Une trajectoire philosophique.* Paris: Les Belles Letters.

Audi, Robert. 1993. *The Structure of Justification.* Cambridge: Cambridge University Press.

—. 2001. *The Architecture of Reason: The Structure and Substance of Rationality.* Oxford: Oxford University Press.

Ayer, Alfred Jules. 1952. *Language, Truth, and Logic.* 2nd edn. New York, NY: Dover Publications.

Backhouse, Stephen. 2011. *Kierkegaard's Critique of Christian Nationalism.* New York, NY and Oxford: Oxford University Press.

Barnett, Christopher B. 2011. *Kierkegaard, Pietism, and Holiness.* Burlington, VT and Farnham: Ashgate.

Barrett, Justin L. 2004. *Why Would Anyone Believe in God?* AltaMira Press.

Batnitzky, Leora. 2006. *Leo Strauss and Emmanuel Levinas: Philosophy and the Politics of Revelation.* Cambridge: Cambridge University Press.

Bello, Angela Ales. 2009. *The Divine in Husserl and Other Explorations. Analytica Husserliana* 98. Dordrecht: Springer.

Benson, Bruce Ellis. 2008. *Pious Nietzsche: Decadence and Dionysian Piety.* Bloomington and Indianapolis, IN: Indiana University Press.

—. 2013. *Liturgy as a Way of Life: Embodying the Arts in Christian Worship.* Grand Rapids, MI: Baker Academic.

Benson, Bruce Ellis and Norman Wirzba, eds. 2005. *The Phenomenology of Prayer.* New York, NY: Fordham University Press.

Bernasconi, Robert. 1997. "The Violence of the Face: Peace and Language in the Thought of Levinas." *Philosophy and Social Criticism* 23(6): 81–93.

—. 1999. "The Third Party: Levinas on the Intersection of the Ethical and the Political." *Journal of the British Society for Phenomenology* 30(1) (January): 76–87.

Bernet, Rudolf, Iso Kern, and Eduard Marbach. 1993. *An Introduction to Husserlian Phenomenology.* Evanston, IL: Northwestern University Press.

Bloechl, Jeffrey. 2002. "Translator's Introduction." In *The Unforgettable and the Unhoped For.* By Jean-Louis Chrétien. New York: Fordham University Press, vii–xv.

Blume, Anna. 2010. "Hermann Schmitz (1928–)." In *Handbook of Phenomenological Aesthetics.* Ed. Hans Rainer Sepp and Lester Embree. Dordrecht: Springer, 307–9.

Boeve, Lieven, Joeri Schrijvers, Wessel Stoker, and Hendrik M. Vroom, eds. 2006. *Faith in the Enlightenment? The Critique of the Enlightenment Revisited.* Amsterdam and New York: Rodopi.

Bourdieu, Pierre. 1977. *Outline of a Theory of Practice.* Trans. Richard Nice. Cambridge: Cambridge University Press.

—. 1991. *The Political Ontology of Martin Heidegger.* Trans. Peter Collier. Stanford, CA: Stanford University Press.

Braver, Lee. 2009. *Heidegger's Later Writings.* London: Continuum.

Brown, Peter. 1983. "The Saint as Exemplar in Late Antiquity." *Representations* 1(2): 1–25.

Budick, Sanford and Wolfgang Iser, eds. 1987. *Languages of the Unsayable: The Play of Negativity in Literature and Literary Theory.* Stanford, CA: Stanford University Press.

Burggraeve, Roger. 2002. *The Wisdom of Love in the Service of Love: Emmanuel Levinas on Justice, Peace, and Human Rights.* Milwaukee, WI: Marquette University Press.

Butler, Judith. 2005. *Giving an Account of Oneself.* New York, NY: Fordham University Press.

Cahn, Steven M., ed. 2009. *Exploring Philosophy of Religion: An Introductory Anthology.* New York, NY and Oxford: Oxford University Press.

Caputo, John D. 1982. *Heidegger and Aquinas: An Essay on Overcoming Metaphysics.* New York, NY: Fordham University Press.

——. 1986. *The Mystical Element in Heidegger's Thought.* New York, NY: Fordham University Press.

——. 1993a. *Demythologizing Heidegger.* Bloomington and Indianapolis, IN: Indiana University Press.

——. 1993b. *Against Ethics: Contributions to a Poetics of Obligation with Constant Reference to Deconstruction.* Bloomington and Indianapolis, IN: Indiana University Press.

——. 1997. *The Prayers and Tears of Jacques Derrida: Religion without Religion.* Bloomington and Indianapolis, IN: Indiana University Press.

——. 2000. "For the Love of the Things Themselves: Derrida's Hyper-Realism." *Journal for Cultural and Religious Theory* 1(3).

——, ed. 2002a. *The Religious.* Malden, MA and Oxford: Blackwell.

——. 2002b. "Who Comes After the God of Metaphysics?" In *The Religious.* Ed. John D. Caputo. Malden, MA and Oxford: Blackwell, 1–19.

——. 2005. "Methodological Postmodernism: On Merold Westphal's Overcoming Onto-Theology." *Faith and Philosophy* 22(3) (July): 284–96.

——. 2006. *The Weakness of God: A Theology of the Event.* Bloomington and Indianapolis, IN: Indiana University Press.

——. 2012. "On Not Settling for an Abridged Edition of Postmodernism: Radical Hermeneutics as Radical Theology." In *Reexamining Deconstruction and Determinate Religion: Toward a Religion with Religion.* Ed. J. Aaron Simmons and Stephen Minister. Pittsburgh, PA: Duquesne University Press, 271–353.

Caputo, John D. and Michael J. Scanlon, eds. 1999a. *God, the Gift, and Postmodernism.* Bloomington and Indianapolis, IN: Indiana University Press.

——. 1999b. "Apology for the Impossible: Religion and Postmodernism." In *God, the Gift, and Postmodernism.* Ed. John D. Caputo and Michael J. Scanlon. Bloomington and Indianapolis, IN: Indiana University Press, 1–19.

Carlson, Thomas A. 1999. *Indiscretion: Finitude and the Naming of God.* Chicago, IL: University of Chicago Press.

Cerbone, David R. 2008. *Heidegger: A Guide for the Perplexed.* London: Continuum.

Chrétien, Jean-Louis. 1989. *L'antiphonaire de la nuit*. Paris: Eds. De L'Herne.

——. 1990. *La Voix nue: Phénoménologie de la promesse*. Paris: Éditions de Minuit.

——. 2000. "The Wounded Word: Phenomenology of Prayer." In *Phenomenology and the "Theological Turn": The French Debate*. By Dominique Janicaud, Jean-François Courtine, Jean-Louis Chrétien, Jean-Luc Marion, Michel Henry, and Paul Ricoeur. New York, NY: Fordham University Press, 147–75.

——. 2002. *The Unforgettable and the Unhoped For*. Trans. Jeffrey Bloechl. New York: Fordham University Press.

——. 2004. *The Call and the Response*. Trans. Anne A. Davenport. New York: Fordham University Press.

Christensen, Carlton B. 2008. *Self and World: From Analytic Philosophy to Phenomenology*. Berlin: Walter de Gruyter.

Clark, David K. 1993. *Dialogical Apologetics: A Person-Centered Approach to Christian Defense*. Grand Rapids, IL: Baker Books.

Clark, Kelly James, ed. 1993. *Philosophers Who Believe: The Spiritual Journeys of 11 Leading Thinkers*. Downers Grove, IL: InterVarsity Press.

Clark, Timothy. 2002. *Martin Heidegger*. New York and London: Routledge.

Cohen, Richard A. 2010. *Levinasian Meditations: Ethics, Philosophy, and Religion*. Pittsburgh, PA: Duquesne University Press.

Connolly, William E. 2008. *William E. Connolly: Democracy, Pluralism, and Political Theory*. Ed. Samuel A. Chambers and Terrell Carver. New York, NY: Routledge.

Coward, Harold and Toby Foshay, eds. 1992. *Derrida and Negative Theology*. Albany, NY: State University of New York Press.

Craig, William Lane. 1994. *Reasonable Faith: Christian Truth and Apologetics*. Wheaton, IL: Crossway Books.

Crisp, Oliver D. and Michael C. Rea, eds. 2009. *Analytic Theology: New Essays in the Philosophy of Theology*. Oxford: Oxford University Press.

Crowell, Steven and Jeff Malpas. 2007. *Transcendental Heidegger*. Stanford, CA: Stanford University Press.

Dahl, Espen. 2010. *Phenomenology and the Holy: Religious Experience after Husserl*. London: SCM Press.

Dallmayr, Fred. 1993. *The Other Heidegger*. Ithaca, NY and London: Cornell University Press.

Dalton, Drew M. 2009. *Longing for the Other: Levinas and Metaphysical Desire*. Pittsburgh, PA: Duquesne University Press.

Davenport, Anne A. 2004. "Translator's Preface." In *The Call and the Response*. By Jean-Louis Chrétien. New York: Fordham University Press, vii–xxix.

De Beistegui, Miguel. 1998. *Heidegger and the Political*. New York, NY and London: Routledge.

De Paulo, Craig, ed. 2006. *The Influence of Augustine on Heidegger: The Emergence of an Augustinian Phenomenology*. Lewiston: The Edwin Mellen Press.

Derrida, Jacques. 1973. *Speech and Phenomena and Other Essays on Husserl's Theory of Signs*. Trans. David B. Allison. Evanston, IL: Northwestern University Press.

—. 1978. *Writing and Difference*. Trans. Alan Bass. Chicago and London: The University of Chicago Press.

—. 1982. *Margins of Philosophy*. Trans. Alan Bass. Chicago and London: The University of Chicago Press.

—. 1987a. "How to Avoid Speaking: Denials." Trans. Ken Frieden. In *Languages of the Unsayable: The Play of Negativity in Literature and Literary Theory*. Ed. Sanford Budick and Wolfgang Iser. Stanford, CA: Stanford University Press, 3–70.

—. 1987b. *The Truth in Painting*. Trans. Geoff Bennington and Ian McLeod. Chicago, IL and London: The University of Chicago Press.

—. 1988. *Limited Inc*. Trans. Alan Bass, Samuel Weber, and Jeffrey Mehlman. Evanston, IL: Northwestern University Press.

—. 1992a. *Given Time: I. Counterfeit Money*. Trans. Peggy Kamuf. Chicago, IL and London: The University of Chicago Press.

—. 1992b. "The Force of Law: The 'Mystical Foundation of Authority.'" In *Deconstruction and the Possibility of Justice*. Ed. Drucilla Cornell, Michel Rosenfeld, and David Gray Carlson. New York: Routledge, 3–67.

—. 1992c. *The Other Heading: Reflections on Today's Europe*. Trans. Pascale-Anne Brault and Michael Naas. Bloomington and Indianapolis, IN: Indiana University Press.

—. 1993. *Circumfession: Fifty-nine Periods and Periphrasses*. In *Jacques Derrida*. By Geoffrey Bennington and Jacques Derrida. Trans. Geoffrey Bennington. Chicago, IL and London: University of Chicago Press, 3–315.

—. 1994. *Specters of Marx: The State of the Debt, the Work of Mourning, and the New International*. Trans. Peggy Kamuf. New York and London: Routledge.

—. 1997a. *Of Grammatology*. Trans. Gayatri Chakravorty Spivak. Baltimore, MD and London: The Johns Hopkins University Press.

—. 1997b. *The Politics of Friendship*. Trans. George Collins. London and New York, NY: Verso.

—. 1998. "Faith and Knowledge: The Two Sources of 'Religion' at
the Limits of Reason Alone." In *Religion*. Ed. Jacques Derrida and
Gianni Vattimo. Stanford, CA: Stanford University Press, 1–78.

—. 2000. *Of Hospitality: Anne Dufourmantelle Invites Jacques
Derrida to Respond*. Stanford, CA: Stanford University Press.

—. 2002. *Negotiations: Interventions and Interviews 1971–2001*. Ed.
and trans. Elizabeth Rottenberg. Stanford, CA: Stanford University
Press.

—. 2005. *Rogues: Two Essays on Reason*. Trans. Pascale-Anne Brault
and Michael Naas. Stanford, CA: Stanford University Press.

—. 2008a. *The Gift of Death (second edition) and Literature in Secret*.
Trans. David Wills. Chicago and London: The University of Chicago
Press.

—. 2008b. *The Animal that Therefore I am*. Ed. Marie-Louise Mallet.
Trans. David Wills. New York, NY: Fordham University Press.

Derrida, Jacques and Gianni Vattimo, eds. 1998. *Religion*. Stanford,
CA: Stanford University Press.

Derrida, Jacques, Richard Kearney, and Jean-Luc Marion. 1999. "On
the Gift: A Discussion between Jacques Derrida and Jean-Luc
Marion." In *God, the Gift, and Postmodernism*. Ed. John D. Caputo
and Michael J. Scanlon. Bloomington and Indianapolis, IN: Indiana
University Press, 54–78.

De Vries, Hent. 1995. "Adieu, à dieu, a-Dieu." In *Ethics as First
Philosophy: The Significance of Emmanuel Levinas for Philosophy,
Literature and Religion*. Ed. Adriaan T. Peperzak. New York and
London: Routledge, 211–20.

—. 1999. *Philosophy and the Turn to Religion*. Baltimore and London:
The Johns Hopkins University Press.

—. 2002. *Religion and Violence: Philosophical Perspectives from Kant
to Derrida*. Baltimore and London: The Johns Hopkins University
Press.

—. 2005. *Minimal Theologies: Critiques of Secular Reason in Adorno
and Levinas*. Trans. Geoffrey Hale. Baltimore and London: The
Johns Hopkins University Press.

Dole, Andre and Andrew Chignell, eds. 2005. *God and the Ethics
of Belief: New Essays in Philosophy of Religion*. Cambridge:
Cambridge University Press.

Dooley, Mark. 2001. *The Politics of Exodus: Kierkegaard's Ethics of
Responsibility*. New York, NY: Fordham University Press.

Dreyfus, Hubert L. and Mark A. Wrathall, eds. 2005. *A Companion to
Heidegger*. Malden and Oxford: Blackwell.

Dudiak, Jeffrey. 2001. *The Intrigue of Ethics: A Study of the Idea of Discourse in the Thought of Emmanuel Levinas*. New York, NY: Fordham University Press.

Durfree, Harold A., ed. 1976. *Analytic Philosophy and Phenomenology II*. The Hague: Martinus Nijhoff.

Edwards, Paul. 2009. *God and the Philosophers*. Amherst: Prometheus Books.

Eliade, Mircea. 1959. *The Sacred and the Profane*. Trans. Willard R. Trask. San Diego and New York: Harcourt Brace & Company.

Elveton, R. O., ed. 1970. *The Phenomenology of Husserl: Selected Critical Readings*. Chicago, IL: Quadrangle Books.

Evans, C. Stephen and Merold Westphal, eds. 1993a. *Christian Perspectives on Religious Knowledge*. Grand Rapids, IL: Eerdmans.

—. 1993b. "Introduction: Christian Perspectives on Religious Knowledge." In *Christian Perspectives on Religious Knowledge*. Ed. C. Stephen Evans and Merold Westphal. Grand Rapids, IL: Eerdmans, 1–14.

Fantl, Jeremy. 2003. "Modest Infinitism." *Canadian Journal of Philosophy* 33: 537–62.

Faulconer, James E., ed. 2003. *Transcendence in Philosophy and Religion*. Bloomington and Indiana, IN: Indiana University Press.

Fitzgerald, Timothy. 2000. *The Ideology of Religious Studies*. Oxford: Oxford University Press.

Fóti, Véronique M. 1992. *Heidegger and the Poets: Poiesis, Sophia, Technē*. New Jersey and London: Humanities Press.

Gadamer, Hans-Georg. 1989. *Truth and Method*. 2nd and rev. edn. Trans. J. Weinsheimer and D. G. Marshall. New York: Crossroad.

—. 1997. "Reflections on My Philosophical Journey." In *The Philosophy of Hans-Georg Gadamer*. Ed. Lewis Edwin Hahn. Chicago: Open Court, 3–63.

Gall, Robert S. 1987. *Beyond Theism and Atheism: Heidegger's Significance for Religious Thinking*. Dordrecht: Martinus Nijhoff.

Gallagher, Shaun and Dan Zahavi. 2012. *The Phenomenological Mind*. 2nd edn. London and New York, NY: Routledge.

Gelven, Michael. 1970. *A Commentary on Heidegger's Being and Time*. New York and Evanston: Harper and Row.

Gély, Raphaël. 2012. "Towards a Radical Phenomenology of Social Life: Reflections from the Work of Michel Henry." In *Michel Henry: The Affects of Thought*. Ed. Jeffrey Hanson and Michael R. Kelly. London: Continuum, 154–77.

Goodchild, Philip, ed. 2002a. *Rethinking Philosophy of Religion: Approaches from Continental Philosophy*. New York: Fordham University Press.

—. 2002b. "Continental Philosophy of Religion: An Introduction." In
    *Rethinking Philosophy of Religion: Approaches from Continental
    Philosophy.* Ed. Philip Goodchild. New York: Fordham University
    Press, 1–39.
Greaves, Tom. 2010. *Starting with Heidegger.* London: Continuum.
Greisch, Jean. 1998. "The Same and the Other: Philosophy and
    Theology in the Twentieth Century." Trans. Fiona Greenbwood.
    In *The Return of God: Theological Perspectives in Contemporary
    Philosophy.* Ed. Niels Grønkjær. Denmark: Odense University Press,
    49–73.
Grønkjær, Niels, ed. 1998. *The Return of God: Theological Perspectives
    in Contemporary Philosophy.* Denmark: Odense University Press.
Gschwandtner, Christina M. 2007. *Reading Jean-Luc Marion:
    Exceeding Metaphysics.* Bloomington and Indianapolis, IN: Indiana
    University Press.
—. 2012. *Postmodern Apologetics? Arguments for God in
    Contemporary Philosophy.* New York, NY and Oxford: Oxford
    University Press.
Guardini, Romano. 2000. "The Playfulness of the Liturgy." In *Primary
    Sources of Liturgical Theology: A Reader.* Ed. Dwight W. Vogel.
    Collegeville, MN: The Liturgical Press, 38–45.
Guignon, Charles, ed. 2006. *The Cambridge Companion to Heidegger.*
    2nd edn. Cambridge: Cambridge University Press.
Gutting, Gary. 2012. "Bridging the Analytic-Continental Divide."
    New York Times, Opinionator (February 19).
Hadot, Pierre. 1995. *Philosophy as a Way of Life.* Ed. Arnold I.
    Davidson. Oxford: Blackwell.
—. 2004. *What Is Ancient Philosophy?* Trans. Michael Chase.
    Cambridge, MA: Harvard.
Hanson, Jeffrey and Michael R. Kelly, eds. 2012. *Michel Henry:
    The Affects of Thought.* London: Continuum.
Hart, James. 1994. "The Study of Religion in Husserl's Writings."
    In *Phenomenology of the Cultural Disciplines*, Contributions to
    Phenomenology 16. Ed. Mano Daniel and Lester Embree. Dordrecht:
    Springer, 265–96.
Haverkamp, Anselm. 1995. *Deconstruction is/in America: A New Sense
    of the Political.* New York, NY: New York University Press.
Hefty, Karl. 2012. "Introduction to the English Edition." In *Words of
    Christ.* By Michel Henry. Grand Rapids, MI: Eerdmans, xi–xxix.
Hegel, G. W. F. 1977. *Phenomenology of Spirit.* Trans. A. V. Miller.
    Oxford: Oxford University Press.
Heidegger, Martin. 1969. *Identity and Difference.* Trans. Joan
    Stambaugh. Chicago and London: The University of Chicago Press.

—. 1971. *Poetry, Language, Thought*. Trans. Albert Hofstadter. New York: Harper Colophon Books.

—. 1974. "Preface." In *Heidegger: Through Phenomenology to Thought*. 3rd edn. By William Richardson. The Hague: Martinus Nijhoff, viii–xxiii.

—. 1982. *The Basic Problems of Phenomenology*. Rev. edn. Trans. Albert Hofstadter. Bloomington and Indianapolis, IN: Indiana University Press.

—. 1993. *Basic Writings, Revised and Expanded Edition*. Ed. David Farrell Krell. New York, NY: HarperCollins.

—. 1996. *Hölderlin's Hymn "The Ister."* Trans. William McNeill and Julia Davis. Bloomington and Indianapolis, IN: Indiana University Press.

—. 1998. *Pathmarks*. Ed. William McNeill. Cambridge: Cambridge University Press.

—. 1999. *Contributions to Philosophy (from Enowning)*. Trans. Parvis Emad and Kenneth Maly. Bloomington and Indianapolis, IN: Indiana University Press.

—. 2003. *Four Seminars*. Trans. Andrew Mitchell and François Raffoul. Bloomington and Indianapolis, IN: Indiana University Press.

—. 2004. *The Phenomenology of Religious Life*. Trans. Matthias Fritsch and Jennifer Anna Gosetti-Ferencei. Bloomington and Indianapolis, IN: Indiana University Press.

—. 2010. *Being and Time*. Trans. Joan Stambaugh. Rev. by Dennis J. Schmidt. Albany and New York: State University of New York.

Held, Klaus. 2003. "Husserl's Phenomenology of the Life-World." In *The New Husserl: A Critical Reader*. Ed. Donn Welton. Bloomington and Indianapolis, IN: Indiana University Press, 32–62.

Hemming, Laurence Paul. 2002. *Heidegger's Atheism: The Refusal of a Theological Voice*. Notre Dame, IN: University of Notre Dame Press.

Henry, Michel. 1963. *L'essence de la manifestation*. Paris: Presses Universitaires de France.

—. 1973. *The Essence of Manifestation*. Trans. Girard Etzkorn. The Hague: Martinus Nijhoff.

—. 1975. *Philosophy and Phenomenology of the Body*. Trans. Girard Etzkorn. The Hague: Martinus Nijhoff.

—. 1990. *Phénoménologie matérielle*. Paris: Presses Universitaires de France.

—. 2000a. "Speech and Religion: The Word of God." Trans. Jeffrey L. Kosky. In *Phenomenology and the "Theological Turn": The French Debate*. By Dominique Janicaud, Jean-François Courtine, Jean-Louis Chrétien, Jean-Luc Marion, Michel Henry, and Paul Ricoeur. New York, NY: Fordham University Press, 217–41.

—. 2000b. *Incarnation: Une Philosophie de la chair*. Paris: Éditions du Seuil.

—. 2003. *I am the Truth: Toward a Philosophy of Christianity*. Trans. Susan Emanuel. Stanford, CA: Stanford University Press.

—. 2004a. *Phénoménologie de la vie III: De l'art et du politique*. Paris: Presses Universitaires de France.

—. 2004b. *Phénoménologie de la vie IV: Sur l'éthique et la religion*. Paris: Presses Universitaires de France.

—. 2008a. *Material Phenomenology*. Trans. Scott Davidson. New York, NY: Fordham University Press.

—. 2008b. *Le Socialisme selon Marx*. Cabris: Éditions Sulliver.

—. 2009. *Seeing the Invisible: On Kandinsky*. Trans. Scott Davidson. London: Continuum.

—. 2012a. *Words of Christ*. Trans. Christina M. Gschwandtner. Grand Rapids, MI: Eerdmans.

—. 2012b. *Barbarism*. Trans. Scott Davidson. London and New York: Continuum.

Hermberg, Kevin. 2006. *Husserl's Phenomenology: Knowledge, Objectivity and Others*. London: Continuum.

Hodge, Joanna. 1995. *Heidegger and Ethics*. New York and London: Routledge.

Holley, David M. 2010. *Meaning and Mystery: What It Means to Believe in God*. Malden, MA and Oxford: Wiley-Blackwell.

Horner, Robyn. 2001. *Rethinking God as Gift: Marion, Derrida, and the Limits of Phenomenology*. New York, Fordham University Press.

—. 2005. *Jean-Luc Marion: A Theo-Logical Introduction*. Aldershot: Ashgate.

Horowitz, Asher and Gad Horowitz, eds. 2006. *Difficult Justice: Commentaries on Levinas and Politics*. Toronto: University of Toronto Press.

Husserl, Edmund. 1931. *Ideas: General Introduction to Pure Phenomenology*. Trans. W. R. Boyce Gibson. New York: Macmillan.

—. 1950. *Idées directrices pour une phénoménologie*. Trans. Paul Ricoeur. Paris: Gallimard.

—. 1970a. *The Crisis of European Sciences and Transcendental Phenomenology*. Trans. David Carr. Evanston, IL: Northwestern University Press.

—. 1970b. *Logical Investigations*. Trans. J. N. Findlay. Ed. Dermot Moran. New York, NY and London: Routledge.

—. 1975. *The Paris Lectures*. Trans. Peter Koestenbaum. The Hague: Martinus Nijhoff.

—. 1981. "Philosophy as a Rigorous Science." Trans. Quentin Lauer. In *Husserl: Shorter Works*. Ed. Peter McCormick and Frederick A. Elliston. Notre Dame, IN: University of Notre Dame Press, 166–97.

—. 1982. *Ideas Pertaining to a Pure Phenomenology and to a Phenomenological Philosophy: First Book*. Trans. F. Kersten. The Hague: Kluwer.

—. 1991. *On the Phenomenology of the Consciousness of Internal Time (1893–1917)*. Trans. John Barnett Brough. Dordrecht: Kluwer.

—. 1999a. *Cartesian Meditations: An Introduction to Phenomenology*. Trans. Dorion Cairns. Dordrecht: Kluwer.

—. 1999b. *The Idea of Phenomenology*. Trans. Lee Hardy. Dordrecht: Kluwer.

—. 2001. *Logical Investigations, Vols. 1 and 2*. Trans. J. N. Findlay. Ed. Dermot Moran. London and New York: Routledge.

—. 2003. *Philosophy of Arithmetic: Psychological and Logical Investigations—With Supplementary Texts 1887–1901*. Trans. Dallas Willard. The Hague: Kluwer.

Janicaud, Dominique. 2000. *The Theological Turn of French Phenomenology*. Trans. Bernard G. Prusak. In *Phenomenology and the "Theological Turn": The French Debate*. By Dominique Janicaud, Jean-François Courtine, Jean-Louis Chrétien, Jean-Luc Marion, Michel Henry, and Paul Ricoeur. New York, NY: Fordham University Press, 16–103.

Janicaud, Dominique, Jean-François Courtine, Jean-Louis Chrétien, Jean-Luc Marion, Michel Henry, and Paul Ricoeur. 2000. *Phenomenology and the "Theological Turn": The French Debate*. New York, NY: Fordham University Press.

Jonkers, Peter. 2005. "God in France: Heidegger's Legacy." In *God in France: Eight Contemporary French Thinkers on God*. Ed. Peter Jonkers and Ruud Welton. Leuven: Peeters, 1–42.

Jonkers, Peter and Ruud Welton, eds. 2005. *God in France: Eight Contemporary French Thinkers on God*. Leuven: Peeters.

Joshi, A. T., ed. 2000. *Atheism: A Reader*. Amherst, NY: Prometheus Books.

Kant, Immanuel. 1987. *Critique of Judgment*. Trans. Werner S. Pluhar. Indianapolis, IN: Hackett.

—. 1996. *Critique of Pure Reason*. Trans. Werner S. Pluhar. Indianapolis, IN: Hackett.

Katz, Claire Elise. 2003. *Levinas, Judaism, and the Feminine: The Silent Footsteps of Rebecca*. Bloomington and Indianapolis, IN: Indiana University Press.

Kearney, Richard. 2001. *The God Who May Be: A Hermeneutics of Religion*. Bloomington and Indianapolis, IN: Indiana University Press.

Kierkegaard, Søren. 1980. *The Sickness unto Death*. Ed. and Trans. Howard V. Hong and Edna H. Hong. Princeton, NJ: Princeton University Press.

—. 1985. *Philosophical Fragments* and *Johannes Climacus*. Ed. and Trans. Howard V. Hong and Edna H. Hong. Princeton, NJ: Princeton University Press.

—. 1992. *Concluding Unscientific Postscript to Philosophical Fragments, Vol. 1: Text*. Ed. and Trans. Howard V. Hong and Edna H. Hong. Princeton, NJ: Princeton University Press.

Kisiel, Theodore. 1993. *The Genesis of Heidegger's Being and Time*. Berkeley, CA: University of California Press.

Klein, Peter. 1999. "Human Knowledge and the Infinite Regress of Reasons." *Philosophical Perspectives* 13: 297–325.

—. 2000. "Why Not Infinitism." In *Proceedings of the Twentieth World Congress of Philosophy*, vol. 5. Ed. Richard Cobb-Stevens. Bowling Green, OH: Philosophy Documentation Center, 199–208.

—. 2003. "When Infinite Regresses Are Not Vicious." *Philosophy and Phenomenological Research* 66(3): 718–29.

Kosky, Jeffrey L. 2000a. "Contemporary Encounters with Apophatic Theology: The Case of Emmanuel Levinas." *Journal of Cultural and Religious Theory* 1(3) (Fall).

—. 2000b. "Translator's Preface: The Phenomenology of Religion: New Possibilities for Philosophy and for Religion." In *Phenomenology and the "Theological Turn": The French Debate*. By Dominique Janicaud, Jean-François Courtine, Jean-Louis Chrétien, Jean-Luc Marion, Michel Henry, and Paul Ricoeur. New York, NY: Fordham University Press, 107–20.

—. 2001. *Levinas and the Philosophy of Religion*. Bloomington and Indianapolis, IN: Indiana University Press.

Large, William. 2008. *Heidegger's Being and Time*. Bloomington and Indianapolis, IN: Indiana University Press.

Lauer, Quentin, S. J. 1978. *The Triumph of Subjectivity: An Introduction to Transcendental Phenomenology*. 2nd edn. New York: Fordham University Press.

Levinas, Emmanuel. 1961. *Totalité et infini: Essai sur l'extériorité*. The Hague: Martinus Nijhoff.

—. 1969. *Totality and Infinity: An Essay on Exteriority*. Trans. Alphonso Lingis. Pittsburgh, PA: Duquesne University Press.

—. 1985. *Ethics and Infinity: Conversations with Philippe Nemo*. Trans. Richard A. Cohen. Pittsburgh, PA: Duquesne University Press.

—. 1986. "Dialogue with Emmanuel Levinas." In *Face to Face with Levinas*. Ed. Richard A. Cohen. Albany, NY: State University of New York Press, 13–34.

—. 1987. *Time and the Other*. Trans. Richard A. Cohen. Pittsburgh, PA: Duquesne University Press.

—. 1990a. *Difficult Freedom: Essays on Judaism*. Trans. Seán Hand. Baltimore, MD: The Johns Hopkins University Press.

—. 1990b. *Nine Talmudic Readings*. Trans. Annette Aronowicz. Bloomington and Indianapolis, IN: Indiana University Press.

—. 1994. *Beyond the Verse: Talmudic Readings and Lectures*. Trans. Gary D. Mole. Bloomington and Indianapolis, IN: Indiana University Press.

—. 1996. *Basic Philosophical Writings*. Ed. Adriaan T. Peperzak, Simon Critchley, and Robert Bernasconi. Bloomington and Indianapolis, IN: Indiana University Press.

—. 1997. *Otherwise than Being or Beyond Essence*. Trans. Alphonso Lingis. Pittsburgh, PA: Duquesne University Press.

—. 1998a. *Of God Who Comes to Mind*. Trans. Bettina Bergo. Stanford, CA: Stanford University Press.

—. 1998b. *Discovering Existence with Husserl*. Trans. Richard A. Cohen and Michael B. Smith. Evanston, IL: Northwestern University Press.

—. 2000. *God, Death, and Time*. Trans. Bettina Bergo. Stanford, CA: Stanford University Press.

—. 2001. *Is It Righteous to Be? Interviews with Emmanuel Levinas*. Ed. Jill Robbins. Stanford, CA: Stanford University Press.

Lewis, C. S. 1961. *A Grief Observed*. New York, NY: HarperSanFrancisco.

—. 1996. *The Problem of Pain*. New York, NY: Simon & Schuster.

Lewis, Michael and Tanja Staehler. 2010. *Phenomenology: An Introduction*. London and New York, NY: Continuum.

Mahn, Jason A. 2011. *Fortunate Fallibility: Kierkegaard and the Power of Sin*. New York and Oxford: Oxford University Press.

Marion, Jean-Luc. 1991. *God without Being*. Trans. Thomas A. Carlson. Chicago and London: The University of Chicago Press.

—. 1998. *Reduction and Givenness: Investigations of Husserl, Heidegger, and Phenomenology*. Trans. Thomas A. Carlson. Evanston, IL: Northwestern University Press.

—. 2000. "The Saturated Phenomenon." Trans. Thomas A. Carlson. In *Phenomenology and the "Theological Turn": The French Debate*. By Dominique Janicaud, Jean-François Courtine, Jean-Louis Chrétien, Jean-Luc Marion, Michel Henry, and Paul Ricoeur. New York, NY: Fordham University Press, 176–216.

—. 2002a. *Being Given: Toward a Phenomenology of Givenness*. Trans. Jeffrey L. Kosky. Stanford, CA: Stanford University Press.

—. 2002b. *Prolegomena to Charity*. Trans. Stephen E. Lewis. New York: Fordham University Press.

—. 2002c. *In Excess: Studies of Saturated Phenomena*. Trans. Robyn Horner and Vincent Berraud. New York: Fordham University Press.

—. 2007. *The Erotic Phenomenon*. Trans. Stephen E. Lewis. Chicago and London: The University of Chicago Press.

—. 2008. *The Visible and the Revealed*. Trans. Christina M. Gschwandtner and others. New York: Fordham University Press.

—. 2012. "The Invisible and the Phenomenon." Trans. Christina M. Gschwandtner. In *Michel Henry: The Affects of Thought*. Eds. Jeffrey Hansen and Michael R. Kelly. London: Continuum, 19–39.

Marsh, James L., Merold Westphal, and John D. Caputo, eds. 1992. *Modernity and Its Discontents*. New York, NY: Fordham University Press.

Martinich, A. P. and David Sosa, eds. 2001. *Analytic Philosophy: An Anthology*. Malden, MA and Oxford: Blackwell.

McCutcheon, Russell T. 1997. *Manufacturing Religion: The Discourse on Sui Generis Religion and the Politics of Nostalgia*. Oxford: Oxford University Press.

McGreal, Wilfrid. 1996. *John of the Cross*. Liguori, MO: Triumph.

McQuillan, Martin, ed. 2007. *The Politics of Deconstruction: Jacques Derrida and the Other of Philosophy*. London: Pluto Press.

Minister, Stephen. 2012. "Faith Seeking Understanding." In *Reexamining Deconstruction and Determinate Religion: Toward a Religion with Religion*. Ed. J. Aaron Simmons and Stephen Minister. Pittsburgh, PA: Duquesne University Press, 75–111.

Mohanty, J. N. 2008. *The Philosophy of Edmund Husserl: A Historical Development*. New Haven and London: Yale University Press.

Morris, Thomas V., ed. 1994. *God and the Philosophers: The Reconciliation of Faith and Reason*. New York and Oxford: Oxford University Press.

Mouffe, Chantal, ed. 1996. *Deconstruction and Pragmatism*. London and New York, NY: Routledge.

—. 2000. *The Democratic Paradox*. London and New York, NY: Verso.

Murray, Michael J., ed. 1999. *Reason for the Hope Within*. Grand Rapids, IL: Eerdmans.

Nagel, Thomas. 1989. *The View from Nowhere*. Oxford: Oxford University Press.

Nancy, Jean-Luc. 2000. *Being Singular Plural*. Trans. Robert D. Richardson and Anne E. O'Byrne. Stanford, CA: Stanford University Press.

Olthuis, James H., ed. 2002. *Religion with/out Religion: The Prayers and Tears of John D. Caputo.* New York: Routledge.

Oppy, Graham and Michael Scott, eds. 2010. *Reading Philosophy of Religion: Selected Texts with Interactive Commentary.* Malden, MA and Oxford: Wiley-Blackwell.

Paci, Enzo. 1970. "Towards a New Phenomenology." *Telos* (Spring): 58–81.

Patton, Paul. 2007. "Derrida, Politics, and the Democracy to Come." *Philosophy Compass* 2 (November): 766–80.

Peperzak, Adriaan T., ed. 1995. *Ethics as First Philosophy: The Significance of Emmanuel Levinas for Philosophy, Literature and Religion.* New York and London: Routledge.

—. 1997. *Beyond: The Philosophy of Emmanuel Levinas.* Evanston, IL: Northwestern University Press.

Perpich, Diane. 2008. *The Ethics of Emmanuel Levinas.* Stanford, CA: Stanford University Press.

Peterson, Michael, William Hasker, Bruce Reichenbach, and David Basinger, eds. 1996. *Philosophy of Religion: Selected Readings.* New York, NY and Oxford: Oxford University Press.

Pinnock, Clark, Richard Rice, John Sanders, William Hasker, and David Basinger. 1994. *The Openness of God: A Biblical Challenge to the Traditional Understanding of God.* Downers Grove, IL: InterVarsity Press.

Plantinga, Alvin. 1998. *The Analytic Theist: An Alvin Plantinga Reader.* Ed. James F. Sennett. Grand Rapids, IL: Eerdmans.

—. 2000. *Warranted Christian Belief.* New York and Oxford: Oxford University Press.

—. 2011. "Response to Nick Wolterstorff." *Faith and Philosophy* 28(3) (July): 267–8.

Plantinga, Alvin and Nicholas Wolterstorff, eds. 1983. *Faith and Rationality: Reason and Belief in God.* Notre Dame, IN: The University of Notre Dame Press.

Podmore, Simon D. 2011. *Kierkegaard and the Self before God: Anatomy of the Abyss.* Bloomington and Indianapolis, IN: Indiana University Press.

Pojman, Louis and Michael Rea, eds. 2012. *Philosophy of Religion: An Anthology.* 6th edn. Boston, MA: Wadsworth.

Polt, Richard F. H. 1999. *Heidegger: An Introduction.* Ithaca, NY: Cornell University Press.

Prusak, Bernard G. 2000. "Translator's Introduction." In *Phenomenology and the "Theological Turn": The French Debate.* By Dominique Janicaud, Jean-François Courtine, Jean-Louis Chrétien,

Jean-Luc Marion, Michel Henry, and Paul Ricoeur. New York, NY: Fordham University Press, 3–15.

Purcell, Michael. 2006. *Levinas and Theology*. Cambridge: Cambridge University Press.

Quinn, Philip L. and Charles Taliaferro, eds. 1999. *A Companion to Philosophy of Religion*. Malden, MA and Oxford: Blackwell.

Raffoul, François and David Pettigrew, eds. 2002. *Heidegger and Practical Philosophy*. Albany and New York, NY: State University of New York Press.

Richardson, William. 1974. *Heidegger: Through Phenomenology to Thought*. 3rd edn. The Hague: Martinus Nijhoff.

Ricoeur, Paul. 1967. *Husserl: An Analysis of His Phenomenology*. Trans. Edward G. Ballard and Lester E. Embree. Evanston, IL: Northwestern University Press.

—. 2000. "Experience and Language in Religious Discourse." In *Phenomenology and the "Theological Turn": The French Debate*. By Dominique Janicaud, Jean-François Courtine, Jean-Louis Chrétien, Jean-Luc Marion, Michel Henry, and Paul Ricoeur. New York, NY: Fordham University Press, 127–46.

Robinson, James M. and John B. Cobb Jr, eds. 1963. *The Later Heidegger and Theology*. New York, NY: Harper and Row.

Rorty, Richard. 1989. *Contingency, Irony, and Solidarity*. Cambridge: Cambridge University Press.

—. 1999. *Philosophy and Social Hope*. London: Penguin.

Rubenstein, Mary-Jane. 2003. "Unknow Thyself: Apophaticism, Deconstruction, and Theology after Ontotheology." *Modern Theology* 19(3) (July): 387–417.

Ruf, Henry, ed. 1989. *Religion, Ontotheology and Deconstruction*. New York, NY: Paragon House.

Rush, Fred. 2001. "The Availability of Heidegger's Later Thought." *Inquiry* 44: 201–22.

Russell, Matheson. 2006. *Husserl: A Guide for the Perplexed*. London: Continuum.

—. 2011. "Phenomenology and Theology: Situating Heidegger's Philosophy of Religion." *Sophia* 50: 641–55.

Sanders, John. 1994. "Historical Considerations." In *The Openness of God: A Biblical Challenge to the Traditional Understanding of God*. By Clark Pinnock, Richard Rice, John Sanders, William Hasker, and David Basinger. Downers Grove, IL: InterVarsity Press, 59–100.

—. 1998. *The God Who Risks: A Theology of Divine Providence*. Downers Grove, IL: InterVarsity Press.

—. 2007. *The God Who Risks: A Theology of Divine Providence*. 2nd edn. Downers Grove, IL: InterVarsity Press.

Schaap, Andrew, ed. 2009. *Law and Agonistic Politics*. Farnham and Burlington, VT: Ashgate.

Schilbrack, Kevin, ed. 2004. *Thinking through Rituals: Philosophical Perspectives*. New York, NY and London: Routledge.

Schmitz, Hermann. 2002. "Hermann Schmitz: The 'New Phenomenology'." In *Phenomenology World Wide: Foundations, Expanding Dynamics, Life Engagements—A Guide for Research and Study*. Ed. A. T. Tymieniecka. Dordrecht: Springer, 491–3.

—. 2003. *Was ist Neue Phänomenologie?* Rostock: Ingo Koch.

Sebbah, François-David. 2012. *Testing the Limit: Derrida, Henry, Levinas, and the Phenomenological Tradition*. Trans. Stephen Barker. Stanford: Stanford University Press.

Shaw, Teresa M. 1998. "*Askesis* and the Appearance of Holiness." *Journal of Early Christian Studies* 6: 485–99.

Simmons, J. Aaron. 2006. "Finding Uses for Used-Up Words: Thinking *Weltanschauung* 'After' Heidegger." *Philosophy Today* 50(2) (Summer): 156–69.

—. 2011. *God and the Other: Ethics and Politics after the Theological Turn*. Bloomington and Indianapolis, IN: Indiana University Press.

—. 2012. "Apologetics after Objectivity." In *Reexamining Deconstruction and Determinate Religion: Toward a Religion with Religion*. Ed. J. Aaron Simmons and Stephen Minister. Pittsburgh, PA: Duquesne University Press, 23–59.

—. 2013 (forthcoming). "On Shared Hopes for (Mashup) Philosophy of Religion: A Reply to Trakakis." *The Heythrop Journal*.

Simmons, J. Aaron and David Wood, eds. 2008. *Kierkegaard and Levinas: Ethics, Politics, and Religion*. Bloomington and Indianapolis, IN: Indiana University Press.

Simmons, J. Aaron and Scott F. Aikin. 2012. "Prospects for a Levinasian Epistemic Infinitism." *International Journal of Philosophical Studies* 20(3) (July): 437–60.

Simmons, J. Aaron and Stephen Minister, eds. 2012. *Reexamining Deconstruction and Determinate Religion: Toward a Religion with Religion*. Pittsburgh, PA: Duquesne University Press.

Smith, David Woodruff. 2007. *Husserl*. London and New York: Routledge.

Smith, David Woodruff and Amie L. Thomasson, eds. 2005. *Phenomenology and Philosophy of Mind*. Oxford: Clarendon Press.

Smith, Jonathan Z. 1982. *Imagining Religion: From Babylon to Jonestown*. Chicago, IL and London: University of Chicago Press.

Swinburne, Richard. "The Vocation of a Natural Theologian." In *Philosophers Who Believe: The Spiritual Journeys of 11 Leading*

Thinkers. Ed. Kelly James Clark. Downers Grove, IL: InterVarsity Press, 179–202.

Talisse, Robert B. 2009. *Democracy and Moral Conflict*. Cambridge: Cambridge University Press.

Talisse, Robert B. and Scott F. Aikin. 2008. *Pragmatism: A Guide for the Perplexed*. London: Continuum.

Thompson, Evan. 2007. *Mind in Life: Biology, Phenomenology, and the Sciences of Mind*. Cambridge, MA: Harvard University Press.

Thomson, Iain D. 2005. *Heidegger on Ontotheology: Technology and the Politics of Education*. Cambridge: Cambridge University Press.

Thrower, James. 1999. *Western Atheism: A Short History*. Amherst, NY: Prometheus Books.

Trakakis, Nick. 2008. *The End of Philosophy of Religion*. London: Continuum.

—. 2013 (forthcoming). "The New Phenomenology and Analytic Philosophy of Religion." *The Heythrop Journal*.

Vanhoozer, Kevin and Martin Warner, eds. 2007. *Transcending Boundaries in Philosophy and Theology: Reason, Meaning, and Experience*. Aldershot: Ashgate.

Vattimo, Gianni. 2002. *After Christianity*. Trans. Luca D'Isanto. New York, NY: Columbia University Press.

Vedder, Ben. 2007. *Heidegger's Philosophy of Religion*. Pittsburgh: Duquesne University Press.

Ward, James F. 1995. *Heidegger's Political Thinking*. Amherst, MA: University of Massachusetts Press.

Welten, Ruud. 2003. "The Night in John of the Cross and Michel Henry." *Studies in Spirituality* 13: 213–33.

Welton, Donn, ed. 2003. *The New Husserl: A Critical Reader*. Bloomington and Indianapolis, IN: Indiana University Press.

Westphal, Merold. 1973. "Prolegomena to Any Future Philosophy of Religion which Will Be Able to Come Forth as Prophecy." *International Journal for Philosophy of Religion* 4: 129–50.

—. 2001. *Overcoming Onto-theology: Toward a Postmodern Christian Faith*. New York, NY: Fordham University Press.

—. 2002. "Divine Excess: The God Who Comes After." In *The Religious*. Ed. John D. Caputo. Malden, MA and Oxford: Blackwell, 258–76.

—. 2003. "Whose Philosophy? Which Religion: Reflections on Reason as Faith." In Transcendence in Philosophy and Religion. Ed. James E. Faulconer. Bloomington and Indiana, IN: Indiana University Press, 13–34.

—. 2004. *Transcendence and Self-Transcendence: On God and the Soul*. Bloomington and Indianapolis, IN: Indiana University Press.

—. 2005. "Reply to Jack Caputo." *Faith and Philosophy* 22(3) (July): 297–300.

—. 2008. *Levinas and Kierkegaard in Dialogue*. Bloomington and Indianapolis, IN: Indiana University Press.

—. 2013 (forthcoming). "Must Phenomenology and Theology Make Two? A Response to Trakakis and Simmons." *The Heythrop Journal*.

Wildman, Wesley J. 2010. *Religious Philosophy as Multidisciplinary Comparative Inquiry*. Albany, NY: State University of New York Press.

Wingenbach, Ed. 2011. *Institutionalizing Agonistic Democracy: Post-Foundationalism and Political Liberalism*. Farnham and Burlington, VT: Ashgate.

Wittgenstein, Ludwig. 1974. *Tractatus Logico-Philosophicus*. Trans. D. F. Pears and B. F. McGuinness. London and New York, NY: Routledge.

Wolin, Richard. 1990. *The Politics of Being: The Political Thought of Martin Heidegger*. New York, NY: Columbia University Press.

Wolosky, Shira. 1998. "An 'Other' Negative Theology: On Derrida's how to Avoid Speaking: Denials." *Poetics Today* 19(2) (Summer): 261–80.

Wolterstorff, Nicholas. 1984. *Reason within the Bounds of Religion*. 2nd edn. Grand Rapids, MI: Eerdmans.

—. 1987. *Lament for a Son*. Grand Rapids, MI: Eerdmans.

—. 1995. *Divine Discourse: Philosophical Reflections on the Claim that God Speaks*. Cambridge: Cambridge University Press.

—. 2011. "Then, Now, and Al." *Faith and Philosophy* 28(3) (July): 253–66.

Wood, David. 2002. *Thinking after Heidegger*. Cambridge: Polity.

Young, Julian. 1998. *Heidegger, Philosophy, Nazism*. Cambridge: Cambridge University Press.

—. 2002. *Heidegger's Later Philosophy*. Cambridge: Cambridge University Press.

Zagzebski, Linda and Timothy D. Miller, eds. 2009. *Readings in Philosophy of Religion: Ancient to Contemporary*. Malden, MA and Oxford: Wiley-Blackwell.

Zahavi, Dan. 2003a. *Husserl's Phenomenology*. Stanford, CA: Stanford University Press.

—. 2003b. "Husserl's Intersubjective Transformation of Transcendental Philosophy." In *The New Husserl: A Critical Reader*. Ed. Donn Welton. Bloomington and Indianapolis, IN: Indiana University Press, 233–51.

INDEX